Developing Global Executives

Developing Global Executives

The Lessons of International Experience

Morgan W. McCall, Jr.
George P. Hollenbeck

Harvard Business School Press
Boston, Massachusetts

Requests for permission to use or reproduce material from this book should be directed to permissions@hbsp.harvard.edu, or mailed to Permissions, Harvard Business School Publishing, 60 Harvard Way, Boston, Massachusetts 02163.

Library of Congress Cataloging-in-Publication Data

McCall, Morgan W.
     Developing global executives : the lessons of international experience / Morgan W. McCall, Jr., George P. Hollenbeck.
        p. cm.
     Includes index.
     ISBN 1-57851-336-7 (alk. paper)
        1. Executives—Training of. 2. Executive ability. 3. Globalization.
     4. Industrial management. I. Hollenbeck, George P. II. Title.

     HD30.4.M42 2002
     658.4'07124—dc21

                                                                    2001039434
                                                                    CIP

The paper used in this publication meets the requirements of the American National Standard for Permanence of Paper for Publications and Documents in Libraries and Archives Z39.48-1992.

To Esther and Ruth, whose love and support encouraged us to undertake this project, and whose patience allowed us to finish it.

Contents

For the last two or three years, I could not help noticing Morgan and George, huddled in global whispers in Morgan's office, no doubt talking about their new book. Naturally, I was more than a little curious about it since they had already asked me to write the foreword. Every once in a while I would query them about their progress: When would they finish? I received the typical author response: "Soon." On occasion, I shamelessly stuck my ear against the office wall and eavesdropped, hoping to pick up some juicy tidbits. (Full disclosure: Morgan occupies the office next to mine and the walls, fortunately, are splendidly porous.)

Well, finally, here it is. And the outcome: an imaginative, unique, wonderfully lucid, and elegantly written book that not only demystifies what "global leadership" is all about, but also, and equally important, clarifies how global companies can, should, and must *develop* this type of extraordinary talent.

This is not your armchair study, not your meta-analysis of variance of all the literature on globalization or a factor analysis of 300,000 questionnaires of international senior executives. This is an in-depth study of 101 real global leaders from thirty-six countries working in sixteen leading global firms such as ABB, Hewlett-Packard, IBM, and Unilever. All 101 of these remarkable people agreed to participate in a lengthy, substantial interview (God knows how long each took!), which covered all manner of topics in their professional and personal lives. Here are a few examples of these global leaders: An executive from Holland, living in London, with twelve years of experience as an expatriate and ten jobs that involved crossing country borders, who is now charged with pulling together sixty "orphan" businesses into a single

· · · · ·

global business; another executive, based in Beijing, born in Singapore, has lived in Australia and Xian, and is now responsible for the China subsidiary of a U.S. company; or a Swedish-born executive, now based in Zurich, with fourteen expatriate years in countries from Germany to Singapore, who said, "Home is where I am"; or the one born in India, who now lives in Singapore and is responsible for operations in eight countries as diverse as Pakistan and Korea. One hundred and one remarkable stories, 101 deeply nuanced reflections about leaders and cross-cultural stereotypes and conflicts, and a few myth-breaking conclusions—all of which are carefully conceptualized and astonishingly useful for strategic global leadership–development initiatives.

As a reader, I know you'll be interested in the seven major competencies of the global executive, the five key developmental experiences that lead to global executive maturity, and the challenges facing organizations and individuals in selecting and leveraging these experiences. You will also be interested in why some managers fail or get derailed (one of Morgan's life-long interests) and why *re*patriation turns out to be so surprisingly difficult. You may also learn some fascinating things about which personal qualities are important in a global executive, especially integrity and "openness to learning and experience"; why everything seems to take so damned long in "other" cultures; how relevant (or not) knowing the native language is; what "culture shock" is all about; and, as they say in TV commercials, "much, much more."

What especially intrigued me—and is of fundamental significance in this book—is the critical difference between *business-crossings* and *culture-crossings*. The "what" of doing business—the basic functional requirements—is increasingly convergent for all companies around the globe. However, there are important differences from country to country in the "how" of doing business; for example, there is no gainsaying that a "yes" in Japan could mean something quite different from a "yes" in the U.K. But to get to their fundamental, most seminal point, they vividly illustrate that mastering the context of *business*-crossing pales in comparison to grasping the *cultural/human* aspects of leading in a global society. The latter requires One Big Thing and that is, *transformation of the self.* Yes, they're talking about change, not just cultural, but deep, personal change.

As the authors point out, the time has passed for breathless recitations of how quickly the world is changing—the imperative for organizations and individuals "to 'become global' is now self-evident." So, be prepared and *don't leave home without this book*!

Warren Bennis
University of Southern California

Ever since the first photograph of earth rising as seen from the moon, we've been awed by how small our planet really is. So it is with business—the very idea of national boundaries has been replaced by "boundaryless-ness," and the need for organizations to become global is now self-evident. So, we thought, writing a book on contemporary business wouldn't even require one of those tiresome recitations of how fast the world is changing, how the pervasive presence of the Internet is evaporating distance, how competition is now on a global scale, and how not even the corner mom-and-pop store (should one be left) can escape the impact of the global economy. We knew that the need for effective international executives was large and growing, but research on how to do it was spotty. "So," we naively said to ourselves, "let's go find out how to develop international executives."

We say "naively" because we had no idea of what would be involved. Both of us had done research on executives, and one of us had even been one. Between us we boasted well over half a century of experience in the field, so we thought we knew what to do and how to do it. "Two years, maximum," we confidently said to ourselves, as we embarked on our own adventure in the world of global leadership.

Three years later we started this book. It took the first year to raise the money, and the second year and then some to identify the executives, set up interviews, travel almost around the world, and bring home the completed interviews. It took the third year to code and analyze the data, prepare and deliver the reports to the participating companies, and just begin putting the findings on paper. What we hadn't realized was the complexity of it all. We knew that we wanted to meet and talk with global executives, not just read about them in other people's articles or send out another massive survey. After all, if you want to understand people's careers in some depth, you have to let them tell their stories in their own ways, without confining them to a questionnaire with its multiple-choice answers.

First, though, we needed executives to interview. Five major international corporations, one based in the United States and four based in Europe, and two consortia of organizations, one based in the United States and one based in Asia, provided not only 101 executives to interview, but also the financial and logistical support needed to carry out the project.

We visited the executives in their habitats to see what their worlds were like, to ask questions, and, most of all, to listen. What, we wanted to know, could their collective 4,844 years all over this planet tell us about how to select and develop global executives? Could we glean from their experiences what was important for success in global work, what experiences taught the important lessons, and why such talented executives so often derail in international settings? Perhaps we could use this accumulated wisdom to help aspiring international executives develop the skills they need for international work, and to help organizations more effectively design and manage global development processes.

Meeting these executives took us on a journey to thirty-four cities and three continents. We found ourselves lost in big cities (Zurich, São Paulo, Tokyo), alone in romantic places (Paris, London, Hong Kong, Buenos Aires), intrigued in parts of the world we had to find on a globe (Sarawak, Hertzogenrath), and slightly insecure in troubled parts of the world (Bogotá, Jakarta). We were struck, though, that wherever we went, we were treated with the utmost kindness and courtesy. When things went wrong, which they often do in international travel, it always worked out. Even in Bogotá, a city torn by civil war and plagued by kidnappings, we spent an evening with former students and other local young people, dancing and laughing and seeing another side of life.

As we met these executives, we quickly saw that international executives were not like the domestic executives we both had studied for so long. They had something of the hero about them, in the Joseph Campbell sense of a transformational journey.[1] Nor were they all like each other. Some were thoughtful, even gracious, in the Old World style. Others, regardless of their nationality, were obviously products of the peripatetic Internet age. Though held together by a common fluency in

. . . . .

English, the people we interviewed represented a veritable Tower of Babel of languages, many of which we had not known existed (for example, neither of us had ever met an executive who spoke Fukienese). They came from everywhere, from a small farm in Scotland to the Bronx in New York. They had been everywhere, from refineries in the outback to skyscrapers in São Paulo. They seemingly had seen everything, from brutal ethnic warfare in Africa to high-tech joint ventures in China. And they had eaten things we had never even imagined might be turned into food. Perhaps as they had been when they first ventured abroad, we were stunned by our own parochialism!

Back home, after more than a year of collecting frequent-flyer miles, we faced the daunting task of making sense out of a mass of interview data. We called for help, adding to our team Turkish and Indian research assistants, who brought both international perspective and boundless energy to the task of analyzing each question in depth. Slowly but steadily we developed an elaborate process for categorizing experience, and what were once rich stories told by real people and embedded in our personal experience became quantifiable data. In the computer, quantified and manipulatable, the information made us feel more comfortable. We proceeded to count things: the number of different kinds of experiences and different kinds of lessons learned, and how often each lesson was associated with each experience. A different, version of reality began to emerge, a "scientific" one, and we were on solid ground at last!

Ultimately, though, it was not the numbers and the statistical tests that told the truth of this research—it was the stories. Lives, it turns out, are tapestries woven of many threads, and diving into the details, though interesting in its own right, sheds little light on the whole cloth. The powerful connection between the lives we heard about and our own experience in doing the interviews made the point with us. The numbers made us feel objective, but the lessons of these experiences were tales of flesh and blood—vivid, emotional, and anything but objective. We began to understand what John Steinbeck was talking about when he returned from his biological expedition with Ed Ricketts to the Sea of Cortez.[2] Having explored the gulf as Darwin had, experiencing the reality of the pace as well as the place, Steinbeck and Ricketts returned both with pickled specimens and with their visceral experience. The contrast between the two realities led Steinbeck to reflect on

· · · · ·

the difference between the gulf of their experience and the objective biology of counted spines and species classification. Without denying the value of objectivity, Steinbeck described the "new generation" of technical biologists, "tearing off pieces of their subject, tatters of the life forms, like sharks tearing out hunks of a dead horse, looking at them, throwing them away." Like Steinbeck's biologists we will report on the quantifiable, to be sure. Ironically, as we went through the editorial process, more and more of that reality was relegated to the appendices. The other truth, the one that forever transformed us, is also the one that intrigues and challenges others. Each person is a unique story, lost somehow in the collective tale, but unique nonetheless.

Changed though we might have been by our experience, we realize how "American" we remain. Try as we might, and as international as our sample is—U.S. executives represent only 16 percent of our group—our style and our ideas still betray our origins. We don't apologize for those origins; after all, we had no choice about that. Nor can we go back and change the lenses produced by our origins which obviously influenced how we went about this research. But now at least we've become painfully aware of our own cultural biases and the myriad of betrayals that repeatedly pop up and of which we are often unaware. It is our hope that the message of the global executives is so strong that even when told through newly opened American eyes, it is still their tale.

Acknowledgments

While only two names appear on the book jacket, it took the efforts of many other people and organizations to make the book happen. We cannot adequately express our gratitude to the 101 executives who gave us their time and shared with us the lessons of their experience. Not only did they answer our long list of questions, but they also showed remarkable patience with us as we tried to understand the world as they saw it. Many of them went out of their way to make our visit special by providing cars and drivers to get us efficiently through strange (to us) cities, showing us their facilities and operations, hosting lunches or dinners, giving suggestions on how to enjoy our time in their countries, and providing the many small and thoughtful actions that make a stranger's stay more comfortable. We feel honored to have met them.

This research would have been impossible without the support of Asea Brown Boveri (ABB), Ericsson, the PDI Global Research Consortia (GRC), the Human Resources Futures Association (HRFA), Johnson & Johnson, Royal Dutch/Shell Group of Companies, and Unilever. Our colleagues in those organizations tirelessly supported and encouraged us throughout the effort: Anne-Christine Carlsson, Par-Anders Pehrson, and Britt Reigo at Ericsson; Charley Corace at Johnson & Johnson; Brian Dive, then at Unilever; Steve Fitzgerald at HRFA; John Hofmeister at Royal Dutch/Shell; Bill Mobley at GRC; and Arne Olsson at ABB. (It was Arne Olsson's tireless efforts, endless wisdom, and belief in and support of the work that initially got this project off the drawing board.) Without all of them, the research and ultimately this book could never have happened. We appreciate their patience while waiting for the results, a process that took, as one of them noted, longer than the gestation period of the Indian elephant.

We also appreciate the efforts of the unsung heroes behind the scenes in these companies who spent many hours arranging all the logistics, especially Margareta Andersson, Maureen Bayless, Y. Y. Choy, Linell Griffin, Anneke Herder, Kathy Mak, Connie Sardellitto, and Anita Yeung. Hilde Wesselink played a special role in coordinating the project feedback meeting for our sponsors in Soestduinen.

We thank the people in the participating member companies in the GRC and HRFA and from Toyota who helped and supported us. They included, from the GRC, Ann Tidball at AlliedSignal (now Honeywell), Elaine Wang at Amoco (now BP Amoco), Phil Read at Dow Chemical, Doug Thompson at Hewlett-Packard, and Isabell Yen, formerly at Mobil (now ExxonMobil); from HRFA, Bob Silverforb (retired) and Dave Roxburgh at Bechtel, Colleen Norwine and Steve Fitzgerald at Ford, Linn Minella at IBM, Wes Coleman at SC Johnson, and Ted Runge (retired) at Xerox; and at Toyota, Karen Arden (with Toyota at the time of the study) and Kirk Edmondson. In passing, we note the incredible pace of change, as reflected in the multitude of changes in such a short period for the people and companies involved in this work.

We appreciate the ongoing support from our administrative home at University of Southern California's Center for Effective Organizations, with special thanks to Ed Lawler for taking us in and to Annette Yakushi and Lydia Arakaki for working so hard to keep everything in order. The Marshall School of Business at USC provided course relief, summer support, and a research assistant.

Many tasks involved in this research can best be described as sheer drudgery. Imagine trying to develop and agree on coding categories using the interview notes from 101 interviews, then coding 952 lessons into twenty-seven categories so that four people agree! And that was for starters. Such tasks fell to our stalwart, dedicated, and patient research assistants, Murat Aspalan (from Turkey) and Azfar Hussein (from India), whose own international experiences certainly qualified them to understand the data they were dealing with. Murat deserves special recognition for creating the database and providing much of the statistical analysis.

When we discovered how deeply we were in over our heads with a hundred-plus interviews to conduct around the world, we needed help. The first to answer our plea was Esther Hutchison, who had been involved in earlier research on executive development at the Center for

Creative Leadership and agreed to help us with the interviews, eventually conducting nineteen of them in England and Sweden. We are also grateful to Karen Otazo and JoJo Fresnedi, who conducted interviews for us in Belgium and England, and in the Philippines, respectively.

As we moved into the preparation of the manuscript, our debt expanded yet again. As we moved into preparation of the manuscript, our debt expanded yet again. Our friend and colleague Tim Hall devoted part of a meeting of the Executive Development Roundtable to a discussion of our work, and the feedback from that group provided a very valuable perspective on the implications of our findings. Thanks, too, to Warren Bennis for his eloquent foreword. His work always has been an inspiration to us, so we are especially pleased that he liked our book.

We are indebted to six anonymous reviewers, who provided us and the Harvard Business School Press with detailed comments on an earlier draft of the manuscript. At the Press, Jeff Kehoe's careful reading and advice made this a better book. Our manuscript editor, Amanda Elkin, and our copy editor, Patty Boyd, did a remarkable job of saving us from ourselves . . . we owe them! Also at the Press, we appreciate the support we received from Marjorie Williams, Erin Korey, and a host of others who worked behind the scenes to create the final product.

When it comes to support, special thanks go to Ruth Hollenbeck, who tirelessly read and reread the manuscript, improving it each time.

And last but certainly not least, thanks to Esther and Ruth—for their patience with us during the years it took to do this project.

Developing Global Executives

1

Introduction: A World of Possibilities

Out of clutter, find Simplicity.
From discord, find Harmony.
In the middle of difficulty lies Opportunity.

—*Albert Einstein, Three Rules of Work*

In 500 B.C. Heraclitus wrote *On Nature,* a book that exists today only in bits and pieces.[1] In his efforts to understand nature's ways, he observed that nature likes to hide its truths and that its principles are elusive. After spending eighteen months flying around the world hearing the stories and the insights of global executives, we reached a similar conclusion about global executive development. We had set out to discover the "truth" about how global executives develop and then to translate that truth into simple and usable form for aspiring executives and global organizations. Like Heraclitus, we found that reality is a bit more complicated than we had anticipated and that many of the readily accessible truths were the obvious ones.

Yes, all business is now global to some degree and organizations can't hide from it; they have been forced to develop strategies and structures appropriate to the international context. Scholars have also paid considerable attention to global strategy and structure, which has resulted in an increasingly differentiated understanding of the issues involved. There are many different types of global corporations, many different strategies for doing global business, and many different structures for carrying out those strategies.[2] Aligning these forces appropriately has become the golden ring of international competitiveness.

These new realities are driven home virtually every day in the business press, where the unfolding corporate struggles are reported. The twists and turns of megamergers, joint ventures, and forays into new markets and the life-and-death struggles against international competitors make exciting reading, involving every industry, from automobiles to cell phones.

But while approaches to strategy and structure have become increasingly sophisticated, our understanding of the kinds of executives required in such a complex setting has remained simple and simplistic. Yes, leading in an international context is more difficult than doing it on your home turf, and yes, it requires more sophisticated skills, but what does that mean? A growing case-study literature exalting the CEOs of admired global firms uses legendary figures like Percy Barnevik and Richard Branson to draw conclusions about what all global leaders should look like.[3] An even larger movement believes that a small list of competencies can adequately describe the successful global executive. Though such lists consistently fail to capture the great variety of challenges for global leadership, they continue to proliferate. Even Jay Galbraith's definitive book on organizational design only touches on leadership issues, leaving implicit most of the leadership implications of strategy and structure choices.[4]

Although many would agree that successful global executives must be flexible, sensitive to cultural differences, able to handle complexity, willing to think globally, and the like, such generalities are not very helpful when it comes to specific developmental strategies. Stewart Black and colleagues, for example, suggest using foreign travel, joining international teams, training programs with a global flavor, and international transfers to develop global executives.[5] It's hard to argue with that, but is that all there is to it? If so, it is hard to imagine why there is a perceived shortage of talent.

Where does this leave us? We can say with some certainty that there are many different kinds of global corporations, varying along all sorts of dimensions, from the degree of their international presence, to how they are designed, to how multinational their work forces are. Since different situations require different executive talents and skills, there must be many kinds of global executives. But if there are many kinds, can an organization come up with a single strategy to develop all of them?

Such is the world of possibilities that we faced as we approached this study. We needed a methodology capable of bringing simplicity to some of the complexity, and capable of providing useful, if perhaps not universal, answers. We arrived at the following: First, we used a methodology that, since the early 1980s, has proved exceptionally useful in understanding how executives develop. Then, we took that approach to the executives in situ, that is, to their offices. We believed that we could understand global executive development more readily by putting ourselves in the global arena than by sitting in our offices analyzing numbers. Finally, and perhaps what was most important, we sought that understanding from global veterans themselves, executives who had "been there, done that," who knew both the excitement and anxiety of being a stranger in a new land with responsibilities that might well exceed their abilities. We describe in the next section just how we did the research. Borrowing again from Heraclitus, who observed that "the beginning is the end," we then include in this introductory chapter eight preliminary conclusions about developing global executives.

The Research Sample

. . . . .

We knew that the success of our method—interviewing executives about their developmental experiences—would depend on the quality of our sample of executives. We interviewed 101 executives, handpicked by their companies because they were considered extremely successful, even exemplary, global executives. The 92 men and 9 women hailed from thirty-six different countries (not counting the many multiple citizenships) and worked for sixteen global companies (see tables 1-1 and 1-2). Their positions were quite diverse, including multiple variations of such titles as chairman, chief executive, president, executive vice president, managing director, country manager, business unit manager, controller. At an average age of forty-eight, they had substantial business experience and averaged nine years of expatriate service. They collectively spoke every major language and had worked in every major country in the world. Highly regarded by their companies, these people by any criterion were a remarkable group, well positioned to provide the kind of information that we would need to address the difficult questions.

Table 1-1 Nationalities of the Global Executives in the Study

Nationality	Number in Study
European (Austria, Belgium, England, Finland, France, Ireland, Italy, Netherlands, Norway, Scotland, Sweden, Switzerland, Wales)	46
North American (Canada, United States)	19
Asian (China, Hong Kong, India, Indonesia, Japan, Malaysia, Philippines, Singapore)	18
Central and South American (Brazil, Colombia, Ecuador, Mexico, Uruguay)	8
African and Middle Eastern (Lebanon, Morocco, Nigeria, Tanzania, Turkey)	6
New Zealander and Australian	4

Table 1-2 Organizations Participating in the Study

Organizations in the Study	Number of Executives from Each Type of Organization
Corporate Sponsors and Independents • ABB • Ericsson • Johnson & Johnson • Royal Dutch/Shell • Toyota • Unilever	72
From the Global Research Consortia • AlliedSignal • Amoco • Dow • Hewlett-Packard • Mobil	16
From the Human Resources Futures Association • Bechtel • Ford • IBM • SC Johnson • Xerox	13

The Approach to the Interviews

· · · · ·

In developing the interview questions, we reviewed the existing literature on global leadership.[6] Although many topics relevant to international corporations have received considerable attention, the available
research on the *development* of global executives is relatively sparse. If
the literature agrees on anything, it is that experience is the primary
vehicle for developing global leadership skills.[7]

Given the centrality of experience, we drew on a study that identified specific developmental experiences that had shaped a large sample
of primarily U.S. managers.[8] The interview protocol and qualitative ana-
lytic methods developed for that study were helpful guides to the current one. This earlier work and subsequent research formed the basis
for Morgan McCall's *High Flyers: Developing the Next Generation of Leaders*,
which provided a conceptual framework and a useful starting point for
understanding the development of high-potential global executive talent.[9] If domestic executives were high flyers, then it wasn't much of a
leap to see global executives as frequent flyers.

The high-flyers framework identifies five fundamental components
in the developmental process. It begins with the assumption that whatever attributes a company desires in its leaders, they are the *outcome* of
the developmental process rather than an input to it. Whatever those
qualities (or competencies) might be for a particular company or executive job, a talented person, given the appropriate experience, might
develop them. In figure 1-1, we labeled the end state of development
"the right stuff," borrowing from Tom Wolfe's book by the same name.
Rather than focus on specific qualities of gifted people, however, the
approach in *High Flyers* focuses instead on the *experiences* that prepare a
person for the leadership challenges inherent in the business strategy.
It is the business strategy, not a theoretical model of leadership, that
determines what experiences are developmentally significant. Only if
we know what the organization is trying to achieve can we talk intelli-
gently about the kinds of experiences its talented people will need to
lead it successfully.

As figure 1-1 also suggests, if experience is the teacher, then who
gets the important experiences is a key issue. Logically, one would hope
to give such valuable experiences to the people most likely to learn from

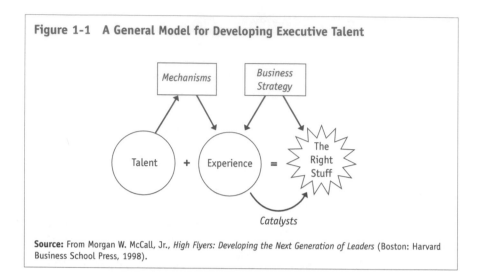

Figure 1-1 A General Model for Developing Executive Talent

Source: From Morgan W. McCall, Jr., *High Flyers: Developing the Next Generation of Leaders* (Boston: Harvard Business School Press, 1998).

them. Thus, talent, or more precisely, potential, can be viewed as the ability to learn from experience.

Talented people, however, don't always have access to the experiences that would best develop their executive abilities, so organizations need some mechanism or process that determines who gets what experience. Whoever gets the experience has the opportunity to grow; the person who determines who gets what job controls development. How this plays out in an organizational context ranges from the decision of a single hiring manager to a formal process of succession planning.

For a variety of reasons, even a talented person may not learn the lessons that an experience has to offer. Talented people frequently are given developmental assignments without knowing specifically what they are expected to learn, without adequate feedback or coaching, or without being held accountable for the learning. Figure 1-1 labels as "catalysts" the things an organization or a boss can do that facilitate learning (which at times may be doing nothing!).

As we designed the current research project, we hoped that this basic framework would be relevant in the global arena even though much of the research underlying it was done with U.S. executives. On the other hand, we did not rule out a priori that something entirely different was going on with non-U.S. executives in international companies. So we revisited the original underpinnings of the framework by including some of the preframework questions: We asked the executives to describe at least three events or episodes that shaped them as executives and the lessons they learned from those key events, and to tell us about a situation they had witnessed in which a talented global executive derailed. In addition, we covered the various components of the framework through open-ended questions about what to look for in choosing people for global jobs (the talent component), and what the organization had done to help them (the catalyst component). We incorporated questions based on other research and theory relevant to global executives, including queries about background experiences and the role of family. Finally, we added some questions aimed at identifying the distinctions they saw between domestic and international jobs, including specific questions about working with bosses and subordinates from cultures other than their own. (The interview protocol, sent to the participants in advance of the actual interview, is in appendix A.)

Our intention, then, was to include an array of questions broad enough for us to tell whether the existing framework or some modification of it was translatable to global executive development. At the same time, we remained open to the possibility that some other approach was more parsimonious.

Introductory Conclusions
. . . . .

This book will lay out in detail what we were told and our recommendations for developing global executives. As the story unfolds we will overuse words such as "complex" and "complexity" as we attempt to describe what we have learned. Because of this complexity it may help if we begin with a few assertions to foreshadow what lies ahead. Though these assertions are more fully developed in the pages to come, knowing generally where we are headed may provide some guidance when the trail gets a bit difficult.

Business Strategy Drives Development

What work must get done? This is what drives (and should drive) development in any organization. It is conceptually clear and hardly controversial. The business strategy and the structure of a global corporation directly affect how many and what kinds of international jobs will exist, how many global executives with what kinds of skills will be needed, and what experiences are available to teach them what they need to know.

The problem is that few organizations have so clear a picture of their global business strategy that it can be translated into specific development needs. Responding to the vicissitudes of the international environment seldom results in logical strategies implemented in an orderly fashion. For example, haphazard efforts to expand internationally (that in hindsight can best be described as naive) often begin with "Who can we send to China (or wherever)?" If the business subsequently fails, the failure is too often interpreted as a deficiency in the person sent to lead the effort rather than what the endeavor was—a high-risk, ill-advised attempt to grow the business. As they go from pillar to posting, it is no surprise that global organizations lose talented leaders with invaluable experiences.

Systematic development of global leaders requires an even stronger, more focused commitment than does a domestic effort. You have to know what you are doing, why you are doing it, and what you want to get out of it. Without that clarity of commitment, the complexity of the global environment will swamp the effort.

What Global Executives Need to Know Can Be Learned, but It's Not All Business

The executives we interviewed described almost a thousand lessons they had learned from their experiences, covering every imaginable skill, ability, and knowledge base. Though some individuals may have some of these abilities as "natural" gifts, global executives, in telling us *what* they learned, were also telling us that such things *can be* learned.

Focusing exclusively on the business side, some executives suggested that the lessons of domestic and international experience weren't all that different. Business is business wherever you are: No matter what country you are in, you still need to concoct strategy, make decisions, handle customers, work with business drivers. People need to be motivated, bosses placated, conflicts mitigated, wherever you find yourself.

Indeed, comparing the lessons described by global executives to the lessons learned by U.S. executives, we clearly see a common core of learning about leading and doing business.

Once beyond that core, however, the cultural context in which the business takes place has a profound effect on the content of the lessons learned. First, culture does affect *how* business is done, if less so *what* must be done. Second, the impact of cultural differences can be so powerful that learning about business becomes secondary. As a result, what people may learn about doing business is less predictable in an international setting and can be culture specific.

Although learning to run a business on the global stage is certainly one objective of global executive development, learning to adapt to different cultures turns out to be both more important and more difficult than acquiring the business lessons. In fact, our data indicate that many business lessons can be learned without expatriation, whereas most cultural adaptability lessons cannot.

Learning to work across cultures is an essential competency of the global executive, and it is for most people an emotional education as well as an intellectual one. In other words, the lessons are both professional and personal—often profoundly personal. We believe that one reason companies consistently have difficulty with repatriation is precisely that so much of what is learned is personal, that the personal learning can be more powerful than the business learning, and that those personal lessons are not always or obviously relevant to the next business setting.

Considering the intellectual complexity of the business lessons and the transformational quality of the personal lessons, we conclude that global executives do indeed have a broader perspective than their domestic counterparts. This unique perspective underlies the elusive quality called a *global mind-set*.

Global Executives Learn Their Trade the Same Way That Other Executives Do

The basic *process* of learning is the same regardless of the executive's country of origin or whether the development is for global, expatriate, or local executive work. In other words, if you give talented people challenging and relevant experiences, if they are open to learning from their experience, and if they get the necessary support, then they can learn many of the lessons needed. That the process is the same is a great relief, because it means that executives, whether international or domestic and regardless of nationality, learn from the same kinds of experiences: challenging assignments, significant other people, perspective-changing events, and the like.

However, when those experiences take place in a different culture, they take on a decidedly different tone, are clearly more complex, and may even teach different lessons. Trying to run a business in a country significantly different from one's own is essentially an experience for which there is no substitute. Doing it a second time, in a substantially different culture, can be transformational.

The experience that most starkly differentiates global from domestic development is what we have described with the term *culture shock,* the result of entering a radically different culture. An executive cannot learn cultural adaptability and the competencies associated with it without actually living and working in another culture and successfully coping with the accompanying discontinuities. This seems to be equally as true for Swedes as for French, for Americans as for Filipinos, for Malays as for Italians.

Finally, other people—as mentors, role models, or examples—play a prominent role in all development; but for global executives, their significance is even more pronounced. Because the environment of another culture is so much more complex, and the nuances so much more subtle, the guidance provided by others (either actively or simply by example) can make the difference between success and failure.

There Is No Magic Bullet for Developing Global Executives

A vast and growing library focuses on the global economy and global business. Stewart Black and his colleagues describe it as a "Tsunami of globalization," asserting that "globalization is not a trend; it is not a fad; it is not an isolated phenomenon. It is an inescapable force. If anticipated and understood, it is a powerful opportunity. If not, it can swiftly destroy businesses and drown careers."[10] What does this tell us about the executives we need in this global arena?

At one level, people are people, and learning is learning, so things are much the same wherever one goes on the world. For senior executives of international companies, English is the common language; the Jakarta Hilton is not much different from the China World or the Shanghai Ritz Carlton or the London Savoy. Despite these similarities, the world of global leadership is much more complex (interesting) and dangerous (exciting) than leading in a domestic organization. There are many more ways to succeed, many more variables impacting success or failure, and likewise many more opportunities to step on a land mine. "Serious students of cross-border organization have arrived at the position that keeping it simple is stupid; the world is complex, and simple organization in a complex world becomes less and less viable."[11] The development of executives who operate effectively in this kind of environment is complicated.

In the long run, it is far better to accept the reality that even under the best of circumstances development is not an exact science and that an organization cannot "make" people develop, even when it "knows" what they need. Many—maybe even most—of the forces that influence the development of global executives are not under an organization's direct control. For this reason, it is all the more important to do well at whatever is within the organization's purview. Sorting out what is within the domain of realistic action, for both an individual and an organization, is an important goal of this book.

A "Global Executive" Is Not One Thing

To say "global leader" or "international executive" is to imply that all beasts thus labeled are the same. Either the jobs they hold or the people holding them, or both, must be similar. It is true that companies operating outside of their domestic environments require executives with something in common: they all must be capable of working outside of their home countries. This required competency was a central feature of our results. The question is no longer whether everyone will have to be globalized; the question is how much, and in what ways?

That said, it is equally obvious that all global jobs are not alike. There are many different types of global corporations, many different strategies for doing global business, and many different structures for carrying out those strategies. Differences may exist in scope of responsibility (e.g., country manager versus manager of a global line of business); in geographic location (e.g., expatriate versus residing in the home country); in type of industry (e.g., consumer goods, for which the cultural differences in the marketplace are paramount, versus oil production, for which the production processes are very similar and highly automated, wherever they are located); in level in the organization (e.g., relative homogeneity at the topmost levels may give way to great cultural diversity at lower levels); and a host of other factors. To the extent that the global nature of an executive's position lies in the work and not in the person the global economy clearly produces many kinds of global executives.

Even if the jobs are not the same, perhaps a "global executive" is found in the similarities among the people who hold those jobs. It was clear from our interviews, however, that all global executives are not cut from the same cloth. One might suppose, to take an obvious example, that people who end up as international executives have background elements in common. Many of the executives did in fact have something in their early lives that inclined them to explore international careers; for example, they had parents from different countries, or they grew up moving to different places around the world. But just as many did not. We found no uniformly shared background experience that predisposed the executives we studied to international work or that uniformly predicted their success. Variety, not homogeneity, was the rule among our executives.

So, neither global jobs nor the people in them are all alike. They come in many shapes.

Global Careers Are Hazardous

At one level, people have always known that leaving home is risky. So too with global work. From a career perspective, going global adds significantly to the possibility of derailment. Moving into a different culture creates more, and more dramatic, opportunities for a particular pattern of strengths and weaknesses to shift from effective in one setting to disastrous in another. Because of differences in norms and values, and misunderstandings due to language, behavior that is acceptable in one culture can become a derailer in another. The effect of cultural differences is felt in a variety of other ways, for example, in increased stress that can result in derailments for other than professional reasons. Alcohol and drug abuse, sexual peccadilloes, and personality changes also show themselves.

Although global executives are in general more talented than their domestic counterparts, they are also more susceptible to things going wrong because of numerous contextual and organizational factors. The international context is multifaceted and includes many things beyond the obvious cultural differences. Family stability is a more central issue, the organization makes more mistakes, and support and monitoring are harder to provide. International work has many more critical danger points—going out, coming back, working for a boss from a different culture, and so on. These changes offer greater possibilities for learning, but also greater opportunities to fail. Clearly global careers can be fraught with risk, terror, and elation. Global executives are indeed adventurers, and their careers are adventures.

Developing Global Executives Is Difficult, but Not Impossible

Although global executive development is more complicated and uncertain than its domestic counterpart, it is not impossible. The most common reason that organizations do not have exceptional global leadership is a lack of commitment to the process of developing it. The problem is not a lack of know-how—in fact, many processes for managing the difficulties of cross-border assignments have been well known for years. The problem is that with the complexity and risk, few organizations have adopted a model robust enough to fit the challenge and then committed the time and resources necessary to implement it.

Global Executives Must Take Much More Responsibility for Their Own Development

Given the added challenge of developing global talent, a substantial burden for development falls on the person who aspires to a global career. Individuals with such aspirations need to seek out international exposure, not wait for it to find them, and the earlier the better; they must approach opportunities to work in different cultures with a sense of adventure, openness to differences, and a penchant for listening and asking questions. Seasoned veterans we talked to advised potential international managers to take some risks, stay open to learning, stay connected to the home office and former colleagues, and take care of the family.

In Sum . . .

We conclude, as have others before us, that people learn to be global from doing global work. Period. In contrast to developing executives for domestic assignments, however, organizations have considerably less control over the process. Despite this handicap, organizations can dramatically increase the probability of successfully developing executives by:

1. being clear on what kinds of global executives with what kinds of skills are needed from a strategic perspective;
2. using experience as a teacher by providing relevant opportunities to those the organization is trying to develop;
3. providing the appropriate levels of feedback, resources, and support to help people learn from the experiences they have; and
4. providing international perspectives and exposure starting early in people's careers.

Experience is still the teacher, but its outcome is less certain in global situations because of the interaction of the assignment, the cultural context in which it occurs, and the background of the person in it. It is harder to predict with certainty what people will learn from a particular kind of experience, and the lack of predictability casts doubt on the very idea of creating generic development programs for all members of a diverse high-potential pool. One size does not fit all.

Assessing a person's potential for success as an international executive presents its own special challenges. Even if development is emphasized, an organization still must *select* those who will be developed for particularly difficult roles. In that regard, there may be certain prerequisites worth considering in choosing candidates for development as international executives. These include the intellectual capacity to deal with the complexity of the global world; emotional openness to find excitement and challenge rather than fear and defensiveness in engaging other cultures and peoples; and the personal stability to survive the rigors of a global career. Most important of all are the capacity and willingness to learn from experience.

Getting the right people into the right experiences at the right times is a large part of the development challenge, but ensuring that they actually learn from them (or that they will learn the "right" things from them) requires additional effort. Finally, the physical and psychological distance associated with global assignments makes it significantly more labor-intensive to provide feedback, monitoring, support, and resources.

An Overview of the Book

What we learned from the interviews with the international executives is laid out in ten chapters. We begin in chapter 2 by addressing the ambiguity surrounding the term *global executive*. We develop the idea that what a global executive is is determined by the interaction between person and job, that crossing cultural borders is at the heart of it, and that there is no single entity that can be called a global executive. Global executives are those who do global work, and global work is found at the intersection of business complexity and cultural complexity.

If chapter 2 points out the interaction of person and job, and deals mostly with the job, then chapter 3 focuses on the person. We discuss the different origins of global executives and show some important differences between *traveling* to other countries to do business and *living* in them while doing business. We introduce three people, using their stories to show how the tapestries of their lives were woven.

In chapter 4 we go beyond the individual cases to lay out the huge variety of knowledge, skills, abilities, and values that this group, collectively, claimed to possess. We reduce the myriad lessons to six basic themes: (1) how to work with cultures different from one's own,

. . . . .

(2) how to run a business that is international in scope, (3) how to lead and manage people unlike oneself, (4) how to handle a complex array of often difficult relationships, (5) how to develop the skills and attitudes necessary for effective personal behavior, and (6) how to know oneself to preserve and enhance one's family relationships and to manage one's own career.

Hiring people who already have mastered these important lessons is an option available to any organization, but it is a source of competitive advantage to an organization to have its own process to develop talent. In chapter 5 we describe the experiences that taught the lessons of chapter 4. The 332 experiences that our sample of successful global executives told us about include foundation assignments that tend to occur early in a career; line assignments that involve leading business initiatives and usually last one to several years; shorter-term experiences that typically involve a focused task carried out in a limited period; and perspective-changing experiences that do just that but are not part of the "official" job. The culture in which an experience takes place directly affects its complexity and intensity, its emotional impact, and the learning that it produces.

Chapter 6 explores in greater depth some of the events that play a uniquely important role in the development of global leaders. Culture shock, for example, is certainly at the heart of global experience. But what is culture shock, exactly? Although people play a significant role in global development, what kinds of people make a difference, when do they make a difference, and what difference do they make? Various formal programs and educational experiences are important, too, but what makes some more valuable than others? Finally, we visit that highly salient, uniquely international, and frequently discussed topic— the role and impact of family on an international career.

Chapter 7 looks at the soft underbelly of global work. This chapter describes the tangled web of international derailments, documenting that just as there are many paths to success in the global arena, there are many ways to lose one's way.

Chapters 8 and 9 further explore the implications of our findings. First, we turn our attention to the part that organizations play in developing global executives. Without offering a magic bullet, we present a framework for understanding how global executives develop and identify the specific actions implied by the framework. Then, in chapter 9, we focus on helping the individual who seeks a career as an international executive. We suggest a number of actions that improve, but do not guarantee, a successful international career. Finally, in the epilogue, we consider how the lessons of the past may have to change as we move into the future.

Back to Heraclitus

In his struggle to decipher nature's ways, Heraclitus did not throw up his hands, and neither shall we. When he persevered, some of nature's secrets slowly revealed themselves.

We acknowledge that the collective wisdom of these successful executives has not produced a simple solution for the challenge of developing global executive talent. Perhaps the hope for a simple solution is only the dream of those who have not yet taken the journey. Although there is no simple solution, organizations can adopt various principles of development, processes of executive learning, and other steps that, if done effectively in the global context, can go a long way to meeting the challenge.

In this book, we use the insights of the executives we interviewed to craft an approach that is realistic and has the requisite variety to address the complexity of issues. We begin by tackling the first tough question: What is a global executive?

What Is a Global Executive?

> The global organization is a complex, multi-dimensional network. Some businesses, such as the Norwegian firm that has 70 percent of the world market for fish hooks, can remain relatively simple. But for the IBMs and Deutsche Banks of this world, complexity is the name of the game to be mastered.
>
> —*Jay Galbraith,*
> Designing the Global Corporation

When we began our study, we sidestepped the issue of what an international or global executive is. In identifying executives to participate in the study, we left it up to the companies to use *their* definitions, whatever they might be. Our tactic was successful in producing a wide range of talented participant executives. We continued in that vein in our interviews when we asked, "What are the most important differences between managing in international work and in domestic assignments?" If the executive responded, "What do you mean by international?" we turned the question back to the interviewee. When we asked, "What are the special challenges of having a boss (or a subordinate) from a different culture than yours?" we let the executive provide the meaning. We tried to withhold our own interpretation until all the data were in.

Eventually we could finesse it no longer. At gatherings of our sponsors we were met with, "What do you mean by a global executive? An international executive?" Our review of the literature of international leadership development and global business found as many definitions as we found articles and books. The interviews with our 101 executives provided an abundance of examples. The time had come to

. . . . .

pull together all our readings and interviews and decide what the terms meant. Before giving our final answer, however, here is a bit about how we got to it.

Expatriate to Transnational

. . . . .

For most of business history the term *international* sufficed; its meaning was clear—"outside the home country of the organization." An international executive, for the most part, was an expatriate, someone who lived and worked "overseas." Wherever and whenever the term *expatriate* originated, the notion has been with us for thousands of years. Didn't the Romans send out expatriates to "manage" their subsidiaries in the corners of the empire? The responsibilities of those early expatriates were not too different from how companies use expatriates today. They were charged with control, making sure that the provinces operated according to Roman law and sent in their taxes. These early expats were also responsible for knowledge transfer, bringing the province new administrative and technical skills, and in those days, perhaps, new gods, language, and culture. Accomplishing those duties required that some knowledgeable and trustworthy executive go there to live and work. It is easy to imagine that the motivations of those early expatriates were similar to those of today's executives who go to live and work in another country—building a set of skills, accumulating wealth, getting one's ticket punched for a promotion, escaping a bad situation, or perhaps just for the adventure itself.

As communication and transportation evolved, being international grew to include more than simply moving to a new land. Executives could travel away from home and return, still residing in their home countries, leaving behind "grass widows," families who stayed home while the executive did a stint in a faraway land. The apparent ease of travel between countries enabled these so-called "corporate seagulls" to fly out from headquarters to manage overseas operations. Although the term *global leader* appeared in the 1960s and 1970s describing a company's market position (e.g., "the global leader in agricultural chemicals"), by the end of the 1980s, the term *global leadership* was applied to executives and to jobs. Globalization took on a new meaning.

In *Managing Across Borders,* Christopher Bartlett and Sumantra Ghoshal described a transnational business model that attempts to cope with the increasing competitive demands of an interconnected world by building global efficiencies and national responsiveness while leveraging learning across markets.[1] The transnational organization took the form of a multiple matrix, business × country × function. Bartlett and Ghoshal defined a global manager in the context of their transnational organization: "[T]here is no such thing as a universal global manager. Rather, there are three groups of specialists: business managers, country managers, and function managers." Managing these three groups is a smaller group of corporate managers "who manage the complex interactions of the three."[2] These four types of executive jobs are defined by their roles in the organization and by what tasks they must get done. Confronted with the difficulties of implementing and managing within such a triple-matrix structure, Bartlett and Ghoshal declared that the essence of the transnational or global organization is not the organization structure per se but a global mind-set.[3]

With the 1987 combination of the Swedish company Asea and the Swiss company Brown Boveri into Asea Brown Boveri (ABB), ABB became the model of the transnational organization, and its CEO, Percy Barnevik, the model of the transnational executive. Since then, the word *global* has been used interchangeably with *transnational* in describing an organization characterized by working across borders. With crossing borders—whether virtually or physically—easier and faster, organizations have increasingly followed their markets outside of their borders. What *forms* these organizations have taken and what types of executives they needed have depended, ideally at least, on what tasks had to be performed across borders.

Crossing Cultures

Based on our work, we believe that Bartlett and Ghoshal were right on several counts. There is indeed no one kind of global executive; there are many. These global executives work *across* borders—borders of business, of product, of function, and of country. All of those "border crossings" contribute to the complexity of the global job. We take Bartlett and Ghoshal's work one step further, however, in concluding that in developing and defining global executives, *crossing country and cultural borders is the determining piece.*[4] Crossing business borders—borders of business unit, of market, of product, of function, and of customer—although important, is fundamentally different from crossing borders of country and culture. Dealing with multiple business elements, however arranged, adds layer upon layer of complexity and contributes to ambiguity, anxiety, and uncertainty, but the impact on executives is primarily cognitive or intellectual. Although the problems may be more complex, they are, at bottom, business problems, not personal problems. It is the crossing of cultural lines that is an assault on the identity of the person. When the task becomes managing differences of country, culture, language, and values, the assumptions we make about ourselves and other people are brought into question. Effective executive performance when crossing country and cultural borders often demands a kind of transformation of who we are and how we see ourselves. Such is the stuff of *global* executive development.

We arrived at our argument after many hours of poring over interview transcripts and notes. After first analyzing the responses to our question about key experiences that changed our executives (described in chapters 5 and 6), we then looked at the examples of international executive derailment (described in chapter 7). We concluded that differences in the *context* of international jobs was the critical factor. In describing contextual effects, executives sometimes focused on business differences, sometimes on customs differences, and sometimes on differences among people. But the common theme was this: Executives cannot function effectively until they understand the context they are operating in. This conclusion was further corroborated in the responses to our interview question about the difference between international and domestic work. We found that the aspects of context that are most challenging and that most clearly differentiate domestic from global work are the country and cultural differences. But what does that really mean?

Changing Contexts

. . . . .

Changing the context of one's work, especially when crossing cultures but also when crossing businesses or functions, has almost inevitable results. Some are good, stimulating, and invigorating; some debilitating, frustrating, and potentially career limiting. Other things being equal, how much difficulty people experience will depend on how different the new context is from the one they came from. People who have changed countries especially, but also those who have changed jobs, will recognize the experience:

- Things take longer.
- Old ways won't work.
- We make mistakes and realize it.
- We make mistakes and don't realize it.
- We feel awkward.
- We have no credibility.
- We have to think about everything; nothing is automatic.
- We have to work much harder.
- Nothing is simple.
- Nobody understands us.
- We don't understand what people are telling us.
- Everything is fuzzier.
- Things don't make sense.

People changing contexts are likely to experience some of these things (and more), whether going to a new function or a new country. But it is going to new countries and cultures that looms large when we attempt to understand international work.

When an executive moves to another culture, the problem is not that doing business or living in one country or culture is inherently more difficult; the problem is the *difference* in contexts, rather than the contexts themselves. Doing business and living in Germany is not necessarily more difficult than doing business in Spain (and, in fact, may be easier in some ways), but to the German in Madrid or the Spaniard in Düsseldorf, the difficulty lies in the difference.

. . . . .

The Cultural Context

. . . . .

Our executives provided vivid testimony to the importance of the culture context. Their responses illustrate not only the experience of crossing cultures, but also the impact of their own (widely differing) backgrounds and responsibilities on what aspect of cultural difference they experienced.

An executive from Holland, living in London, with twelve years as an expatriate and ten jobs that involved crossing country borders, now charged with pulling together sixty orphan businesses into a global business, described his experiences this way:

> In international work, the cultural aspects are critical. You must understand the frame of reference: What is allowed in one place may not be allowed in another. In France, nuances in language can convey subtle meanings. Brits are seldom candid about the bad side of things and you have to read between the lines. The Dutch are blunt— they have to be very sensitive when they are in other cultures.

One executive, now living in Beijing, was born in Singapore, had lived in Australia and Xian, and is responsible for the China subsidiary of a U.S. company:

> The most important difference is the cultural diversity, and sometimes the hardship that comes with living in another place. I have subordinates from Singapore, Hong Kong, and Taiwan. The issue with holding them together is managing diversity. Managing in another culture requires that you dig out the local culture and incorporate it to give credibility to what you do.

An executive born in Sweden, now based in Zurich, said, "Home is where I am." With fourteen expatriate years from Germany to Singapore, all his jobs have been international. Now responsible for a worldwide business segment, he went on to say:

> It is the cultural aspects that are at the heart of it. You need readiness to accept various views. The biggest mistake a person can make

is to go into a new culture and "do it my way." You need to listen and consider their point of view. If you show a bit of yourself—give trust—some people will come forward and you can build on that.

Another executive, a native Brit living in London, spent eight years in three international assignments. He worked first as a sales manager for Europe, then took on worldwide product responsibility, and later assumed total responsibility for Europe, the Middle East, and Africa. His only expatriate experience was a global product job at headquarters in the United States. Here are his observations:

> You have to understand the differences in the culture and be able to adapt your dominant working style. You must recognize that we are not all the same, and you must apply different styles. In the U.S., people are more outwardly optimistic, but it is false optimism; the UK is closest to the U.S., but in France they begin by looking at the problems.

Working and living in Hong Kong, a U.S. executive had functional responsibility for Asia Pacific:

> You must understand that culture, values, and morals are not always shared. If you can identify and understand the differences, you can then decide what to do with [them]. You can't operate on assumptions based in domestic values and motivations. In domestic, you can understand what goes wrong because you know a lot about cause and effect. In international, those assumptions are often wrong—political, legal, physical, and cultural things can be different. Don't assume you will have electricity every day, that there will be roads to the site, et cetera. You must understand the important drivers in your own country, and what they are in this country.

Born in India, where he started his career, and now living in Singapore after a dozen years as an expatriate throughout Asia, a regional executive responsible for operations in eight countries, as diverse as Pakistan and Korea, described international work this way:

International work requires much more sensitivity to the individual cultures. Culture can have an influence sometimes, and when it does, it can be decisive. You must understand the differences . . . in customers, the markets, the individuals, and, in our business, how the doctors operate in each culture. You must spend time in the environment where you will work most often. The first time I go, I go to listen, and not to advise. I keep asking, What are the things people think will work here, and what things will not?

These descriptions leave little doubt about the importance of crossing cultures, whether working across cultures or living in a different culture, or sometimes both. One of our executives, a Japanese living and working in the United States, described life in Japan to illustrate how different Japan is from the U.S.:

Domestically, Japan is one tribe. There are no real cultural differences, no time zone differences. We eat the same food; it is easy to communicate; our education is homogeneous; there is not much difference in backgrounds. Entertainment is a means for building relationships; karaoke clubs are part of doing business; international business runs on meetings and off-sites. The Japanese are more "behind the scenes." Japan is still a masculine society.

As seen through this executive's eyes, Japan seems like a very foreign country indeed for most of us. For an interesting exercise in "country-centricity"—whatever your country may be—imagine how foreign San Francisco must have seemed to this executive!

Here is a slightly different slant that emphasizes working across borders while *living* at home, versus *living and working* in a different country. This executive found that the difference was not so much what she did during the day, which was mostly the same wherever she was posted in this global company, but the life outside of work:

The big difference is where you go home to. If you are in an international assignment outside your home country, you go home and you become a part of the other culture. Our headquarters culture here is very much an international culture at work, but of course, it becomes domestic for me at home. In some ways it is easier there, because the people are more themselves both at work and in their nonwork lives.

The cultural difference that our executives found most challenging was communication and language. Describing her first international assignment, to Brazil, an Australian executive in Jakarta eloquently described the frustration and isolation of not knowing the language:

> The most difficult thing was coming to terms with effective communication. The biggest challenge was communicating, understanding people and what they want, and motivating them. I have always been a very verbal person and I can get people enthusiastic about things, but I couldn't do it, because I could not understand it. I learned the language as quickly as I could, but I had a recurring nightmare that I still have sometimes that I could not speak and could not communicate. I was surprised at how difficult communication was with the business operated in Portuguese and me speaking only English.

As companies have become more global, having a common language—usually English—has relieved a measure of this frustration (the aforementioned executive pointed out that now her business in Brazil is conducted in English). Communication problems run deeper than simply understanding the words and the language, however, with cultural patterns making meaning obscure and requiring much more effort. Here is how several different executives described it:

- "Sometimes I understand what people tell me, but I do not understand how to interpret it because of the cultural differences."

- "In your own culture much of what goes on is automatically understood; the level of communication is deeper without much work."

- "When you tell a person this is what we are going to do, if he doesn't understand he will not tell you. It is a part of the Latin culture, not the language, that they will never tell you bad news and never tell you that they don't understand."

- "It takes more time for people to understand what I am saying. My analogies, the ones I am accustomed to using, don't work in Japan. I realized quickly they were falling on deaf ears."

Leadership issues are closely related to communication issues, of course, and our executives gave domestic versus global context examples as well as highlighting differences from one specific culture to another. "Commanding" styles that may work in one culture won't work in others, the sources of motivation may be different from one culture to another, and how the executive gets things done must be adapted. If operating in a culture other than one's own adds complexity, then operating across several cultures dramatically increases complexity and the demands on the leader who has to face it. Several executives commented on how they learned to cope:

- "In the worldwide arena, you need to be very open. You have to listen, you have to be honest, and you have to work toward a consensus within each country. Many people will resist global initiatives, and you can't make people do things."

- "It's easier to motivate people locally. You can frame an external enemy and draw on nationalism. A global job forces integration across value sets, and you must find more common ground."

- "The work, the efficiencies, et cetera, are about the same, but how you manage people to get the most out of them is different. Although [I am] ethnic Chinese and born in Hong Kong, I am more American than Chinese, and I must adapt to people and manage differently."

- "The corporate life in the U.S. is more hierarchical than in other countries. In Europe, you cannot command—you have to sell your ideas. I don't know of a single country within Europe where commanding would work."

Our executives also told us about differences between domestic and international work that we labeled business processes. Doing business presented international executives with a prodigious learning task that included specific knowledge of countries, their laws or business customs, their decision processes, different companies and customers, perspectives on risk and organization structure, and how business relationships are developed. Although some of these differences have run through the examples given above, we add some brief ones here, in their words, to emphasize the point:

- "You don't know what the law is, what the business practices are; negotiations can be subtle."

- "Business is not done the same way in other countries. . . . England is more functional and sequential. You shouldn't make judgments too early; the pace is slower in other countries."

- "I have to know a lot about how things work in other countries. For example, to standardize an incentive program, I must know what we have in Germany and what is required to change that, and I must do that around all the countries."

- "You must understand the differences in customers and the markets. One's perspective on managing risk, on people and cash, is influenced by whether it is domestic or international. What a domestic perspective sees as risky may not seem to be risky from an international perspective. Things foreign seem riskier to people who have never been in the culture, who don't understand."

- "In a domestic assignment you have the network. You know the ministers and the customers; your network develops over time, and you feel comfortable in how to get things done. But building networks in another country, as a foreigner, is very difficult. I still had no network—even after two years of a five-year assignment. You simply can't develop such a network, you must depend on locals. I can twist arms, but I can't fight the battles."

Only a few executives mentioned the importance of the family as a distinguishing factor in international assignments. We attribute the small number to the order of our questions rather than to lack of importance of the family. As described in chapter 6, the critical importance of the family came through loud and clear in our findings, as it has in most other studies of international executives.[5]

Furthermore, a few executives discounted the differences between international and domestic work, sometimes thinking at a level up from the specific, sometimes reflecting the view that globalization has and will dilute any differences that exist, or questioning our question itself. Their responses, printed below, serve as a background for the epilogue's discussion about the future.

- "It's not all that different. In a new country you have to work on getting the frame of reference right. The challenges are similar in an international company, whether you are in your own or another country."

- "In the end, people are people. You don't have worse people [one place] than [you do] anywhere else. There are good people everywhere."

- "I'm not sure they are so different. I can't identify what's so different. International business is domestic when you get to where you are."

- "It's different, but more and more the same. At least in countries of similar nature—Sweden, Europe, Australia. Is this a relevant question today? Look at clients and suppliers—they are all global."

- "The international environment is the real one. There is no premium for a domestic mentality. Becoming international involves multicultural, multisocial, multibusiness experiences. You must stay long enough in the other culture to become immersed in it."

In sum, according to these experienced executives the primary difference in international jobs is the difference in context, and the primary context change is the difference in cultures. Executives from widely different cultures each experienced the difference from her or his own perspective. What is global work? What is a global executive? We are now ready to answer those questions.

The Dimensions of Global Work

Global work combines two dimensions of complexity: business complexity and cultural complexity. Business complexity derives from the

Figure 2-1 Dimensions of Global Work

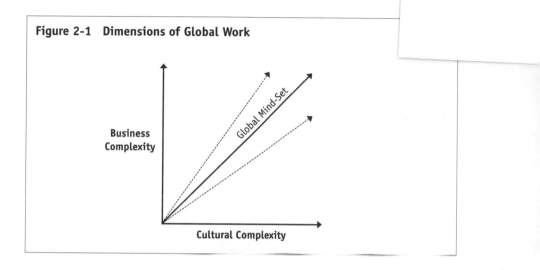

number of functions, products, suppliers, organization units, locations (our list is only illustrative) that make up the scope and scale of the business. Although we present these as a continuum, in fact, the business factors may be added to a job successively or in groups, and some factors may be more complicated than others (functions, say, compared to products or locations). But crossing the borders of business is not enough by itself for a job to be global. All these borders, however well defined and difficult to cross, may be crossed (in principle at least) in a domestic company or job. The essential border crossing that makes a job global or international is crossing the border of culture, a border defined at its most basic level by geography, languages, and other divisions that relate to the differences among people and their habits.[6] Adding layers of either business or culture makes jobs more complex, but the crossing of cultural borders makes demands upon executives that are fundamentally different from crossing business borders. Crossing a cultural border requires emotional or self-learning rather than simply intellectual and cognitive learning.

Global work, we contend, is work that involves some combination of these dimensions (figure 2-1). Crossing either of these boundaries, business or culture, alone is not enough; explanations of either, taken separately, miss the point. Business theory, though enlightening, fails to tell us much about doing business in a foreign culture, and cross-cultural studies that enlighten us about what it means to be in another

. . . . .

culture tell us little about what it means to do business there. The *business in situ* (culture) is critical. And it is from doing global work, as we have defined it here, that one can develop a global mind-set.

Executive jobs (and work) may be more or less global, depending on the mix of business and cultural complexity. For example, the CEO job in a single, relatively homogeneous culture, like Finland with a Finnish incumbent, may include all the elements of business and be quite high on our business complexity dimension, but have little cultural complexity. Consequently, the CEO job will not be very global. Likewise, jobs with very narrow business scope, even when they operate across cultures, are not very global as we define them.

Implicit in our description is that "global" resides in the work, not the executive. This subtle but significant distinction saves us from the quagmire of defining how global a job is by the background of the executive who fills it.

The Global Executive

. . . . .

Simply put, global executives are those who do global work. With so many kinds of global work, again depending on the mix of business and cultural crossings involved, there is clearly no one type of global executive. Executives, as well as positions, are more or less global depending upon the roles they play, their responsibilities, what they must get done, and the extent to which they cross borders. We will not distinguish between international and global executives; we use the terms interchangeably. Both terms, as descriptors of both executives and jobs, involve "more or less" rather than absolutes. Even the most global of organizations, the United Nations, does not extend into every corner of the world.

The Global Mind-Set

Since its introduction (the first use we found was by Bartlett and Ghoshal in 1992), the term *global mind-set* has been used to describe the skills of executives who succeed in jobs combining both cultural and business dimensions.[7] As a term, it has become the catchall for the competencies required of global executives. We also will use it in this way, although a global mind-set alone does not necessarily make a global executive. In addition to a global mind-set, an executive must have a global job.

Differences between Domestic and International Jobs

Our executives provided us with a job analysis, albeit an informal one, with great consistency in how global work differs from domestic. We summarize those differences in box 2-1. These differences are almost a recipe for ambiguity, uncertainty, culture shock, and enormous challenge, even considering that executives will experience these differences in their own way, depending on the gap between where they come from and where they find themselves. Given the array of differences, it is no wonder that global work is often cast as a "Hero's Journey," and that one executive suggested that it would be impossible to ever find anyone who had enough qualifications. Nor is it surprising that global executives sometimes resent that people back at headquarters may view their lives as a series of vacations in exotic places.

Another set of differences were sometimes present in global jobs, depending on the structure (and strategy) of the organization in which they were embedded. Frequently, global jobs are physically and psychologically a long way from headquarters, with the attendant goods and bads. On the good side, our executives told of quantum leaps in autonomy and in breadth of responsibility, and of the opportunity to recover from mistakes unnoticed—all of these, of course, contributing to the developmental potential of the job. On the bad side, executives risked losing their networks, becoming organizationally and technically obsolete, missing promotions, and having their work misunderstood, undervalued, or both. These factors figure importantly in explaining why talented international executives sometimes derail, a dynamic that will be discussed in chapter 7.

Global jobs differ in the degree to which they require managing relations between the company, the government, and the society. Dealing with high-level government officials and influential members of the host society again brings both rewards and risks. One executive

. . . . .

Box 2-1   Cultural Differences

- Laws, business practices
- Language, meanings, actions
- Pace (faster or slower)
- Frame of reference, connections
- Levers of change
- Motivations, values
- Politics, social patterns, protocol
- Social/work overlap
- Business drivers

- Actions, behaviors, habits
- Food, transportation, rules
- Decision-making processes
- Problem-solving approaches
- Leadership practices
- Interpersonal styles
- Time frames
- Titles, authority

---

described arriving in Jakarta for the first time to take on a new job, only to be ushered by the Minister of Resources onto a palace balcony and told to "speak to the crowd."

The demands of global work affect the executive's family as well as the executive. Family adjustment to a new culture is a key issue if the executive is an expatriate. If he or she has global responsibility but lives domestically, then family adjustments to the extensive travel and extended absences is required.

Global Competencies

The search for global executive competencies has failed to uncover a universal set of competencies.[8] We contend that no one agrees on a global competency set, because there is no universal global job. Global competencies, like global jobs, must be thought of as a mix, depending on the job. We cannot, however, resist the temptation to derive our own global competency set based on the distinctions that our executives made between domestic and international work, what it takes to do it, and the developing literature of global leadership (box 2-2).

With our emphasis on crossing cultures in defining global work, it will come as no surprise that in defining competencies, we emphasize the cultural rather than the business dimensions of global jobs. We do not deny a basic skill set that executives need, however. In fact, our

> **Box 2-2   Competencies of the Global Executive**
>
> **Open-minded and flexible in thought and tactics:** The person is able to live and work in a variety of settings with different types of people and is willing and able to listen to other people, approaches, and ideas.
>
> **Cultural interest and sensitivity:** The person respects other cultures, people, and points of view; is not arrogant or judgmental; is curious about other people and how they live and work; is interested in differences; enjoys social competency; gets along well with others; is empathic.
>
> **Able to deal with complexity:** The person considers many variables in solving a problem; is comfortable with ambiguity and patient in evolving issues; can make decisions in the face of uncertainty; can see patterns and connections; and is willing to take risks.
>
> **Resilient, resourceful, optimistic, and energetic:** The person responds to a challenge; is not discouraged by adversity; is self-reliant and creative; sees the positive side of things; has a high level of physical and emotional energy; is able to deal with stress.
>
> **Honesty and integrity:** Authentic, consistent, the person engenders trust.
>
> **Stable personal life:** The person has developed and maintains stress-resistant personal arrangements, usually family, that support a commitment to work.
>
> **Value-added technical or business skills:** The person has technical, managerial, or other expertise sufficient to provide his or her credibility.

executives consistently advised global career aspirants to develop these basic business skills as a first priority.

Except for value-added technical or business skills (which remind us that an executive's purpose is to do business in another culture, not just live there), the competencies depicted in box 2-2 are similar to those that others have proposed.[9] These competencies are what enable people to live and work in other cultures.

The How/What Link

Several executives described the challenge of global work in almost the same words: "The *whats* remain the same, but the *hows* are different."

A Belgian expatriate in Germany, responsible for German research laboratories, described it this way:

> The big difference is the link between the what and the how. It is very easy to go from what to how in a domestic organization because your instincts work. I know how to do it in Holland, where I have worked and lived, and it will be my natural behavior. In Germany, the what is the same, but the how is somewhat different. I have to continuously think about the how, and this gets more complex with multiple locations and different cultures. You cannot rely on your natural responses. It will take me another three years until I get this down.

This executive's description is made more interesting because his intercultural background might have misled us into thinking that he would find little cultural challenge—his parents are Belgian and Dutch, his wife is Dutch, he had worked extensively in Holland, and he still resided in Belgium, less than 100 miles from his office.

We found this how/what link in interviews from Germany to Singapore. Mastering that link across one or more cultures and businesses is much of what global executive development is about.

Global Complexity

The common wisdom, both from writing and research in the international area as well as from our interviews, is that global work, as contrasted with the domestic kind, is more complex (and in turn more difficult, challenging, and interesting), and makes greater demands for learning and conceptual abilities. Here is what a few executives said:

- "[International work is] intellectually more challenging. You need to be more flexible, communication is difficult, wider horizons are required. Domestic assignments are fairly narrow minded—they don't see beyond Taiwan."

- "An international assignment has a higher order of complexity, challenge, and learning. I ran the whole operation when I was in

Venezuela. It was small, but I ran it all. Scale and structure are leveraged—I was involved in government affairs, the economy, social issues, et cetera. You get the dynamics of the whole business in an international assignment like that."

- "The international environment is more complex—you must be able to anticipate the impact of various actions. You can't keep a parochial perspective; you have to see connections."

- "It is an order of magnitude simpler in domestic work. Selling a German product to a German client, everybody knows the boundaries. There is not enough room to be very creative. Now, go to Saudi Arabia—then you have to develop more 'fantasy.'"

- "There is an enormous difference in learning—in your own culture you see little that's new. It is much richer in learning."

- "In international [jobs], you are dependent on so many other things. There are so many more variables, and frequently, other companies are involved as well. You have to adapt. In the other companies and other countries, people do things differently."

- "In domestic assignments, you have a common denominator around politics and protocol. You can figure out how things work. In international work the rules are different and you will never know all the rules."

The argument for greater complexity is self-evident in what might be called "Big G" jobs, global jobs that extend far out in both dimensions of business complexity and cultural complexity. These jobs belong in the upper right-hand corner of figure 2-1. Such jobs operate across several businesses and many cultures—the 150 corporate executive positions at ABB immediately come to mind. It is intriguing, however, to find that this experience of global complexity happens to executives who go to live and work in a single culture other than their own as well as to those who cross more than one culture. Our explanation for this experience leads us to a paradox of global executive development and to a final layer of complexity: the executives themselves.

. . . . .

The Executive Layer of Complexity

. . . . .

We have spent some time describing business and cultural differences that define global work, as if these differences were fixed dimensions. In fact, of course, differences are a function of where one comes from. As our Japanese executive so convincingly pointed out, Japan is very different, but not for the Japanese! What one finds different depends on one's background. As we examine global executive development, we see that "development is in the difference." The differences that add to the complexity of global work are also the differences that make the work such fertile ground for executive development. Remember our executive's description of the difference (for him) in doing business in Germany and Saudi Arabia. Unlike the situation in the typical domestic organization, whether German or Chilean or Japanese, in global organizations people come to a much wider variety of tasks from a very wide variety of backgrounds. The individual, then, becomes an important link in "who is a global executive" and in the challenges he or she faces.

Companies try in various ways to capture "where one comes from." *Home-country national, local national, foreign national,* and *third-country national* are some of the terms we heard. Although global work was defined in terms of crossing borders, *where one comes from* defines the fundamental cultural border for a particular person. One company's home-country national (e.g., a Swede working at Ericsson in Stockholm) may be another company's local national (e.g., a Swede working for IBM in Stockholm) or the same company's third-country national (e.g., a Swede working for IBM in Singapore). Our sample of 101 executives included all these categories and some that defy classification— is a Netherlander with offices in Royal Dutch/Shell's headquarters in both London and The Hague a foreign national when she is in London and a home-country national on the days she is in The Hague?

Expatriate is the term, however, that raises the irreconcilable. Nearly all 101 executives were, or had been, expatriates. But is an expatriate an international executive when doing a domestic job? For example, is a Malaysian expatriate a global executive when working for Unilever in London in a UK domestic marketing job? And if she is a global executive, does her successor, a native of the United Kingdom, become a domestic rather than a global executive? We won't attempt to answer that!

Increasingly, some executives claim no home country, and likewise, some companies are identified only tenuously with a particular country. Brian, whose development we describe in the next chapter, was born and reared in Africa by his British parents (who now live in the United States). He attended school in the United Kingdom (but never worked there) and has retired to France with his Japanese wife. As for companies, ABB, we were told, was designed more as an American than a Swiss company. Moreover, former CEO Percy Barnevik asserts that ABB has no geographic center, with only 150 professionals working in its headquarters in Zurich, financial results reported in U.S. dollars, and English as its official language of business.[10]

With the layer upon layer of complexity that make up global executive work, and those layers further complicated by the makeup of the executives and the organization, global executive development becomes a complex process indeed. Small wonder that the "secret of global leadership" is yet to be found.

From This Point of View

. . . . .

We have tried in this chapter to build a bridge from expatriates in earlier times to the complexity of global and international work today. We have presented the view of global business as a transnational activity, and we have examined in detail our executives' perspectives on the differences between domestic and international jobs. Global executive work is work that simultaneously crosses borders of business and culture, but the defining cross is culture. Crossing these borders makes global jobs at once more complex, interesting, rewarding, challenging, exhausting, and frustrating. Global (or international) is not an all-or-nothing thing, but a continuum of complexity. Global executives are executives who do global work; being global resides in the work, not solely within the executive. A global mind-set is the set of competencies required to do global work. Difficulties arise in global work because the differences that define global work depend on the makeup of the individual executives. Those seeking the secret of global leadership will,

. . . . .

we contend, be disappointed when these layers of complexity confound their search.

Given the complexity of global jobs and the talents of global executives, our task ahead is to identify the lessons learned along the way that prepare executives for these jobs, to discover where they learned these lessons, and to put it all together in a model that can guide practice. But we want to do that while never losing sight of the individuality of global executives and the richness of the experiences that developed them. In chapter 3 we frame these experiences by describing the backgrounds of our global executive group and by telling the stories of three of these executives.

Global Journeys: The Lives of Global Executives

I took a good deal o' pains with his education,
sir; let him run the streets when he was very
young, and shift for his-self. It's the only way
to make a boy sharp, sir.[1]

—*Charles Dickens,* The Pickwick Papers

In the spring of each year, Unilever's top 300 executives gather at one of the Unilever headquarters, alternately in London and Rotterdam. They come from all corners of the Unilever world, which encompasses most of the continents and many countries. The executives' countries of origin are quite diverse (e.g., India, United Kingdom, Australia, Italy, France, New Zealand, United States, Brazil). Most have traveled here via jet, and limos have met them at the airport and taken them all to the same or similar hotels offering essentially similar services. The men wear suits and silk ties, the women silk dresses. They are engaged in animated conversations, all speaking and listening in English—which may not seem unusual to our readers, but only a minority of the world's population speaks English, either as a first or a second language.[2]

During their days at headquarters, they will eat the same food (although a few will shun meat) off of china dinner plates with silver knives and forks and will drink the same drinks (although a few will avoid alcohol) out of crystal glasses. All are believed to have the "right stuff," that particular combination of lessons learned that makes them effective global executives. All, or at least most of them, have had experiences—*business in global situ*—that produce the global mind-set. An outsider would find it hard not to notice that they, in many ways, are alike in appearance and behavior.

Despite their similarities, these global executives didn't start out that way. All took different life and career journeys to get here. The similarities disguise the differences in their backgrounds, the experiences they have had, the lessons they have learned, and the skills and talents they have developed.

Without denying the importance of genetic endowment in both mental abilities and personality, we say with some confidence that these executives were not *born* global leaders. We doubt that any of their mothers or fathers leaned over the crib and said, "I see here a global leader." Had we tried at that early age to predict how they would develop, our predictions would almost certainly have been widely off the mark. Their lives have been complex tapestries, each different from the other, woven with some combination of purpose and fate. A few among this global executive group may have taken a simple career path and may even have stayed within their home country, but not many at this senior level. Unilever is a complex global company, and the careers of its executives are complex and global, also. These executives know what "difference" feels like, the ambiguity and uncertainty of crossing cultures and taking on new business challenges. They have been in situations in which they learned by going against the grain of their natural bents, and in situations in which their learning was smooth and easy. They have had towering successes, or they wouldn't be here; they have the skills and talents to work in a major global organization. But most have also experienced at one time or another the disappointment of not getting the results expected or the job they hoped for.

The executives we describe are, of course, particular to Unilever, as is the annual meeting. In fact, we have never attended the meeting. Even if we wanted to go, outsiders wouldn't ordinarily be allowed—we were only told about it. Nor do we have special knowledge of the backgrounds and talents of all the Unilever executives who attended. But Unilever is not our point. Our point is that similar gatherings of executives occur in global companies throughout the world. In purpose and time, the meetings are unique to the company and the executives, but the principle of *seemingly similar executives with such diverse journeys* is evident across the various companies and meetings. The simple fact that these executives didn't start out the same or follow the same path to the top has great implications for global executive development. This chapter takes that principle and these diverse journeys to form a background for the essential thesis of this book.

First, we examine where our executives came from: what they said about their early experiences and how those experiences contributed to their development. Then we give more extended excerpts of interviews with three of our study executives (none from Unilever, we might add). We use these extended stories to emphasize the importance of individual experience in understanding global executive development in a way that no list of executive competencies can provide. The stories also illustrate our methodology—lessons of life learned in the crucible of experiences—and they preview our detailed analyses of the lessons and experiences reported in the following chapters. The stories of Andrew, Jean, Brian, and others will serve as touchstones as we discuss what organizations and individuals should do to develop global executive talent.

The Early Experiences
. . . . .

As we planned our interviews, the opportunity to include a question about the early backgrounds of the executives was too tempting for two behavioral researchers to pass up. We settled on this question: "Was there anything special in the way you grew up or in your early life that caused you to seek out or to be especially effective in an international context?" On the one hand, if there were obvious factors that influenced them, we didn't want to miss those. On the other hand, our study was not intended as an in-depth study of background factors, and we didn't want to spend too much interview time on only one aspect of their lives, regardless of how interesting it might be.

Our executives did not disappoint us in their answers. Altogether, the great majority (68 percent) could identify some background factors that had influenced either their choice of an international career or their effectiveness as an international executive or both.

Backgrounds That Lead to International Careers

Half the executives identified *early influences* that they felt resulted in their going into international work in the first place. Sometimes the

. . . . .

family background and situation while growing up seemed almost to assure that the person was "to the international world born."

Hans is a good example. The son of a Russian mother and Swiss father, Hans was born in Beirut, where his father ran his own business. Hans describes his father as a "strange man" who lived and worked in a corrupt country, but was himself never corrupt. He taught Hans a very important lesson: "Be honest in everything you do, and you will succeed in the long run." A discipline problem in school, Hans was sent to Switzerland at age thirteen to live with a schoolmaster and attend school. Hans describes it as an experience of shock and excitement— away from parents but with strong discipline. The tough control that he experienced turned him from the worst to the best student, setting the stage for his studying physics, inventing several devices, and getting a fast start on a career.

Although Hans didn't set out to have an international career, considering his early experiences, his schooling, and his aptitude for physics and invention, it would be hard to imagine him settling down to a domestic job in a domestic company in a small country. As he puts it, "I am an opportunist. My whole career has been a happening; when I saw opportunities, I took them." At age forty-four, Hans's career included assignments in Indonesia, the Philippines, and Japan, as well as Hong Kong, where we interviewed him. Interestingly enough, none of those places has as its native language one of the six languages he speaks: Arabic, French, English, Swiss German, German, and Russian.

Hans's international background may be more extensive than that of some of our executives, and his early influences involved more upheaval than most, but executive after executive identified influences in their early lives that directed them toward international work. Here is a sampling of what they said:

- "My dad was an engineer, and we lived in Australia from age three to six. The international world was part of the scenery. I got my Ph.D. in Australia. . . . I like being in other cultures; I have always liked traveling" (a Brit in Paris).

- "My father was a government manager, and he moved us around; we moved three times in my twelve years in school. That exposed us to very different parts of the country, with different languages. In high school I was selected to be a foreign student in the U.S. for a year. I came away with the confidence that I could succeed anywhere" (a Filipino in Shanghai).

- "My family in Finland was very important. Dad was a psychology teacher, but he made sure we had science training. He promoted the idea of learning languages and going outside of Finland" (a Finn in Zurich).

- "My father was a physicist with international contacts; my mother had lived in London and encouraged me to study English" (a Hollander back home in Holland).

- "My mother was Swiss and my father was Swedish, although he was born in South Africa. As a family we came to Switzerland regularly. I didn't feel special, although my background was remarkable . . . born in East Africa, raised in South Africa, my father an engineer building bridges" (a Tanzanian in Zurich).

- "My parents were highly influenced by education; they believed that things worked better abroad and they valued going abroad. It was put into my head that it was a good idea to go and see. And our business gurus had been overseas, so I wanted to do that. Another thing is that all my teachers had been abroad and encouraged us to do that" (an Indian in Singapore).

- "I was born in a small city and moved to Stockholm and always liked where I lived, but my mother married a man who worked for the UN and had lived outside Sweden for twenty-five years. I visited them a lot. The more important thing was that I was taught by my mother, who teaches religion at the university, to respect other cultures and religions" (a Swede in Singapore).

- "My father was born in Scotland and spoke with a Scottish accent and was very acceptant of other people. My family had six brothers and a sister, and we always had a 'live-in' from outside the U.S. to help with the kids. We would go to church on Sunday with someone who wore a sari. . . . It made me tolerant" (an American back in the United States).

- "My schooling was important; it was all in Turkey. I attended boarding school from age eleven in an American school where everything except Turkish history and language were taught in English. Being away from home, [I found that] those closest to me were in school, not my family" (a Turk in Holland).

- "My father and his buddies would wake me up singing in Swedish; my mother was born in the Philippines. Growing up thinking in that way, I grew up with an 'aura of international,' if you will" (a Swedish Canadian in the United States).

- "We moved around a lot in India. Fourteen languages were spoken there, and they were always easy for me. My parents exposed me to international culture at an early age. My father was in the diplomatic service and moved around a lot, and I have moved a lot also" (an Indian in Jakarta).

- "I lived in China, Hong Kong, and Canada while I was growing up. That prepared me to deal with different cultures" (a Chinese Canadian in Hong Kong).

- "I had an uncle who was a legend in the family who worked for the company. He worked outside Sweden and he inspired me to have an international career" (a Swede in Jakarta).

- "Ireland is a culture you leave; it was not a big thing. Moving is what you have to do to survive in life. You don't think about it in the same way that other countries do; everyone has cousins in weird and wonderful places" (an Irishman in Belgium).

- "Growing up in two cultures (my parents were French but we lived in Morocco) prepared me. It was not just a foreign land, but a small country—you cannot confine yourself to a single country when you live in a small country. I was in school with people from all over the world. Living in Morocco, I was always meeting different types of people" (a French Moroccan in the United States).

These responses illustrate the range of factors that executives listed as important: parents, uncles, and grandparents; travel; schooling; and an emigrant or small-country culture. One comes away convinced that "history is destiny," that there are identifiable background factors that determine an executive's interest in international work, and these types of factors appear around the world—our executives experienced them growing up in Africa, Australia, Asia, the United States, Sweden, England, Ireland, wherever. Such illustrations lead one to the inescapable conclusion that early influences may well be the primary determinants of global careers. Primary determinants, that is, for one half of our executives. The other half of our executives *could not* identify early influences that propelled them into international careers. Their responses, too, are persuasive; these executives are convincing in the ordinariness of their backgrounds, convincing in the lack of predetermination of their international careers. And they too came from all corners of the world:

- "There was nothing special. My dad was a civil servant, and I was not exposed to international life. I just rolled into this" (a Dutchman in London).

- "I'd be the last person you'd expect to have an international career. I grew up on a farm in Indiana. But I always wanted to see some different things" (an American in Hong Kong).

- "Nothing really relevant. I had an ordinary background, worked on a farm before I went to the university. I had no idea what a multinational company was before I went" (a Brit in Holland).

- "Nothing special. I came from a traditional working family, Dad an electrician, Mom a hospital worker; we didn't go anywhere" (a Swede in Zurich).

- "No, I think it came later. When I was young if anyone had said, 'You'll see the world one day,' I wouldn't have believed them" (a Swede back in Sweden).

- "There was nothing special about my family or childhood. I was interested in cars. I went on my first international assignment because my company ordered me to" (a Japanese in the United States).

- "I always wanted to be a senior manager, but not necessarily an international manager. I went to an international job because it was the only way I could get to the level I wanted, a country manager job" (an Australian in Tokyo).

- "I grew up in Paris, Texas, where my grandfather ran a department store; there was nothing special. This Asian job was thrust on me. . . . They needed someone who could survive" (an American in Hong Kong).

- "I came from a normal, middle-class family in Mexico. There was nothing special, except maybe that I did attend bilingual schools" (a Mexican in Argentina).

- "I don't think so. I'm from a large family, three sisters and one brother. I never left it to go anywhere. My mother is a nurse in a local hospital. I was not exposed to foreigners, but I was exposed to people in general" (a Brit in Paris).

- "My dad was a policeman and my mom a housewife. We had a very strong family with great respect for education. My parents were horrified when I went to Brazil. . . . But I think my mother was really quite proud of her daughter" (an Australian in Jakarta).

- "There was nothing special in my upbringing. I was in the middle of five brothers and sisters. When I was sent to training in Sweden, I had never been abroad" (a Brazilian Italian in Brazil).

- "No, I grew up in East Sarawak. I was always just planning to finish secondary school, but they offered me a scholarship based on my test scores" (an Indonesian back in Indonesia).

- "Nothing special. My father was a steelworker in Kansas City, Missouri. Neither parent had a high school education. But my father was insistent that we go to college, and my mother was a voracious reader. I took my first international job because it was a challenge" (an American in Jakarta).

- "There was nothing special in the way I grew up. I grew up in a small country and it makes you cautious. It instills caution in your mother's milk; it inhibits your thinking. My family is the reverse of me. My father and mother have never left Switzerland, and I have two brothers who live within fifty miles of where we were born" (a Swiss in the United States).

So much for our conclusion that international careers are deter-mined by identifiable early influences. The quotations supporting this conclusion are equally as convincing as those supporting the opposite, and we see similar experiences (or lack of them) from around the world.

There are, of course, methodological problems with both sets of answers. Searching one's background for causes suffers from twenty-twenty hindsight; seldom is life so random that careful scrutiny won't find *some* causes—after the fact. That answer bias, however, adds weight to the fact that half our executives could *not* identify background causes that led them to international careers.

As we saw in the quotations, some executives sought or took inter-national positions not because of a particular interest in international, but because the jobs offered rewards not available at home—rewards such as more responsibility, better pay, increased country-level respon-sibility, a stepping stone to broader corporate responsibility, or a posi-tion at headquarters. Several who might not be able to identify specific early influences told us that they headed out because their small coun-tries (Ireland, Uruguay, Canada, Holland, and Switzerland were men-tioned) did not offer enough opportunity.

A few simply stated that they had always had personal characteris-tics and interests that drew them to international careers. These char-acteristics included a need for variety and change ("I have always hated habits") and interests such as travel, foreign countries, other cultures, history, and languages. These responses, in which an executive claimed to be "always like that" with no apparent reason, raise the age-old lead-ership question of whether they were born or made.

Is there a "global gene" that underlies an interest in being an inter-national executive? As the executive who grew up on a farm in Indiana said, "It is more your personality than your early experience." Increas-ingly, psychologists are recognizing that the different dispositions we see in people, both as adults and as children, may indeed have genetic roots. When executives say, "I have always been interested in travel," or "I have always wanted to see the world," it is difficult not to believe that such an adventurous spirit may have some basic roots. More intriguing perhaps is when only *one* of a family goes out. For example, the U.S. executive whose Scottish father and international childcare providers made his international career seem quite natural pointed out that he was the *only* one of eight children to move out of Chicago. Was that interest born or made? We don't know and will never know. But we do know that, whether born or made, some people's interests and predisposition to an international career began early.

Backgrounds That Contributed to Global Effectiveness

About half (52 percent) of our executives, whether or not they could identify background forces that led them to international careers, could identify background influences that made them *effective* in international work. These influences resulted in personal attributes that read like the list of competencies presented in chapter 2: being open to experience; flexibility; being comfortable with moving; being open to other cultures; an honest, direct style; interest in other people; and eagerness to learn languages. These qualities bear on the question of whether the elements of the global mind-set can indeed develop without leaving home. Here are some illustrations from the interviews:

- "Growing up in a tiny village of one thousand people in Scotland prepared me in a strange way for my work overseas, like in Borneo. In the village, I knew everyone and saw all kinds of people and knew all the things that went on and I learned to relate to all kinds of people. It helped me to understand that people are all different and do all kinds of strange things" (a Scottish executive in London).

- "My father's character was a background factor. He was continuously inquisitive and open-minded to the world. He wanted to learn about the world, would try new things years before anyone else. He was the only one of twelve children who was curious and interested, and he was also the most successful. I have always loved new things. It is part of my basic character" (a Scottish executive in Beijing).

- "My parents left Morocco when the Arabs took over and wanted the French out. We lost everything. As a result of that, I have lots of drive. I always wanted to succeed because of the rough life" (a French Moroccan in Zurich).

- "I was an only child and got lots of attention. My father made a special effort to communicate bad news without being afraid of it. He taught me not to hide bad news, to be open about mistakes, to be honest and get hissed at, and go on. Or, to hide it and go to bed without dinner. That has been an important lesson" (an Ecuadorian in Germany).

- "Growing up in India prepared me for flexibility for myself and my family" (an Indian in Bangkok).

- "It could be that growing up in Hong Kong was important. It has always been a very open, international metropolis, and being born there, educated there, and working there provided me with very good exposure to the outside world. That has helped me a lot in adapting to my international assignments" (a Hong Kong Chinese back in Hong Kong).

- "As a kid I moved eleven times in thirteen years—my father worked for AT&T. I was used to moving around and adapting, so moving was not a foreign concept at all. My wife lived in one place all her life, and she has had a difficult time adapting" (an American in Paris).

- "I grew up in the French colony in Brazil. My parents were divorced when I was ten, and I have basically been on my own since then. They were always direct, open, and clear. I had to negotiate with each parent, make my own decisions. By the time I was twenty-one, I was on my own, earning my own money" (a French Brazilian in São Paulo).

- "My father ran a poultry farm and had eight children. He trained us to aim for the best, no matter what, always striving to do better. He made sure we went to school on a staggered basis so the kids would help run the farm. . . . All of us learned to combine activities. At the end of the day, he did the bookkeeping and I learned from that" (a Filipino in London).

- "I went to seven different schools, and I grew up in a multicultural environment in South Africa. My parents were unbiased in a highly biased society. I knew that I would have to learn to survive as an outsider, no matter where I went" (an Irish South African in London).

. . . . .

- "My wife would say I had a tough childhood. My parents were divorced when I was age thirteen, and I was brought up by my stepmom. She was tough. She was *really* tough. My mom was in a mental institution in my teens and died. I learned a toughness and fortitude from that" (a Brit back in London).

- "I am Flemish and grew up in a border community; it makes you very adaptable. My mother is Dutch, my wife is Dutch, my father is Belgian; I have no strong national feeling" (a Belgian in Germany).

- "My mother was a Christian and my father was a Buddhist; I was surrounded by diversity at all times, at home, and in religion" (a Singaporean in Beijing).

In these stories we not only see what the early influences were, but also get another glimpse at what executives believe is important for success in international work—whatever their origin!

So What of the Backgrounds?

Our analysis of these two sets of responses, one focusing on factors that get executives *into* global careers, one on factors that contribute to effective functioning *once there,* produced nearly fifty-fifty splits in each case—half could identify factors, half couldn't. About a third of our executives could identify *neither* factor in their backgrounds. And, when factors were identified, as our quotations so vividly show, only at the most general level are these common factors. We thus conclude that no single set of background and early experiences, no single background pattern, leads to a global career. Careers are not built on common foundations that lead to linear progressions of planned and predictable events, even within a single organization.

Our results offer no support for those who would design rigid selection systems based on early background or personal characteristics. Such a system would end up screening out half of the successful executives. On the other hand, as our continuing discussion will show, neither can we afford to ignore the natural flow of people's lives that leads them to global careers. Some candidates will arrive on organizations' thresholds with backgrounds that give them a head start on developing a global mind-set, but nearly as many will arrive without it. The stories of Andrew, Jean, and Brian in the following sections show that even backgrounds that would seem to prepare a person for cross-cultural transitions may not be enough. Few are exempt, we argue, from the impact of crossing the borders of business and culture—in fact, that certainty is what makes cross-border experiences such rich developmental soil.

At the same time, we observed striking similarities among the individual cases from around the world. Although the influences that shaped them were as unique as the human condition, there were common *themes* as likely to occur in Hong Kong or Singapore as in Sweden or England. A Singaporean attributed his comfort with other cultures to a Buddhist father and a Christian mother and a next-door neighbor who took him to Sunday school. An American in Chicago attributed his comfort level to a Scottish father and a live-in maid who would accompany the family to Mass in a sari. An Indian was accustomed to moving because his family had moved around India, whereas an American learned that moving was OK when his family moved around the United States fourteen times when he was growing up. The similarity of the underlying dynamics strongly suggests that these dynamics are not limited to one culture or geographical area.

Three Stories: Andrew, Jean, and Brian
. . . . .

To a greater extent than we realized when we started, global executive development is best understood through the stories of the executives themselves. We have selected three stories to highlight some central concepts and assumptions, to illustrate the complexity of global careers, and to provide examples of our methodology.

Our stories suggest a number of questions, assumptions, and conclusions about global executive development. As you read the stories, consider how the experiences of these executives may address the following questions:

- Are global executives born or made? Or both?
- What kinds of experience does it take to change the tools of thinking—the concepts, attitudes, schemas?
- How important is selection for global executives? Is development enough?
- When do executives learn, in easy times or hard?
- Do all executives learn in the same ways, or do they have styles of their own, some learning from some types of situations, some from others, and a few from all?
- Can learning be scheduled and forced, or is it unpredictable?
- Can executives be developed quickly, or does it take a long time?
- How important is crossing borders of culture? Is it really necessary?
- Should executive development be as individual as a career, or can it be done pretty much the same for everyone?
- Whose fault is it when talented global executives derail? Do we ever know? What can be done to prevent it?
- Is there, after all, a secret to global leadership?

Our first two stories are about Andrew and Jean. We first noticed them because of their superficial similarities: Both had the same name (neither Andrew nor Jean); were forty years old; were engineers with M.B.A.s; worked for large, multinational companies; spoke excellent English; and—like us—both were wearing dark blue suits and white shirts when interviewed in their offices. When we met them, both Andrew and Jean were expatriates with global responsibilities, and neither considered himself a "to-the-bone" national in the country of his citizenship. Both were at that career stage called *booming,* or "becoming one's own man" (perhaps "becoming one's own person" would be more appropriate today). Each was about to take career-critical next steps. The coincidences were too many to ignore.

As their stories unfolded, however, the emerging tapestries of their lives were quite different, clearly woven by different hands, with different designs, and with different thread. At age forty, Andrew and Jean were hardly finished products, and we could not help but look at their development, their careers, and their experiences to date and wonder what the world may yet hold for them.

As much as possible, we tell these stories as we heard them, impressions and all. Like all the quotations used in this book, they are taken from our notes and have been edited and in some places modified to protect confidentiality.

Andrew

It was our first trip on the ferry across the harbor to Kowloon, and we weren't sure what to expect. Those who have taken that trip can picture in their minds our ferry ride and pleasant walk on crowded Hong Kong streets to Andrew's modern office building.

Andrew is the vice president of marketing for a thirty-year-old joint venture between a U.S.-based company and a Japanese manufacturer. Although Andrew has worked with the joint venture for five years, he has been the senior representative for only a year. No one ever told us, but we suspect that in Hong Kong, office size matters. If it does, then Andrew has an important job. His parent company is the U.S. partner of the venture, and he is a Canadian citizen; he is the only non-Japanese in the joint venture. His primary task is to provide a bridge between the *similar* companies yet very *dissimilar* executives who make up the joint venture partners. As we see his career unfold, we can ask, "How does one develop the talents to provide that bridge? Are they born and not made? Or maybe both?"

Andrew was born Chinese in Shanghai, and even though he left China to finish high school in Canada, there is "still a lot of Chinese-ness in me," he says. After high school he studied engineering in Canada, obtaining both a bachelor's and a master's degree. He used those years to broaden his experience: "I got to know people there. I could have chosen to stay among the Asians, but I chose to get out and meet others. I had a balanced group of associates, although I leaned toward the Chinese." When Andrew went back to graduate school to get an M.B.A., however, the situation was different; he was the only Chinese:

> So I had to have more association with others. It made me very
> much more comfortable with Canadians, and I had more dealings
> with foreigners. I learned to use English as my mother tongue, I got

in touch with Canadian culture as a participant rather than an observer, and I made personal friends. Having personal friends transcends cultural biases and gives you cultural sensitivity. It's not just knowing about it, but using your knowledge to understand how they feel.

Andrew's first international assignment, a marketing job with a U.S. company, was a key developmental experience for him. The job offered him a chance to expand his horizons beyond engineering to something more business oriented. His job was to live in Hong Kong while opening up the China market. Even though this company was well known for its strong culture of self-reliance, trust, and respect, Andrew was surprised that they threw him into "the deep end of the pool, to sink or swim." Without giving him much help, they said, "Go do it." The job turned out to be quite a challenge, and one of the lessons he learned was the importance of trust in enabling a person to make good use of his or her capabilities and, in turn, to developing self-confidence.

> This was my first dealing with China, and I learned how very different it is from Hong Kong. I had to learn the language—I knew Mandarin, but they spoke Cantonese. On my first trip to China my boss went along and all we had to get started were some phone numbers for possible customers. When we got there, I began making phone calls, but nobody was answering the phone. What neither my boss nor I realized was that it was during the National Days, and the entire country was closed up. I was very embarrassed; I should have known. I learned the lesson of being prepared.

Andrew also listed among his lessons learned in Hong Kong the importance of cultural sensitivity: "Everyone has biases, but I learned to set aside my biases, to listen, and to go in with an open mind. Hong Kong was my first exposure to dealing with ten different cultures."

A second key experience for Andrew took place after he got his M.B.A. Andrew was back again in Hong Kong. This time he had the opportunity to work in a start-up, a joint venture that included Chinese, British, and Americans, designed to provide satellite TV coverage for all of Asia. The start-up was high profile with grand plans, in part because it was the business "coming-out" of the second generation of a local tycoon.

Andrew only stayed for one very tough year, but he learned several lessons. Again, he grew in self-confidence—he could handle the pressure and do things he had never done before. He learned to hire and trust his judgment of others, to build a staff, and then to supervise his cross-cultural team. And, as he usually does when he looks at what he learned from an assignment, Andrew learned a more abstract lesson of business—the importance of strategy. He learned firsthand that short term is not enough: "Without a vision, a strategic direction, people will ask, Why? That is why I left."

Andrew's current position, the joint venture between the United States and the Japanese companies, was the third developmental experience he told us about. Again, this was a tough challenge—he was given a blank sheet of paper and told to go do it. With only six months, he had to prepare a proposal for approval by the U.S. main board concerning whether to expand the joint venture or do it themselves:

> This was my first experience dealing with the Japanese under a tight time line. I had to get up the learning curve quickly and deliver a product in a condition of very high visibility. And the project was controversial with strong views on both sides. There were lots of cultural issues—I am ethnic Chinese and work for a U.S. company. The key lesson from this is learning to listen, to understand, to put down my biases in order to build a bridge between the Japanese and American styles of management. Japan is culturally as different as you can get, and they can be very difficult to deal with. I had to learn about Japanese and how they operate so that I could play interpreter. This was my first time playing a bridging role between cultures, and this will be a permanent skill.

As we saw in Andrew's previous job, he was also learning more abstract lessons of business:

> One lesson is that any organization has challenges because of how it operates. Our company is very American and Midwestern and it will always be U.S.-based with perhaps some organizations in Asia;

the Japanese company is very similar. Here we had two similar organizations trying to work together, but as different as they appeared, they both, as organizations, had similar challenges.

Andrew learned another lesson that is one of the key lessons of managing internationally:

I learned that there are different ways to skin a cat, to achieve the objective. How you do it back home may not work at all, so you have to find another way. The Americans are very direct and straightforward. To a point, that is good, but not if the other guy is different. That style won't work here—you have to be flexible and try to understand the other person and how to get at his mind and heart.

Moreover, Andrew learned a great deal about dealing specifically with another culture, the Japanese:

It is much subtler. The Japanese are not direct and are concerned about saving face. Protocol is very important; they are more formal. They are polite, but a "yes" is not necessarily a "yes." They hate ambiguity; complicated things should be presented in a linear fashion. They place great importance on commitment and giving their word; they respect seniority, so age differences have to be managed.

When Andrew told us about an executive derailment, the theme was cultural sensitivity:

A highly regarded U.S. executive came to Asia in a senior position dealing with many cultures. He was a typical American—very well qualified and very conscientious; he was very focused on getting the job done and had no hidden agendas. It sounds ideal. His focus should have been a strength, but he was too focused on getting the job done and had an acute lack of cultural sensitivity. To adjust to a different mode, you have to lay down your biases and hear. He couldn't do it. He would say, "I hate dealing with those people," based on past experience, and he let those experiences drag him down. "Oh no, we have to go meet with *them*," he would say. He was very effective in getting his message across, and on the surface he seemed to be getting respect. But the issues around his insensitivity got back to the home office. He failed miserably, was shipped back to the U.S., and has since left the company. Was it totally his fault? Not really. He understood very well how things are done at our home base, and a tour in Asia is just a stepping-stone. He had been very successful, but he had succeeded in a narrow culture so that he was not really prepared for the job.

Andrew is still a young executive, but when asked, he explained how he had changed as a result of these experiences:

> My core qualities have not changed, but there are different ways that have been amplified. I am more open-minded, more willing to set aside issues, to listen, to appreciate others' views, and to try to understand why they are saying what they say—I have greater cultural sensitivity. Having lived in China, Hong Kong, and Canada prepared me to deal with different cultures. And my wide range of experiences has given me more confidence in myself.

Key Elements of Andrew's Story

Andrew's experiences provide not only the basic data for our statistical analysis, but also insights into the development of individual executives. Not surprisingly, one of Andrew's strengths is his sensitivity to operating in other cultures, based on his upbringing in China, Canada, and Hong Kong. But even with his multicultural upbringing, Andrew still had important lessons of cultural sensitivity to learn.

Andrew's story presents a picture of someone who has often been an outsider—an Asian in school in Canada, a Mandarin-speaking Chinese Canadian in Hong Kong working for a U.S. company; the lone non-Japanese employee of a U.S./Japanese joint venture with the task of bridging the partners. The challenging, tough assignments that (at least in his eyes) he handled largely alone taught him lessons of self-confidence. Andrew seems to be a keen observer of other people, as evidenced by his listening and openness and by his detailed description of a derailed executive. He is also a keen observer of business situations that he draws lessons from. Although highly talented in his culture-bridging role, Andrew has not yet had experience running a business or in a major operating job. In fact, his cross-cultural expertise is so highly valued in the world of today and tomorrow that he risks being given that assignment again and again, rather than getting assignments that teach additional lessons of business and leadership.

We miss in Andrew's story any mention of teachers who took him under their wing. When asked whom he had learned the most from, he answered that no one person stood out. For that, we turn to Jean. It is difficult to describe Jean without referring back to Andrew, but as we tell the story we will try to leave those references to the reader—at least for now.

Jean

We did not have to look far that cold winter day in suburban Boston to know that we were a long way from Hong Kong. But if office size makes a difference in Boston as it seemed to in Hong Kong, then we were about to interview another executive with an important job.

Jean's office is in the corporate headquarters of a large and respected information technology company. As a marketing vice president with global responsibilities, his job is matrixed in several ways as the company is moving from a U.S. corporate structure to a truly global one. We always find it difficult to understand the scope of these jobs—Jean has 50 people "on his team " and 500 dedicated people in business units. He shares 1,000 salespeople and $15 billion in revenue with the vice president of sales. The details of his current job, however, are less important for our purposes than how he got there.

Jean was born in France, but he points out that his parents were not French—his father was from Tunisia and came to France at age twenty; his mother was born in France but of Hungarian parents. His parents wanted the children to assimilate "and we did—I *feel* French—but nothing French is in our genes." In addition to speaking French, he adds, "I understand Spanish fully; growing up we had a Spanish nanny." Jean's English is excellent with a touch of a French accent, which most Americans would find charming.

After engineering school in Paris, Jean worked as an engineer for a year with a consulting firm while getting an M.B.A. He then joined his current company as a sales engineer. Jean interpreted our key-events questions to mean milestones in his career, and for our interview he was prepared to talk about five of these milestones, all of which, he pointed out, involved working closely with strong personalities. His first milestone took place early in his job as a sales engineer:

> After about a year, they assigned me to a very big French customer. Although it was a huge French company, we had never had much success with them, so it was a small account. Soon the customer changed CIOs [chief information officers] and put in place a very demanding, tough IT [information technology] executive. Within a few months, he and I had built a great business relationship—our share of the business increased tremendously.
>
> It was very exciting. I was young, and I was driving the business. This tough CIO relied on me, had a lot of confidence in me—I helped him become successful, and he was very committed to my career. He wanted me to be the next GM [general manager] for France, and he became sure I would. We were so successful that, when it came time for me to transfer, he managed to have me stay, replacing my boss. I worked directly with him for four years, and I still keep in touch.
>
> I learned a lot from him. I learned the importance of technical skills, of knowing what you are talking about, of deep analytical work, and of an in-depth understanding of what you tell the customer. Often you tell the customer as much as you know, but he was always checking to make sure that I knew what I was talking about.

Jean's next key experience was his job as executive assistant to the general manager in France. He described several types of learning both from the *person* he worked for and *where* the job was. The job provided an overview of the business that Jean had not seen before: "This was a very different job; it enabled me to see how the company worked at that level." But most of Jean's lessons came from the general manager himself:

> He was an incredible executive, very bright, but with terrible people skills. He was unbelievably fast, always very well prepared, but still he did not work night and day—only from 8:30 in the morning till 10:30 at night, and never on weekends. He could switch from one

project to another instantaneously. I saw what skills an executive at
that level should have, and he set the standard for me in many
areas. The amount of work he would put into a speech or presentation was remarkable; I had no idea. I saw the work behind the stage
presentation. He taught me how to communicate.

The second thing I learned from him was fast decision making
and moving on to other things. And the third thing was how to
organize your life so that you don't have to work all the time—this
is related to being able to work fast, and the ability to move quickly
from one thing to another.

Jean's third "event" was unique among the 332 events that we collected. Although several executives mentioned their spouses as critical
in their careers, Jean was the only one to list the spouse as a key event:

My third event is my wife. She is unique, exceptional, completely
different from me, and she brings a completely different perspective
on everything. I don't look to her for advice, but at critical times in
my career she has always given excellent advice. She is faster moving than I, less conservative, always pushing to try new things. From
her I learned that I need to see things in a larger context, to look
beyond what is, to have a larger vision.

A small software subsidiary provided Jean's first international
assignment, not as an expatriate, but a job he could do while traveling
out of Paris. Although he was advised not to take the job—general
manager of a small French company, a subsidiary scattered across
twelve countries—Jean decided to take it because it was "real operating experience in a totally new business, and an opportunity to be in
international." When the subsidiary was originally formed, the owner
had bought the twelve companies and left them intact with their owners in place; those owners were not eager to have an "alien" come in.
The job turned out to be even more exciting than Jean had thought,
and in retrospect, he considers it his most important developmental
experience:

It was a great culture shock when I went there—different people,
different culture, different business; it was very small and French,

rather than large and American like my company. It was as different as night and day from what I was used to. The biggest surprise was seeing our large company from the outside. And the biggest challenge was getting acceptance from these entrepreneurs and getting them working with us, without giving up their own cultures.

Clearly Jean's success would ride on getting these older businessmen, all from different countries, all now with their own money and a great deal of business sense, to work with him and the parent company. We asked him how he did that. As he answered us, it was clear that Jean had a lot of respect for these twelve executives—probably no small part of why he was able to build relationships with them.

I loved working with them. I spent a lot of time with them and listened a lot. I fought their battle in trying to keep us separate. I still have relationships with them, and I call them with questions about business investments because I know they are in touch with the real world.

This was probably my most important key event. I learned to manage a company, to make decisions, to hire and fire. This was the first time I had P&L [profit and loss] responsibility. At the parent company, nothing was real; I was closing deals, not running a business. And in my mind this was international, and I enjoyed the travel and the people. I was amazed by the differences among people in different cultures when there seemed no logical reason for the differences.

I am not sure what prepared me for this. I tried not to be arrogant, I tried to listen, I asked people. I was not so specialized as most of our people, with more business skills. I have good business sense—you either have that or you don't, you get it from your parents—my mother is very successful in a large company, and my father has run several companies.

Exciting and enjoyable as it was, this assignment we suspect may have nearly derailed Jean. He turned out to like the job *too* much; as he continued to fight to keep this company from being absorbed by the parent, Jean couldn't understand why nobody in Paris paid much attention. Finally, when he called his boss's boss seeking help, he was told that the subsidiary was not a part of the larger strategy. Higher up, they intended to kill the company. Although Jean realized that he had missed the big picture, he still felt more a part of the subsidiary than the parent. Should he stay or go back to the parent? This was one of those times when his wife's advice was helpful, and Jean went back to a promotion at the parent. Although he had been successful in the assignment, Jean must have come close to testing the patience of corporate.

Jean's final developmental event was his move to Boston. He took the job to get experience overseas and at headquarters. He got both in ways he didn't quite expect. Our guess would be that once again, Jean very nearly derailed. Well traveled in the international world, Jean did not anticipate any problem in moving to Boston. In fact, he anticipated so few problems that he left his office on Friday in Paris, moved into a home in Newton over the weekend, and went to his new office in suburban Boston on Monday expecting business as usual. It didn't quite work out that way:

> I arrived and had a terrible beginning. I got no advice from anyone, either in France or in the U.S., and we did all the stupid things people do. I took no time to get my life in order or to adapt. I had seriously underestimated the impact of the changes—it was not just moving from one city to another. I was amazed at all the changes outside of work, things like shopping, finding schools, talking to people about schools, et cetera.

And things did not quite work out as Jean expected at work, either:

> I felt under a great deal of pressure because this promotion was a great opportunity to succeed in a very visible role in the U.S. I was in a new and very difficult job in a matrixed world—it was the first job in the company without direct power or operating authority. Many people did not want to move to the new concept, and still don't. And I did not realize how things worked in an office in the U.S.—it is another world and I never thought about that. For example, people would not be in their offices and it took me a month to learn that they were working at home. I didn't know—that doesn't happen in Europe.

Without realizing it, Jean had become ill—he felt bad, but didn't know why. He described a vicious cycle of feeling bad, getting bad results at work, feeling worse, getting worse results. It took him a month to accept going to a doctor, and months longer to find out that he had an unusual virus. Finally, he had to take two months off to get rid of the virus. "This was a big experience for me personally, and I grew a lot from it. Most important was perspective about what is really important in the world. But I also learned a lot about how to be an expatriate, and the mistakes I had made in simply assuming that nothing would be different."

Picking up from ground zero when he returned to the office, Jean began to partner with a peer executive whom he now identifies as the person from whom he had learned the most about international management:

> He was nearly a dozen years older than I and he decided to coach me. We started taking trips together, and he shared everything. He taught me how to work in the U.S.; he was a kind of sponsor who introduced me to a lot of our business partners whom I could not have gotten to know. I learned about people and about business. He had the ability to criticize positively—a rarity in American executives, they are always positive but have seldom thought things through. He taught me the importance of pushing people to talk, to over-dialogue in order to understand. The second learning was the power of teamwork—we worked together and built a strong team across the organization. I saw the importance of other people who had different strengths than you. I learned that by talking and listening you can always build a team. You must put yourself in the other person's shoes, then you can understand and build a team.

Despite his shaky start, Jean is a strong advocate of being an expatriate:

> You can learn twice as much when you go outside your country and live. I value much more my experience here as an expatriate than the experience when I was traveling to other countries. It builds your own personal strengths, and you learn that people are different. You can see those differences, but you can't understand them if

you don't live there. It is an emotional rather than an intellectual understanding, the difference between reading about it and living it. Your book needs to spend some time explaining the key value in doing this.

As we closed the interview, Jean began to engage us about his next steps:

Soon I will have three choices: to stay in the U.S., to go back to Europe and leverage that, or to go to another country. What should I do? Will I learn something in addition to what we have already learned? Every executive will answer this differently, but what are the elements that should guide the decision?

Key Elements of Jean's Story

One thing that stands out in Jean's career is his remarkable ability to relate to and learn from other people. Looking back, we see that his teachers include a customer, a boss, a peer, some subordinates, and his spouse. It is difficult to think of an available source that Jean didn't learn from. And looking at the lessons learned, he has clearly capitalized on the learning opportunities presented. How can we explain this? Did those opportunities come along through luck, or is there something about Jean that attracts the magical friends of the hero's journey?

Despite his wealth of experience and learning, Jean does not seem nearly ready to quit learning—he is already looking for his next experience. Perhaps it is Jean's passion for his job or his talent at describing his adventures, but he often seems to flirt closely with the edge. What's more, how could someone with so international a background, both in family and at work, be so surprised at the shock of crossing cultures? Has anything taught him the big-picture thinking that he admittedly admires in his wife? And can someone who enjoyed running a small business so much resist the temptation to do it again, sooner rather than later?

Before we discuss these questions in detail, we will examine one more story. We include Brian's story, not because of the similarities to Andrew and Jean, but because of the differences.

Brian

Seasoned global executives seem to understand the excitement (and anxiety) of a firsttime visit to Asia. For us, the excitement of our visit to Asia easily overcame the fatigue of the fifteen-hour time difference. Four days of interviewing in Tokyo had exceeded our expectations, both in the richness of the interviews and of the culture. Then we moved on to Beijing, deeper still into the mysterious East. Shell's offer to have a car pick us up at the airport eased our arrival anxiety and allowed us to use the three-hour flight to focus on the task ahead.

Looking over Brian's résumé, we weren't sure what to expect. At age fifty-five, Brian could be nearer the close of his career than the beginning—he might be looking back rather than ahead. We suspected that he would have adventures to relate. Already we had learned that adventure was common on the exploration and production side of the oil business. Apparently, in addition to oil, the business produced executives, sometimes permanent expatriates, who thrived on experiences that to most would seem daunting. The résumé described a British citizen; a UK master's degree in petroleum engineering; assignments in Holland, Norway, Brunei, Sarawak, Oman, Australia, Nigeria (some of these more than once), and, presently, China. But never in the United Kingdom. Brian's title, chairman and CEO of the companies in northeast Asia, was not very revealing, but at least suggested global responsibilities.

The Mercedes that met us at the airport, the China World Hotel where we stayed, and the modern office building where our interviews would take place were a stark contrast to the bicycle-jammed streets that the driver negotiated with no fear. An intriguing thing about interviews halfway around the world is that they are almost never canceled at the last moment, they almost always take place at the appointed hour, and the interviewee is usually well prepared. Brian's interview fit the mold; his experiences did not. When we met Brian, we had two first impressions: He looked older than his fifty-five years, and he had a kind of centeredness that one occasionally finds in people very comfortable with who they are. The demeanor is almost an aura, which we had last seen in a missionary posted in Madagascar.

Brian was born and reared in Nigeria, where his British father and mother ran a tin mine "out in the bush." His father was in fact the person from whom Brian learned the most about international management:

> I saw him handle everything, the community issues, the day-to-day issues. He enjoyed it enormously, and he taught me how to manage people. When I was twelve years old, I got mad at him when I came home from school and saw him being quite rude to someone who had broken a rule. Of course, he was wiser than I—he knew that in that culture they would not respect you unless you showed the force of your intent. He taught me that there is a hard and soft side of getting things done. And I learned a great deal from his friends whose mines I often visited.

Not surprisingly, perhaps, Brian followed in his father's footsteps. The first of the key developmental experiences he told us about took place when he was twenty-four years old, himself now running a tin mine in northern Nigeria. Although Brian learned a business lesson, the most important lesson was one of courage, a lesson that served him well later. To put a complex situation in a nutshell:

> The technical staff mostly came from the south, so eighty percent of our people were southerners. After the political coup, there was great ethnic strife, and the northerners began killing the people from the south. Over two to three weeks, thirty thousand people were killed in the north; I and a friend buried bodies with a bulldozer because nobody else was doing anything. I was in shock and tried to help them. I was one of only a handful of white people there, but I could speak the language and I was running the mine. There was literal mayhem; I had Ibos sleeping on my roof to save them from being killed.

The business lesson Brian learned was to persevere in a crisis—he had a mandate to keep the mine open and he did, albeit "only for half days." But that was not the major lesson.

> One day my fit engineer, Ali, himself a northerner from a nearby part of the mine, showed up in his flowing tribal robes rather than the shorts and flip-flops that we usually wore. I asked him why he

was dressed that way. "There are a hundred layabouts coming to get the southerners, and I am going to stop them. If I get killed, when I meet God I want to be wearing this." That day Ali stood in the road and turned the whole crowd back. This was amazing courage and bravery. That day, I learned to respect people. People are people—that is fundamental. Nothing else matters; your race, et cetera, is irrelevant. I also learned about courage.

Little did Brian know that nearly thirty years later, he would have another key experience back in Nigeria:

> Shortly after I arrived in January 1994, there was a problem. We were producing half the oil in Nigeria, and ours was on land rather than offshore. I had learned over the years to build quick and good relations with the unions and began to do so. Some of my management team opposed me, but I said, "No, I want to know them," and within a few months, I knew both of the unions well.
>
> By June, the president-elect was in jail and one of the ethnic groups was threatening what looked to the government like secession. The unions decided to go on strike to shut us down and to put pressure on the government to install the elected president. They came to me beforehand and asked me to shut down, but I refused and tried to explain to them that it wouldn't work—it would just raise the price of oil. They went on strike, but we continued to produce for some time using expatriates and contractors.
>
> The unions began to break in at night and sabotage the equipment. I got very concerned about safety, not our safety, but that of our striking staff. I was afraid that they might be shot or injured by our security, and I realized that this was just the tip of the iceberg. The real issue was secession. The military government was bound to interfere, and if there was bloodshed, there would be a civil war. I decided to shut down the land-based operations (half of our production). I knew that I would get support from the Shell Center because one of our values is to put people's safety above production, so I informed them of my decision.
>
> Then the head of state called me in. I had met him twice before in the few months since my return to the country, and we had developed a reasonably close relationship, helped by my northern Nigerian

origins and by my knowledge of Hausa, the language of the north. He wanted to know why I shut down production. "Very simple," [I answered him]. "You can't control what will happen, and it will get out of hand if you send the army in. Give me six weeks, and I will negotiate a settlement with the union." He agreed, and with my knowing the people and the unions, I was able to negotiate an end to the strike, and they were back at work. Afterwards, they put the union leaders in jail, but I managed to get our Shell person out following a personal appeal to the head of state.

The learning point is that people must live by their principles. I could very clearly read in our principles what I should do and that I could do it. It taught me complete confidence in my own basic reality, and it all comes back to Ali all those years ago standing in the road—now it was my job to do what he had done so long ago.

Not all of Brian's developmental experiences were quite so dramatic. The next one he told us about occurred when he returned to Malaysia for the third time. He knew the people, so he could focus on the business:

Suddenly I grasped some key things about management. We had the challenge of changing an old company embedded in an old-fashioned society. I learned how to transform a company without destroying the people, how to work with a complicated system. This was a long and complex process, not just one single event.

A key in my doing this was that I had spent nine weeks at MIT [Massachusetts Institute of Technology], where, among other things, I learned about systems thinking. This provided an extremely useful set of tools. We were able to use these tools in the transformation. My wife, who is Japanese, came to some of the classes we put on and floored me when she said, "This is easy stuff; this is the way Asians think."

The key learning point for me was that we must learn and apply new ideas and techniques all the time. Now I always say to people, "Keep learning every day; the day you stop, you will be of little use to me." I tell my son, who is in the U.S., as long as you are adaptable, are willing to keep learning and willing to learn the language, you will be fine. That is what he learned growing up in so many countries and cultures.

Our questions had used up all our time, but another characteristic of interviews in faraway places is that people will often give you more time than allotted. Brian was willing to talk, and we were willing to listen:

> All of my assignments have been international. My first was in Norway, but I have always worked in countries where I am seen as a foreigner. That has some advantages: You are more likely to be taken for what you are than in your home country, and also you get more insight into what is going on—locals will tell an outsider much more than they will tell a local. In fact, I am cautious about leaving a local in place for too long as a managing director. After a while, that person will not be able to tell the truth to other locals.

We then asked Brian what he thinks it takes to succeed as an international executive.

> Assignments vary by country, and what you need will vary, also. In general, you need a sense of adventure. You must be inquisitive and want to learn—you must have this in your blood. You must be flexible and adaptable without giving up your principles. Some people will fit in Africa, or the U.S., or Asia, but not others. In Africa, you must love adversity, not be bothered by chaos; you must not be biased against races, and you must be extremely focused emotionally. You must be open and flexible to enormous inconvenience, and in some places, there are serious issues of safety. If you let that sort of thing get you down on a daily basis, you can't survive.
>
> Asia is different, but it is difficult also because the language is so difficult in China and Japan. You can very easily get cut off from words, and that is quite a shock. Here you cannot be arrogant. Like yin/yang, you must be conscious of your female side and let your sensitivity come through. I tell people when they come here to shut up and listen.
>
> America is different still. There, things are overstated. It is grossly overmechanized, and I do not feel comfortable with that. I was in Houston, and they seemed to have concrete everywhere. Many people are uncomfortable with that unless they are brought up with it.
>
> Learning the language is quite important. It is more important outside of Europe because outside you are a minority if you do not

speak the language, and it limits how much you can understand. I would have been much more efficient in Malaysia and Brunei had I learned the language—I would have if I had known that I would spend ten years there. I studied Chinese for six weeks before I took over the job here. We have a retirement house in France, where I will retire next year in an area where English is not spoken.

We never got around to asking Brian how many languages he spoke, but we can count at least four.

The family is a key with people living outside their home countries. The wife—it is usually a wife—must be a partner and participate with you. If she is over the horizon, psychologically or physically, the executive will be, also. My wife and I are both foreigners. But the trick of adapting is to make where you are your home—both of us do that. I live where I am, otherwise I am homeless. I will commit to a country, and one result of that is that I get lots of concessions because I do.

If the executive has a husband as spouse, that is a very difficult family situation in Asian countries. In these societies, people are simply not accustomed to having a husband at home and it is very unlikely that a second job will be available.

Brian speculated a little about the future and our book:

One issue is that tomorrow's world will be very different from today's. The crucial thing, an adventurous spirit, will still be required. In a world of chaos, you cannot make a plan, but you can have certain characteristics that will help you. The worst thing you could do would be to produce a workbook of what to do and what not to do. It isn't like that. We need a concept, not a set of rules about what to do. Do not tell someone, "Don't fall down the stairs." Tell them to be careful, then let them take that concept and make their own rules. This is the only way you can manage chaos and unexpectedness. And they must be able to get feedback—the early signal that things are changing and to detect the changes among key variables. The worst thing is to have a captain following a compass when the magnetic field has changed—that is the kind of world we are in today.

Key Elements of Brian's Story

One thing that stands out in Brian's interview is the heavy value orientation in his experiences. He projects a clarity of values learned in a cauldron of experience that most executives will not go through. These values guide his perspective on the balance of business, social, and political factors.

Many executives, even those in our study, rooted in their own countries and cultures, might find Brian's "homelessness" unsettling, although it didn't seem to bother him a bit. In fact, he seemed to consider it a positive. These permanent expatriates, who become citizens of the world, who feel at home both anywhere and nowhere, have gone far out on our dimension of crossing borders.

We know that Brian learned the basics of managing people at his father's side, but where did he learn all those other lessons of international experience? He clearly learned both lessons of technique—at MIT, how to use a framework to create transformational change—and maxims for working and living—"keep learning every day." But where did he learn the lessons of working in joint ventures, of negotiation, of relationships with headquarters, of managing scope and scale? And what of the lessons from significant bosses that others in CEO jobs told us about?

Brian's experiences and lessons are quite different from those of Andrew and Jean. Well-prepared as he was, Brian answered all our questions (and then some), but we left shaking our head at the difficulty of capturing these different stories in codes and calculations.

Is the difference in the people? Or the stages of their careers? Both Andrew and Jean are looking ahead to leveraging their experiences into higher-level positions. Brian will leverage his into retirement from Shell and participation in lectures and teaching programs.

Is it their industries? We gained a healthy respect for the importance of working with governments when your only product is a natural resource of another country. Moreover, natural resources such as oil offer a kind of permanence that permits and even promotes a long-term perspective that electronics and consumer products do not. When the product is a major source of the wealth of nations, it is inevitable that executives will face questions of values and the role of the company in that society.

· · · · ·

Brian's key experiences, at least the first two, are so much more dramatic than those of most other executives we interviewed, that we can't help but wonder if the events had disproportionate influence on his development. Are there both positive and negative effects of such fundamental key experiences at such an early age?

Our three interviews serve as the backdrop for our more formal results. The stories of Andrew, Jean, and Brian, only 3 of the 101 who constituted our sample, were selected because of their specific similarities and differences, but they turn out to be surprisingly inclusive. They include elements of all twenty-seven categories of lessons (chapter 4) and all eighteen categories of experiences (chapters 5 and 6) derived from the larger sample. Their stories place these generic lessons and experiences in stark relief. The top five lessons, those listed most frequently—how to run a business; lessons of self-confidence; general lessons of culture; lessons of business strategy; and learning to listen—are all easily identifiable in these three stories. Jean's most important key event taught him to run a business. Andrew learned lessons of self-confidence, business strategy, and the importance of listening. Brian's events included dramatic lessons of perseverance, of respecting others (a culture lesson), and of the importance of listening, as well as additional lessons of dealing with governments and politicians.

In Summary

· · · · ·

A central theme of our book is that the excitement of a global career is some combination of the complex, multifaceted, and unpredictable ways in which global careers evolve, and the complex, multifaceted people who live them. This chapter has tried to capture some of that complexity and uncertainty, as well as some of the excitement.

No single mold fits global executives, their work, the experiences that serve as their teachers, or the lessons they learn. We have emphasized this point through the stories of three executives, Andrew, Jean, and Brian, all quite different, and yet all successful in their own ways. Despite our many hours of executive interviews and the analysis that followed, what stayed in our minds were stories and experiences like these. The stories, by putting a human face on our categories of lessons and experiences, enable people to understand global executive development in a different way.

Executive development, we will show in more detail in the chapters that follow, takes place through experiences that executives, individually, can learn from as they need and as they are ready. Challenge, change, opportunity, and risk are its bywords. Globalization raises the ante, both for organizations and for individuals. It offers combinations and permutations of individuals and experiences not available in "selling a German product to a German customer." It argues for highly individual, tailored development processes that, fortunately, information systems of global companies can make possible. Such processes require that we understand the dynamics of lessons and experiences that grow out of the global context. Those are the concerns of the chapters that follow.

We begin by distilling from the volumes of interview notes the lessons of these executives' experience. We present the lessons first, rather than the experiences, because an organization has a choice. Do you select people who have already learned these lessons, or do you try to design developmental opportunities so that they can get the experiences that will allow them to develop the skills they don't have? Obviously a good plan will incorporate some of both, and at different times and for different people different combinations. But the lessons learned by this group mark a path for the development of global executives.

The Lessons of International Experience

> *Insight,* I believe, refers to that depth of understanding that comes by setting experiences, yours and mine, familiar and exotic, new and old, side by side, learning by letting them speak to one another.
>
> —*Mary Catherine Bateson,*
> Peripheral Visions: Learning along the Way

In the opening chapters we have tried to accomplish two things. First, in chapter 2, we confronted the confusion and complexity inherent in international executive work. Not only are there many kinds of global jobs, but they vary in degree of internationality and exist in a changing world where even the nature of these jobs is shifting. Just as the people we interviewed were unique, so too were the challenges they faced. Despite the uniqueness of the challenges and of the executives themselves, there are important generalities. Clearly there are meaningful differences between executive jobs that involve expatriation, those that entail international responsibilities without expatriation, and those that are primarily or solely domestic. What is needed from a leader varies depending on the situation, as do the kinds of lessons learned from those experiences.

Second, in chapter 3, we presented information and examples of how our executives got into international work, and we provided in some detail the stories of three executives in our sample, Andrew, Jean, and Brian. There is something different in seeing the larger picture of a career—something that analyzing coded data or one or two lines of quotations cannot provide. The reality of our executives' stories is only hinted at by numbers, categories, and generalizations. Each of these people is unique, and if we forget this uniqueness—even though there are some generalities—we lose the deepest of the lessons in this research. That said, this chapter moves away from individual cases and begins to look for generalizations across the sample.

In this chapter, we will review in detail the lessons learned by this group of global executives. We will then enrich the conversation by comparing the lessons of domestic and of international experience, suggesting that they overlap but that the differences make a difference. We will also look at how these lessons relate to research on the early identification of international leaders and to what our executives said they look for when choosing international executives. Triangulating with these sources, we will describe what effective global executives need to learn. We postulate the existence of meta-competencies that make learning possible, and a global mind-set that results from cross-cultural experience.

Some people believe that leaders are born, not made, and the accomplishments and sometimes colorful lives of the people we interviewed might seem to support that perspective. However, to believe that their talents were all in their genes or even in their upbringing is to belittle the accomplishments of their lives. These people *learned* to lead, and they learned through effort and sacrifice. Whatever natural gifts they brought to the scene, those gifts weren't enough. Like the executives who will follow them, they had to *learn* how to operate effectively in an international context. The "what" that they learned are the lessons of international experience, and these lessons paint one portrait of the modern global executive. However, we do not present the lessons as *the* definitive set that any global executive must have. As chapter 2 shows, every global job is different, requires a different mix of talent, and teaches different lessons.

The Lessons of International Experience

In the interviews, we asked each of the executives to tell us about at least three experiences that had shaped them as international executives and what they had learned from those experiences. The result was nearly a thousand lessons. Our research team of four independent coders argued to agreement on two points: (a) the definitions of twenty-seven categories into which the lessons would be sorted, and (b) the placement of every one of the 952 lessons into those categories. Appendix B describes the process we used. To the extent that executives say they learned these lessons, then global executives are made and not born, by their own admission.

Six broad themes emerged from this analysis (see box 4-1). We discuss here the lesson themes and the individual lessons within each.

Lesson Theme: Learning to Deal with Cultural Issues and Different Cultures

Learning to deal with cultural issues and different cultures involves the following three specific lessons:

1. Learning to speak a foreign language
2. Learning about specific foreign cultures and contrasts between specific cultures
3. Learning generic lessons about living and working in foreign cultures

It is not much of a stretch to suggest that the foundation for international success begins with understanding the cultures where one works. As Craig Storti observed, "So long as we are put off by or consistently misconstrue the behavior of the locals and so long as we repeatedly provoke or baffle the locals by our own behavior, we can never expect to feel at ease abroad or to be wholly effective in our work."[1] Understanding cultures, from these executives' perspectives, involved three kinds of lessons. One can almost see these as a progression from the most specific (fluency in a particular language), to a deeper understanding of a particular culture or cultures, to lessons about how to manage in any culture or across multiple cultures (where, incidentally, even the multilingual cannot speak enough languages to converse in all the native tongues involved). These cultural lessons are so important that we will examine them in some detail.

Box 4-1   The Themes and Lessons of International Experience

Learning to Deal with Cultural Issues and Different Cultures
1. Learning to speak a foreign language
2. Learning about specific foreign cultures and contrasts between specific cultures
3. Learning generic lessons about living and working in foreign cultures

Learning to Run a Business—Strategy, Structure, Processes;
Global versus Local; Specialized Knowledge
1. Learning strategies for doing business
2. Learning the specifics of running a business

Learning to Lead and Manage Others—Selection, Development, Motivation,
Team Building, Deselection
1. Learning how to establish credibility
2. Learning to select the right people
3. Learning to build and sustain an effective team
4. Learning to make tough calls about people
5. Learning to stay focused—keeping it simple, setting clear goals
6. Learning to keep people motivated and committed, what to delegate and what not to delegate
7. Learning to develop people and the importance of developing people

Learning to Deal with Problematic Relationships—Headquarters, Bosses,
Unions, Government, Media, Politics
1. Learning to handle immediate bosses and other superiors
2. Learning to manage the interface with headquarters and the larger organization
3. Learning to handle public appearances and the media
4. Learning to deal with governments and (external) politicians
5. Learning to deal with unions and other types of negotiations
6. Learning about internal politics

Learning about the Personal Qualities Required of a Leader
1. Learning to listen carefully, to ask questions, and to see the world through other people's eyes
2. Learning to be open, genuine, honest, fair; to treat other people with respect; and to trust others
3. Learning to be flexible, to adapt to changing situations, to take changing circumstances into account, to manage multiple priorities and complex relationships, and to think on your feet
4. Learning to assess risks and take them, and to act in the face of uncertainty

5. Learning to persevere, to act with discipline, and to stay calm under tough circumstances
6. Learning to be optimistic, to believe in oneself, to trust one's instincts, to take a stand for what one believes is right, and to accept responsibility for the consequences of one's actions

Learning about Self and Career
1. Learning about likes, dislikes, strengths, weaknesses, and preferences
2. Learning what support you need from family or others, and how to manage the family under the pressure of foreign work
3. Learning to manage your own career and development

Whether an international executive needs to speak the local language is a much-debated question for which there is no obvious answer. This is good news and bad news. The good news, for those fortunate enough to speak English, is that English has become the universal language of business. English-speaking people can get by in business situations, if not always optimally, almost anywhere they go, even if they don't know the local language. The bad news is for everyone else: Non–English speakers must learn to speak fluent English if they are to become effective global executives. The lessons of language are, however, more complicated than that.

There are times when it is very important to know a foreign language and times when it is not so critical, and knowing the difference is a significant learning—especially since those who cannot speak the local language frequently are unaware of what they are missing. One executive told us, for example, that "because they spoke English I assumed I knew what they meant" (he didn't). Another discovered that "not speaking a language puts you at a disadvantage" because you can't understand what everyone is talking about. Learning to work in the local language is evidently very important when one's subordinates or major customers speak it and all parties are not equally fluent in English, or when understanding others requires understanding the nuances of their expression (it is a distinct disadvantage in negotiations, for example, to be at the mercy of translators).

The case for knowing the local language was made by one executive who noticed a "step change" in communication with his people when he addressed them in their own language. Another found that "speaking the language enables you to integrate into the society and people accept you more. It makes it much easier to be one of them, and it allows them to raise things with you that they would not be able to get out otherwise." Yet another veteran expatriate pointed out that "if you rely on English, you will be surrounded by people who speak English. You will keep the same circle of people. This will hurt the integration process." Brian told us in chapter 3 that Asia can be particularly difficult if one doesn't speak the language "because the language is so difficult, . . . you can very easily get cut off from words, and that is quite a shock."

When an executive's responsibilities cross multiple cultures and languages, it isn't always possible to be fluent in all of them. As one multilingual executive said when asked about the importance of learning the language, "What language would you suggest I learn? I have subordinates in China, Hong Kong, Vietnam, Korea, Japan, and Jakarta." While not speaking the local language can be a disadvantage, it is not necessarily disabling and can sometimes be used to advantage. If one does not know the language but is willing to try to learn some of it, that effort can earn a great deal of respect from the local people. Not knowing the language, or not knowing it well, also "lets you ask dumb questions."

The truly disabling aspect of not knowing the local language is failing to recognize the limitations created by not being able to communicate, and therefore not ameliorating the potential problems. The situation worsens if an executive does not even try to pick up some of the language—which is perceived by the local people as arrogance.

This was brought up most pointedly as one of us rode the elevator up to an executive's office to conduct an interview. The executive was a U.S. expatriate, newly arrived in the country. The interviewer, being escorted by the man's secretary (who spoke English fluently), was curious about the person he was about to meet. He asked her casually how well the new executive was doing at learning the language. Her response told all, as her expression grew cold and she said, "He doesn't even try." Subsequently in the interview that same executive proceeded to explain why knowing the local language was not important.

Although speaking the language certainly helps, it doesn't by itself guarantee that a culture is understood. Many lessons that the executives learned were about the specific cultures in which they found themselves, and they were often lessons of contrast with the home cultures of the executives. Sometimes stark cultural differences were expected but their reality was still a shock, for example, when Western Europeans worked for the first time in parts of Africa, or when Asians found themselves transplanted to Western Europe or the United States. At other times the executives did not expect stark contrasts, and the differences came as a surprise. Jean's experience of moving from Paris to Boston, described in chapter 3, provides a vivid example of that surprise when he expected—mistakenly, it turned out—that things would be essentially the same in Boston as in Paris.

As we reviewed the interviews, it became clear that most academic models of cultural differences are too general to capture the experience of an executive going into a different culture. Such classic distinctions as "power distance" (acceptance of hierarchically determined power differences) are no doubt real, but to the person on the front line, the experienced differences are finer-grained. They include a long list of very specific country differences along a number of dimensions:

- How narrow and parochial a culture is, versus how worldly
- How direct and open a culture is in its communication and sharing of information, versus how closed or subtle
- The importance of saving face, what it means to treat people with respect, and how trust is developed
- The value placed on close personal relationships as a way of doing business, versus the value placed on a more formal (and distant) attitude
- What motivates people, including the perceived value of money and of respect, as reflected in status, position, and hierarchy
- Work ethic, entrepreneurialism, sensitivity to the customer, action orientation, and the like
- Mental models, ways of thinking, and patterns of logic
- Expectations of how a leader should act
- The state of the economy (e.g., inflation, instability), social organization, and political processes
- Historical underpinnings of attitudes and stereotypes, for example, the relationship between the Germans and the French or the Japanese and the Koreans

· · · · ·

Like knowing a local language, the need for in-depth understanding of a particular country or culture depends upon the nature of the business operation in that country. Running a manufacturing operation in a foreign country to export goods is quite different from selling to consumers in a foreign country. When a deep level of understanding is important, there is a real danger of turning superficial understanding and stereotypes into cultural blinders. While this can be fatal at any level of global responsibility, it can be debilitating when your responsibilities require an intimate working relationship with a particular country that is substantially different from your own. Many executives felt that to be effective in the country they were in, they had to change their behavior in a variety of ways. These changes included learning to be careful of what was said, acting in line with others' expectations, changing management and communication style to fit the new situation, and learning to value other ways of thinking—all of which required in-depth knowledge of the local situation. To be effective in another country, they seem to be saying, you need to change yourself. This stands in stark contrast to our hypothetical Roman expatriate mentioned in chapter 2 whose mission included converting the territories to the Roman way!

At the elementary level of learning about other cultures, you master a single culture that is different from your own. Unless you broaden that specific knowledge, however, you are at a disadvantage at a later stage when you need to deal with multiple countries and cultures. A person can easily become biased for or against a culture as it becomes familiar and, like any expert, allow that frame of reference to overly influence a new experience. Likewise, an executive's mastery of one culture may cause him or her to be labeled by the corporate office as a "country expert" rather than a global manager, with the result of having assignments limited to the same or similar countries. In the former example, the executive stops being an effective learner; in the latter, the executive does not get new opportunities to learn. Both eventualities underline the importance of the third category of cultural lessons, those that involve learning the principles of crossing borders.

We will distinguish these broader culture lessons from learning about specific countries by calling them *generic*. Generic cultural lessons can differ in three ways from their specific cousins. First, generic lessons typically involve dealing with multiple cultures simultaneously, not just with one. One Asian executive, after a successful assignment in Canada, found himself transferred to Hong Kong, where he had to work with ten different cultures. After experiences like these, executives begin to speak of things like a "global presence" and becoming "a citizen of the world," a perspective that recognizes the differences across cultures and gives up a parochial allegiance to any one country. As one executive put it, "Prepare yourself in a way to cut ties to your country—cut them sharply when you go." Another expatriate found his transformation in Australia, "[I] stopped seeing myself as a Singaporean but as a citizen of the world."

Part of becoming global is learning that one's own country and one's own perspective are narrow when placed against the rest of the world. A U.S. executive after an overseas assignment realized "how provincial Americans are." A Norwegian expatriate to the United States "saw that neither Norway nor Kansas is the center of the world."

Generic cultural lessons were often as profound as they were obvious:

- "Don't take for granted that what works in one place will work in another. Make no assumptions."
- "I learned just how deep the mistrust is between nations—never underestimate how deep it is."
- "I was stunned by the nationalism of the individual country managers and their people."
- "The value of life is held differently by different people."

These generic lessons included the impact (or the lack of it) of social or religious values and beliefs on business processes. One telling story involved a European executive assigned to a troubled multicultural operation in Southeast Asia. As in most turnaround situations, the remedy required reducing costs, and one way to do that is by lowering head count. He noticed that the cafeteria had too many chefs for the number of meals that were needed, so, as was customary in his home country, he fired four of them. It turned out that one of those fired was the only Muslim cook, and by terminating him, he had eliminated the only chef who knew how to cook for the Muslim members of the workforce. The executive had inadvertently created a major incident among the large Muslim segment of the workforce. It was a memorable lesson.

The overriding generic lesson, however, was simply a basic respect for, and sincere interest in, cultures other than one's own. No matter where you are, an executive told us, "You must respect the local values. That means accepting that the way people behave is not good or bad compared to what you are used to. You must adapt to that. You cannot change the social structure; there are always positive things in any society. Find the good things." As other executives were quick to point out, respecting local values does not mean you can't make decisions or take action, but it does suggest that context matters.

Generic lessons also differ from single-culture lessons in that they often involve learning to reconcile a *company's* culture with multiple country cultures. This was clearly a major lesson for many executives as they tried to balance the management styles, processes, values, and directives of the corporate office with the culture and values of the various countries in which they found themselves.

Generic lessons by definition contain general rules or conclusions for going into *any* new culture, rather than rules or conclusions aimed at a specific culture. Make sure you understand, make sure you are understood, build new relationships, recognize how people view you as a boss, be patient and tolerant, show some humility, be clear on your own ethics and values—all of these were among the lessons of multicultural experience.

Ironically, many of these conclusions were drawn by expatriates from watching the havoc created by other expatriates: "It wasn't the locals who were causing the trouble. I had to kick out several expatriates, all technical people, because they were abusing the locals and generally couldn't cope with the new environment."

Overall, lessons about cultures swirl around figuring out what you need to change and what not to change, how cultures and their peoples differ, and what is constant across them. As many have observed, people are people wherever you go—with the proviso that, although they are mostly the same, what is different can be critical. Many executives realized that foreigners are not always welcome, or that even when they are, they can't effectively "go native." Always an outsider, an expatriate must learn the art of using his or her foreignness as an advantage while coping with the disadvantages it entails—and not to go so far in the effort to understand and appreciate the culture that it becomes a trap for accepting cultural excuses.

Lesson Theme: Learning to Run a Business—
Strategy, Structure, Processes; Global versus Local;
Specialized Knowledge

As absorbing as adjusting to another culture may be, that is not why an executive is sent to another country or given international responsibilities. The primary reason global executives are needed is to run the business. In this regard, two specific lessons are necessary:

1. Learning strategies for doing business
2. Learning the specifics of running a business

The executives found that, at the strategic level, the emphasis was on learning to find and exploit possibilities. "Business is business, wherever you are," more than one executive observed, but cultural differences could create significant challenges for established practices. While understanding cultures required recognizing and appreciating differences, global business strategy required finding common ground amid the multitude of cultural differences. The executives learned to focus on the similarities offered by business purpose, and, when possible, to exploit the cultural differences to create business advantages. Strategic consistency across cultures, they learned, could be achieved if they focused on the customer, leveraged scope and scale, tapped shared business values, benchmarked against world-class processes, and thought about how to make money on a global (rather than local) basis. "Big picture" perspectives required learning about issues such as creating shareholder value when shareholders are in other countries, managing risk globally, and valuation and international finance. The dilemmas created by strategic perspective included having to balance the global perspective of the firm with the local business situation, and figuring out when it was important to know the details and when to focus on broader issues. Notably, the lessons of strategy often center on *when* to be strategic and how to be simultaneously strategic and appropriately involved in the details of the business.

In contrast to strategic learning, lessons from an operating perspective were the down-to-earth kind about how to run a business. As if to give truth to "business is business wherever you are," these lessons included such universals as mastering the technologies and functions (especially sales and marketing); creating and using various types of systems, structures, and processes; assessing and then managing partnerships and joint ventures; and understanding cash flow, logistics, inventory, cost accounting, law, and so forth. While these all sound like the basics of doing business, extending them to the global context changes them in important ways. Particularly difficult was learning to operate in a global matrix, where multiple interests had to be reconciled and where even the meaning of profit and loss, much less responsibility for it, was subject to multiple interpretations.

The greatest challenge in mastering the details of running a business was to avoid getting lost in them. Just as being strategic did not mean ignoring the details, being operational did not mean losing sight of the larger purpose. The overarching lessons of global business were how to stay on top of the relevant details while simultaneously assuming a strategic global perspective—and, in the midst of this complexity, keeping it simple.

Lesson Theme: Learning to Lead and Manage Others— Selection, Development, Motivation, Team Building, Deselection

Strategy, structure, and processes are all important leadership issues, but leading involves people. Managing subordinates is hard enough when the leader and subordinates are from the same culture, but learning to lead people is increasingly difficult when they come from a different culture or, even more of a challenge, from multiple and very different cultures. Yet the basics of managing people, like the basics of running a business, are essentially the same whether local or international:

1. Learning to establish credibility
2. Learning to select the right people
3. Learning to build and sustain an effective team
4. Learning to make tough calls about people
5. Learning to stay focused—keeping it simple, setting clear goals

6. Learning to keep people motivated and committed, what to delegate and what not to delegate
7. Learning to develop people and the importance of developing people

The lessons our executives learned are fundamental lessons, for example, how to select the right people, or to establish credibility. There is nothing new here, except that these things have to be done in other countries where people may not speak the same language and where religious, social, and cultural values may be dramatically different.

It is in this domain of dealing face-to-face with people that the cultural overlay might be expected to have its greatest impact. But the lessons these executives learned about leading people were not obviously international at all. People are people, they seemed to say with a collective voice, and people are different no matter where they are from. Be sensitive to people, and you will, by definition, also be sensitive to the cultures from which they come. Another universal, perhaps, was this: The executives' lessons were filled with intangibles like earning trust, showing respect, having faith in people, consistently modeling what they believe, proving they aren't biased, building teams, providing clear direction, and understanding that people are motivated by different things. Somehow these intangibles, they learned, establish a leader's credibility, no matter where on the planet the leader found himself or herself.

Lesson Theme: Learning to Deal with Problematic Relationships—Headquarters, Bosses, Unions, Government, Media, Politics

In learning to deal with the myriad relationships in a global job, our executives pointed to the following challenges:

1. Learning to handle immediate bosses and other superiors
2. Learning to manage the interface with headquarters and the larger organization

3. Learning to handle public appearances and the media
4. Learning to deal with governments and (external) politicians
5. Learning to deal with unions and other types of negotiations
6. Learning about internal politics

All executives have to manage numerous relationships, and aligning people other than subordinates is part of every leadership challenge. International work is at least as complicated as its domestic counterpart when it comes to these relationships, and often more so. Most global executives have more types of relationships to manage than do domestic executives. The people they have to work with are more geographically dispersed, and key people are more likely to come from different cultural backgrounds.

When it came to dealing with their superiors, for example, these executives encountered the full gamut of possibilities. They discovered that they needed a boss's agreement, support, or permission, and they had to learn how to get it. They ran into situations that required them to challenge a boss or to justify a decision, and so had to learn how to disagree effectively with someone more powerful than they were. Sometimes they discovered to their dismay that their superiors were flawed ("some senior executives are dumb as rocks") or that they just had to live with a difficult relationship ("do not feel paranoid that he does not like you") and had to learn how to function in spite of it.

Managing these situations at great distances from their superiors might be challenging, but going to headquarters, where the expatriates' superiors often resided, could be even more difficult. It was not unusual for executives to say that they detested working at headquarters or that they "hated the HQ environment." Here they had to learn to deal with politics, or how to cushion their people from the "red tape and scrutiny of headquarters." Some found that people at headquarters didn't understand foreign operations, whereas others were pleasantly surprised to find that they did.

Whether it involves dealing with their bosses, headquarters, peers, or third parties, the life of an international executive is filled with negotiations. Perhaps because of their frequent isolation from corporate office support, global executives find themselves personally negotiating in joint ventures, customer relationships, collective bargaining, government interventions, and media investigations. The lessons they learned corresponded to those groups and those demands.

Lesson Theme: Learning about the Personal Qualities Required of a Leader

Not surprisingly, given all the demands of differing cultures, strategies, and relationships described above, our executives needed to develop a broad range of personal attitudes and skills if they were to survive the trials of international work. The lessons they said they learned about personal behavior were many, but we summarized them into broad categories:

1. Learning to listen carefully, to ask questions, and to see the world through other people's eyes
2. Learning to be open, genuine, honest, and fair; to treat other people with respect; and to trust others
3. Learning to be flexible, to adapt to changing situations, to take changing circumstances into account, to manage multiple priorities and complex relationships, and to think on your feet
4. Learning to assess risks and to take them, and to act in the face of uncertainty
5. Learning to persevere, to act with discipline, and to stay calm under tough circumstances
6. Learning to be optimistic, to believe in oneself, to trust one's instincts, to take a stand for what one believes is right, and to accept responsibility for the consequences of one's actions

Of all the skills that are helpful in an international environment, none seemed more important than learning to listen. Quickly finding out that things weren't always what they seemed to be and that the solutions they had come up with weren't always right, the executives learned to look underneath problems, to ask questions, to dig deeper, to see the world through other people's eyes—above all, to listen, to observe subtle cues, and finally to understand. This general rule was expressed by one executive who had learned it the hard way: "I learned not to impose my point of view early on. In the beginning you listen, observe, and engage the issues. Then you can shape and influence strategy with that knowledge." Another executive pointed out that "being shy was an advantage—they were not put off and it made me listen."

Obviously, many personal attributes are helpful or necessary in global work. For many people, at least some of these qualities were natural gifts or were developed early in life and therefore did not appear as lessons to be learned from their experiences. For others, however, discipline, the ability to listen, flexibility, and openness were not natural gifts and had to be cultivated, often with great difficulty and under intense pressure. But overarching all of these, and accumulating consistently from both successes and failures, was self-confidence. This, we believe, is a fundamental building block for success under the stresses of international work. Tempered by humility—also an abundant lesson in international work—confidence makes it possible to cope with uncertainty and take risks, both of which are prerequisites to learning.

Lesson Theme: Learning about Self and Career

The final category of lessons learned were reflective and personal—international experience taught these executives a lot about themselves.

1. Learning about likes, dislikes, strengths, weaknesses, and preferences
2. Learning what support you need from family or others, how to manage the family under the pressure of foreign work
3. Learning to manage your own career and development

Through the doing, the executives discovered where they found joy, what they were willing to sacrifice and what they weren't, what they were good at and what needed work.

The stresses, strains, joys, and triumphs of international careers also tested, strengthened, or sometimes destroyed families, as these executives discovered what kinds of support they needed from family or others, and what it meant to manage family relationships under the pressures of foreign work and living. If they hadn't known it before, expatriate assignments taught them that it's not just the executive who goes abroad; it is the whole family. The family's experience becomes very much a part of success or failure in international assignments, and learning that is an important lesson (see chapter 6).

Finally, some executives learned how to manage their own careers and development. We were surprised at how few lessons were in this domain. Perhaps through learning to deal with the unexpected and the ambiguity of international assignments, they came to accept that one does not control a career, but rather learns to be flexible and opportunistic.

Making Sense of the Lessons Learned

Cataloging and explaining a long list of lessons, or even the simpler and shorter list of themes, makes everything look logical and precise. It is anything but. To say that we have found the twenty-seven things that all international executives need to learn, or that we have created a list of the competencies a person must have to be effective in global work, is to seriously misrepresent this research. Although the results are consistent with other research on international executives and our executives are a credible source of lessons—lessons that make sense, given what we know about the challenges and demands of international work—all we have provided so far is a way of describing these collective lessons. But having described them, can we now put them into perspective?

There are at least two ways to gain a broader perspective. One is to compare the lessons of global executives with those learned by domestic executives. To do that we will use a study of U.S. executives that used a similar methodology.[2] That study identified thirty-two lessons, which we will compare to the results of our current study. A second way to get perspective is to compare seasoned global executives with people earlier in their careers. One empirical study looked into the early identification of international executives.[3] Those results, combined with our study of what global executives seek when choosing international managers and executives, help identify which lessons form the foundation of international careers.

. . . . .

The Lessons of U.S. versus Global Executives

In the mid-1980s, McCall and his colleagues interviewed or surveyed nearly 200 U.S. executives about the experiences that had shaped them and the lessons they had learned from those experiences.[4] Table 4-1 shows how those lessons compare with the lessons from our study for each of our themes and individual lessons.

The table makes several striking points. First, even though they don't fit perfectly, the types of lessons learned are quite similar. This overlap is even more striking considering the time between the studies (almost fifteen years), and the difference in the samples (almost exclusively from the United States, versus truly global[5]). As we shall see, this surface similarity masks some important differences, but it still provides strong evidence that all effective executives, global or otherwise, learn a common set of skills.

Second, the two studies show clear and dramatic differences in lessons about language and culture. Cultural lessons are learned by global executives and not by domestic executives. These lessons made up over 15 percent of the lessons for the global executives and were not even a category in the U.S. study, even though some of the events described by the U.S. executives took place outside the United States. Finding no culture lessons in the U.S. study may seem obvious in retrospect, and perhaps it is, but this is still more evidence that global executives have to learn a whole additional domain of abilities that their domestic counterparts do not.

There also appear to be differences in the third lesson theme, Learning to Lead and Manage Others. The U.S. executives had many more lessons under this category than did the global executives. On the other hand, the global executives had twice the number of lessons under "Strategies for Doing Business" than the U.S. executives had. While these comparisons are crude at best, they suggest that global executives learn more about big-picture strategy and working across cultural boundaries, whereas the U.S. executives learn more about managing subordinates and specific relationships. In short, the data support the idea that global executives see the world from a broader perspective than that of purely domestic executives. This may help explain why repatriation—which often thrusts executives back into comparatively narrow domestic jobs with peers and bosses who may not have global experience—can be such a problem.

Table 4-1 Lessons of International Executives' Experience Compared to U.S. Domestic Executives' Experience

Lessons from International Executive Study (952 Lessons)	Closest Matching Lessons from the Domestic U.S. Study[a] (1,547 Lessons)

Learning to Deal with Cultural Issues and Different Cultures (15.3 percent versus 0 percent)

1. Learning to speak a foreign language (2.6 percent)	
2. Learning about specific foreign cultures and contrasts between specific cultures (5.6 percent)	
3. Learning generic lessons about living and working in foreign cultures (7.1 percent)	

Learning to Run a Business—Strategy, Structure, Processes; Global versus Local; Specialized Knowledge (16.6 percent versus 15 percent)

1. Learning strategies for doing business (6.7 percent)	15. Seeing organizations as systems (3 percent)
2. Learning the specifics of running a business (9.9 percent)	4. Specific technical knowledge (6 percent)
	5. How the business works (4 percent)
	25. How to build and/or use structure and control systems (2 percent)

Learning to Lead and Manage Others—Selection, Development, Motivation, Team Building, Deselection (19.2 percent versus 24.7 percent)

1. Learning how to establish credibility (2.8 percent)	2. Basic management values (7 percent)
	32. Use and abuse of power* (0.5 percent)
2. Learning to select the right people (2.3 percent)	30. Can't manage it all by yourself** (1 percent)
3. Learning to build and sustain an effective team (3.5 percent)	30. Can't manage it all by yourself** (1 percent)
4. Learning to make tough calls about people (2.3 percent)	16. Learning to be tough (3 percent)
	19. Needing to act on or confront a subordinate performance problem (2 percent)
5. Learning to stay focused—keeping it simple, setting clear goals (2.1 percent)	
6. Learning to keep people motivated and committed; what to delegate and what not to delegate (4.9 percent)	1. Direct and motivate (10.2 percent)
7. Learning to develop people and the importance of developing people (1.3 percent)	26. Develop your people (1 percent)

Learning to Deal with Problematic Relationships—Headquarters, Bosses, Unions, Government, Media, Politics (9.7 percent versus 12 percent)

1. Learning to handle immediate bosses and other superiors (2.2 percent)	13. How to work with executives (3 percent)
	23. What executives are like (2 percent)
2. Learning to manage the interface with headquarters and the larger organization (1.6 percent)	
3. Learning to handle public appearances and the media (0.6 percent)	
4. Learning to deal with governments and (external) politicians (0.9 percent)	

(continued)

Lessons from International Executive Study (952 Lessons)	Closest Matching Lessons from the Domestic U.S. Study[a] (1,547 Lessons)
5. Learning to deal with unions and other types of negotiations (2.7 percent)	18. Strategy and tactics of negotiation (3 percent)
6. Learning about internal politics (1.7 percent)	8. Politics is part of organizational life (4 percent)

Learning about the Personal Qualities Required of a Leader (31.4 percent versus 33.7 percent)

1. Learning to listen carefully, to ask questions, and to see the world through other people's eyes (6.7 percent)	6. Dealing with people (4 percent)
	24. Management is different from technical* (2 percent)
2. Learning to be open, genuine, honest, fair; to treat other people with respect; and to trust others (5.5 percent)	11. Basic human values* (3 percent)
3. Learning to be flexible, to adapt to changing situations, to take changing circumstances into account, to manage multiple priorities and complex relationships, and to think on your feet (3.7 percent)	7. Comfort with ambiguity, stress, and uncertainty** (4 percent)
	17. Finding alternatives in solving and framing problems (3 percent)
4. Learning to assess risks and to take them, to act even in uncertain conditions (2.3 percent)	7. Comfort with ambiguity, stress, and uncertainty** (4 percent)
	31. Be ready to take opportunities* (0.7 percent)
5. Learning to persevere, to act with discipline, and to stay calm under tough circumstances (4.6 percent)	12. Persevering under adverse conditions; singleness of purpose (3 percent)
	20. Strategies for coping with situations beyond your control (2 percent)
6. Learning to be optimistic, to believe in oneself, to trust one's instincts, to take a stand for what one believes is right, and to accept responsibility for the consequences of one's actions (8.6 percent)	3. Self-confidence (7 percent)
	10. Standing alone (4 percent)
	29. Dealing with conflict* (1 percent)

Learning about Self and Career (7.7 percent versus 8 percent)

1. Learning about likes, dislikes, strengths, weaknesses, and preferences (5.8 percent)	14. Recognition of personal limits and weaknesses (3 percent)
	21. Discovering what you really want to do (2 percent)
2. Learning what support you need from family or others, how to manage the family under the pressure of foreign work (1.1 percent)	28. Perspective on life and work* (1 percent)
3. Learning to manage your own career and development (0.8 percent)	22. You have to take control of your own career (2 percent)

[a] Esther H. Lindsey, V. Holmes, and Morgan W. McCall, Jr., *Key Events in Executives' Lives,* technical report no. 32 (Greensboro, NC: Center for Creative Leadership, 1987).

* Not a perfect match, but close.

** Matched with more than one lesson; percentages split accordingly.

Note: Lessons from the U.S. study with no close match: (9) Getting lateral cooperation (4 percent), (27) How to manage people with more experience than you or who used to be your peer or boss (1 percent), (33) Management models (<1 percent), and (34) Doing it is more important than thinking about it—practice over theory (<1 percent).

At least on the theme level, the global and U.S. executives learned similar things about the personal qualities required of an executive and in the learning about self and career. Specific lesson categories do apparently show some differences, such as learning to listen carefully and the importance of the family in global work. Certainly any executive would need to gain knowledge in these areas, regardless of the scope of the particular executive job. A close examination of the actual interviews, however, reveals that the international executives learn these same lessons in a way that reflects the complexity of the cultural context in which they are learned. As a result, the lessons tend to be deeper and broader than when the same kinds of lessons are learned in less complex situations. One might say, for example, that any executive needs to learn to be flexible and to adapt to changing circumstances. However, the degree of flexibility required in a global job, where so many additional variables are in flux and where control over circumstances may be quite limited, can be both greater and different.

Early Identification of High Potentials

Yet another way to get perspective on the lessons of global executives is to look at an independent study of the qualities that distinguish high-potential from solid performing international managers. Our argument is this: There should be some overlap between the qualities that organizations use to select high-potential global executives with the qualities that our executives said they looked for in people to do global work. Moreover, some of those qualities should be represented in the lessons of our study.

Table 4-2 compares the attributes of high-potential executives from the early-identification study, the lessons learned by the executives in our global study, and the global competencies executives in our study look for in those they choose for international work. The early-identification study was based on boss's ratings of nearly 800 international managers.[6] The researchers statistically derived the qualities that differentiated between high potentials and "solid performing" global executives. The column entitled Lessons from Global Study shows how lessons from table 4-2 were similar to the high-potential qualities

Table 4-2 Comparison of the Lessons Learned by International Executives with Early-Identification Variables and with the Competencies International Executives Look for When Choosing International Executives

Lessons from the International Executive Study	Early-Identification Study	Global Competencies (What Global Executives Look for)
I. Learning to Deal with Cultural Issues and Different Cultures		
1. Learning to speak a foreign language		
2. Learning about specific foreign cultures	Adapts to cultural differences	Cultural interest and sensitivity
3. Generic lessons about culture		
II. Learning to Run a Business—Strategy, Structure, Processes; Global versus Local; Specialized Knowledge		
1. Learning strategies for doing business	Seeks broad business knowledge	
2. Learning the specifics of running a business		Technical/business skills
III. Learning to Lead and Manage Others—Selection, Development, Motivation, Team Building, Deselection		
1. Learning to establish credibility	Acts with integrity*	Honesty and integrity*
2. Learning to select the right people		
3. Learning to build and sustain an effective team	Brings out the best in people*	
4. Learning to make tough calls about people		
5. Learning to stay focused—keeping it simple		
6. Learning to keep people motivated	Brings out the best in people*	
7. Learning to develop people		
IV. Learning to Deal with Problematic Relationships—Headquarters, Bosses, Unions, Government, Media, Politics		
1. Learning to handle superiors		
2. Learning to manage the interface with headquarters		
3. Learning to handle the media		
4. Learning to deal with governments and politicians		
5. Learning to deal with negotiations		
6. Learning about internal politics		

V. Learning about the Personal Qualities Required of a Leader

1. Learning to listen and see through other people's eyes		Open-mindedness
2. Learning to be open, to treat other people with respect	Acts with integrity*	People skills
		Honesty and integrity*
3. Learning to be flexible, to adapt to changing situations	Is insightful; sees things from new angles	Flexibility in thought and tactics
		Ability to deal with complexity
4. Learning to assess risks, to act in the face of uncertainty	Has the courage to take risks	Self-motivation and resourcefulness
		Ability to deal with ambiguity
		Ability to take risks
5. Learning to persevere, to act with discipline, to stay calm	Is committed to making a difference**	Resiliency and perseverance
6. Learning to be optimistic, to trust one's instincts		Optimism

VI. Learning about Self and Career

1. Learning about likes, strengths, weaknesses	Seeks and uses feedback	Curiosity and adventurousness**
	Is open to criticism**	
	Learns from mistakes**	
2. Learning what support you need from family		Stable personal life
3. Learning to manage one's own career and development	Seeks opportunities to learn**	

* Matched with more than one lesson.
** Not a perfect match, but close.
Note: Global Competencies with no match: Energetic and healthy; Motivated to help others.

and to the global competencies. The global competencies in column three are our executives' answers to the question "What would you look for in selecting someone for global work?"

The convergence among the results of these studies is striking. All three sets of data suggest that in choosing people for international work, we should look for the following qualities:

• Interest in, and willingness to adapt to, cultural differences
• Knowledge of some aspect of the business, possibly technical
• Demonstrated ability to work effectively with people
• A constellation of personal qualities reflecting confidence, flexibility, integrity, and courage
• A constellation of qualities best described as an openness to learning and experience

The "other stuff," things like selecting the right people, learning to make tough calls, staying focused, developing people skills, learning how to handle all the problematic relationships—all these can be learned if the basic attributes are there to begin with.

Although our study showed that these qualities were also learned through experience and were not natural gifts, the implications for selection are clear: The likelihood of having executives who succeed in another culture can be increased by selecting carefully in the first place.

In Conclusion

· · · · ·

In this chapter, we have described the six themes and twenty-seven lessons that the global executives we interviewed said they had learned from their experiences. We attempted to make sense of what is otherwise just another list of desirable qualities by contrasting our present study with a study of U.S. executives, showing that although the lessons are alike, there are also some significant differences. We also looked at how the lessons fit with other work on early identification and selection, suggesting that some of the lessons look a lot like foundation qualities that make learning other lessons more likely.

As we close the chapter, we return to Andrew, Jean, and Brian from chapter 3 to see how their stories fit into this new framework. We conclude by building on the idea of meta-competencies that may underlie the development of international executives and by looking at one end product of that development process, a global mind-set.

Complex Tapestries of Talent

The problem with typologies is that they suck the lifeblood from the reality they are intended to represent. This list of lessons learned is no exception—no executive has mastered all these lessons, and to portray the perfect global executive as having all these qualities, however desirable they may be, is to create a false god. These executives' lives are complex tapestries; their lessons are hard-won and woven into a unique fabric that reflects who they are, where they have been, and what they have learned. Global executives are amalgams of strengths and weaknesses, and they remain works in progress. As long as they stay open to learning, what they have not yet learned is still a possibility.

As with any tapestry, the threads don't make a lot of sense if examined separately—the picture only emerges after the weaving. So we followed Andrew in chapter 3 as he acquired yet another language, refined his cultural sensitivity in Hong Kong, developed self-confidence over a series of pressure-filled events, built a staff and formed a business strategy, and learned to balance corporate culture with country cultures. His journey stands in contrast to Jean's. Jean was talented in his ability to time and time again form relationships that helped him learn. As he learned the lessons of a specific culture, however, he also acquired cultural blinders that almost kept him from seeing the worldwide strategic perspective he needed to develop. Neither Andrew nor Jean followed the same path as Brian, who learned to lead and developed perseverance and courage while facing life-and-death situations in Nigeria.

But to celebrate uniqueness is not to deny the similarities. There is no question that international work makes heavy personal demands and that global executives must learn effective ways to meet those demands. As different as these executives' paths were, each of the three in his own way confronted all six of the learning themes we have identified: adapting to different cultures, running an international business, leading people, handling multiple and multifaceted relationships, growing personally in ways that enhance adaptation and growth under tough circumstances, and developing a realistic understanding of self.

Many of the dimensions comprising the themes can be seen as extensions of lessons that any executive in a complex organization would have to learn. All types of executives have to deal with other people, for example; it's just more difficult when those people come from different cultures, you can't speak their language, or you are in a multicultural alliance in which you have little formal authority. But other dimensions are uniquely international—they seem to be transformational lessons rather than extensions of more modest ones. The most obvious of these are the lessons about culture. It seems only logical that if dealing with culture is a continuum, then one should be able to learn about it gradually. But many people say that it is *qualitatively* different to live in another country, that it is an assault on one's mental models of such magnitude that change doesn't happen a little at a time.

The question of evolution or transformation aside, it is tempting just to hold up this list of lessons and say, "There you have it. This is the competency list for global executives; now let's go find us some." But the importance of any of these lessons is a product of the person (his or her natural gifts, what the person has already learned and is capable of learning), the type of global job he or she is in, the business strategy of the company, and the country or countries the executive is responsible for. And those are just for starters. It gets even more complicated when we consider the convoluted paths that international careers can take, and how what is learned in one assignment (say, how to run a business as a country manager) can actually get in the way in the next one (for instance, running a worldwide business in which particular countries may be suboptimized).

So, with an almost endless list of unrealistic expectations about what executives need to know, how do we tackle the issue of development? We argue here, as we have argued before, that the essential ingredient is the capacity to learn from experience.[7] Only through whatever qualities make a person an effective learner in a global context can the necessary abilities be acquired (or their absence be managed) as the demands of the job constantly change. Thus we can use our data to better understand what Tim Hall and Philip Mirvis have described as meta-competencies, the skills of learning how to learn.[8]

Meta-Competencies

Two major streams of work lend support to the idea that successful global executives not only need numerous specific competencies for dealing with the cultures, tasks, and relationships characteristic of international work, but also need the underlying skills and abilities that allow them to acquire those competencies. One of us (McCall), using McCall, Spreitzer, and Mahoney's research with high-potential and solid-performing international managers, postulated that "the heart of development lies in the ability to learn from an accumulation of experiences."[9] He suggested that the ability to learn is reflected in four dimensions or behaviors of executive learners:

1. They pay the price of admission (they get organizational attention and investment through their commitment and accomplishments).
2. They have a sense of adventure (they take, when offered, and make, when not offered, opportunities to learn more).
3. They learn more (by creating an effective, feedback-rich context for learning).
4. They take the learning to heart (by changing as a result of the experiences they have).

These dimensions of ability to learn sound very much like the two meta-competencies that Tim Hall, Gurong Zhu, and Amin Yan have proposed from their analysis of global executives: adaptability and identity.

If a person has adaptability, he or she is able to identify for him or herself those qualities that are critical for future performance and is also able to make personal changes necessary to meet those ends. But adaptability is not enough. The person also has to change his or her awareness of self, so that he or she internalizes and values that

. . . . .

change. Thus the second metacompetency is identity: the ability to gather self-related feedback, to form accurate self-perceptions, and to change one's self-concept as appropriate.[10]

The convergence of these two perspectives is apparent, but how does our current study relate to these hypothesized underlying factors? First, adaptability is heavily represented in the lessons our executives learned. A quick look at table 4-1 reveals that seeing the world through others' eyes, being flexible and adapting to changing situations, acting in the face of uncertainty, and trusting one's instincts—all of which are arguably part of adaptability—constitute a hefty 21 percent of the lessons learned. Second, self-awareness, a lesson also identified by the executives in our sample, made up almost 6 percent of all lessons learned (which made it the sixth most frequent of the twenty-seven categories).

These results raise at least two basic questions about developing global executives. The first question is, Where are meta-competencies learned? The second is, If these are underlying abilities, does it make more sense to select for them rather than to develop them? In the next chapter, we will look at where these underlying abilities come from when, indeed, they are learned, and will explore the selection-versus-development dilemma in more depth. Before that discussion, however, we will consider the global mind-set.

Developing the Global Mind-Set

Does the accumulation of lessons like those described in this chapter lead to anything larger than the sum of the parts? Efforts to identify and categorize the knowledge, skills, and abilities required of successful international executives are legion and growing.[11] Are we simply contributing to the endless lists of the specific skills required to run a business in another culture?

A number of people have argued that in the end a global executive is not described by a list of attributes that are largely extensions of the knowledge, skills, and abilities needed by domestic executives. Indeed, the evidence is accumulating that at some point a fundamental transformation takes place for successful global executives—a transformation that can be described in shorthand as the acquisition of a global mind-set. Transformed executives "become more 'cosmopolitan,' they extend their perspective, they change their 'cognitive maps.'"[12] Hall, Zhu, and Yan take it even further:

> Out of this deep change, the individual develops *a new perspective or mindset*. This is not just a view of oneself (identity) but a new view of one's organizational and professional role. This change goes far beyond a change in the skill set—it is a change in the *person*. We know that these deep changes in personal identity occur as a result of being confronted with a higher level of complexity in the environment, . . . and that is precisely what happens in an international assignment. . . . Not only does the person develop new perspectives, but he or she also *develops skills in the taking of new perspectives, and developing and holding multiple perspectives*. This ability to acquire and hold multiple, perhaps competing, perspectives (i.e., the ability to see a situation through another person's eyes) is a quality of a more "evolved" identity.[13]

We believe that this mind-set comes not from home-country leadership challenges, but rather from experiences in other cultures. To reach this level of understanding, executives should be fluent in at least one language other than their native one, and need to live *and* work in at least one, and probably two, other cultures.

An organization has a strategic choice. It can select for certain qualities that these lessons of experience represent, or it can create processes to develop them in the people it believes have potential. Obviously any organization will have to do both. If people come having mastered some of the lessons already, then development can be about other things. But all the lessons discussed in this chapter were, according to these executives, learned. Now we describe the experiences that taught them.

Experiences That Teach Global Executives

> Through the years I have encountered people and been involved in events that have had a huge impact, knocked off rough corners, lifted me to heights of joy, plunged me into the depth of sorrow and anguish, taught me to laugh, especially at myself—in other words, my life experiences and the people with whom I shared them have been my teachers.
>
> —*Jane Goodall,* Reason for Hope

The most powerful tool available to organizations trying to develop global executives is their control over the experiences their talented people will have. These experiences are the classrooms that teach the lessons of leadership, to the extent that these lessons are learned. This is certainly not a new idea—job rotation and career paths have been around for a long time—but it is difficult to do effectively. Systematic use of experience has rarely reached the sophistication evident in many corporate training and structured educational programs, even though formal programs are a relatively small part of an executive's education, in terms of both the time spent and the lessons learned.

One reason experience receives less attention than it deserves is that under the best of circumstances organizations have limited control over a person's experiences and the lessons taken from them. However, organizations have considerable influence over some experiences, notably the kinds of assignments people get and when, what is done to help them learn, and to whom they are exposed. Using experience for development therefore requires a deep level of understanding about what experiences are important, what makes them significant, and what can be learned from them.

This ground is not entirely unplowed. As mentioned in chapter 4, Morgan McCall and his associates tried to learn more about developmental experiences by interviewing executives with U.S. companies. In referring to those data, McCall later observed that:

> To say that development is the result of experience leaves a lot open
> to interpretation. In the broadest sense, experience is what happens
> every day. Each Monday morning is an experience, but not all are
> equally powerful. Though most people emerge from the vast major
> ity of their experiences unchanged in any significant way, some
> experiences do have a significant impact on one's understanding of
> oneself, one's view of the world, one's sense of right and wrong, and
> one's subsequent behavior. All experiences are not equal.[1]

Because of this earlier work on the experiences that shaped U.S. domestic executives, a parallel study of largely non-U.S. global executives promised to be a win-win situation, no matter how it turned out. If the key developmental experiences for an international sample are the same as those already identified, then we would need not reinvent the wheel; development of global executives could be based on the same foundation. If, however, global executives were shaped by different experiences, or if they learned different things from the same kinds of experiences, then the study would provide a new foundation on which to build. Either way, something valuable would be learned.

The Dynamics of Learning from Experience
· · · · ·

Heraclitus, whose struggle to understand nature was mentioned in chapter 1, postulated that all learning comes through strife. As we will see in this chapter, the kinds of experiences that shaped these global executives still fit the observation he made in 500 B.C. Even when an experience was described in positive terms, for example, when a good boss was central or when great success was achieved, it almost always happened in the context of a broader challenge. It boils down to a simple conclusion: Challenging experiences force people to learn new things; bland experiences don't. This raises the question of what constitutes a challenging experience.

What makes an experience significant enough for an executive to choose it as among the most significant of his or her career? There seem to be universal principles operating. John Steinbeck put it this way: "If an animal is good to eat or poisonous or dangerous the natives of the place will know about it and where it lives. But if it has none of these qualities, no matter how highly colored or beautiful, he may never in his life have seen it."[2] Steinbeck's observation, made during his biological expedition to the Sea of Cortez, says what we all know—that for an experience to be memorable, for it to affect our behavior, it must first get our attention. And usually the things that rivet our attention are those that challenge, even threaten, us. As if to document that across cultures and time, Joseph Campbell pulled together a "world literature of miraculous tests and ordeals" in his work on the myth of the hero's journey. Throughout recorded history, the true test of the hero always has been to "survive a succession of trials."[3] What is true for mythical heroes seems also true for contemporary executives:

> The essence of development is that diversity and adversity beat out repetition every time. The more dramatic the change in skills demanded, the more severe the personnel problems, the greater the bottom-line pressure, and the more sinuous and unexpected the turns in the road, then the greater the opportunity for learning. Unappealing though it may seem, shocks and pressures and problems with other people are the best teachers.[4]

In this chapter we bring together these challenging experiences that are the essence of development. Our global executives described 332 developmental experiences that we placed into eighteen categories of experiences within four broad categories, presented in table 5-1.

What strikes one immediately about table 5-1 is that the experiences, with one exception (culture shock), look much like the experiences that we might expect for domestic executives. At first glance, the development of global executives does not appear significantly different from the development of primarily domestic executives. After all, aren't business turnarounds, significant other people, and first managerial assignments important in the global environment also? As we defined a global executive in chapter 2, we will argue that the compelling reason that

. . . . .

Table 5-1   The Developmental Experiences of Global Executives

Event	Number of Events	Percentage of Events	Percentage of People Describing Event
Foundation Assignments			
Early work experiences	12	4	12
First managerial responsibility	7	2	7
Major Line Assignments			
Business turnarounds	35	11	30
Building or evolving a business	19	6	16
Joint ventures, alliances, mergers, or acquisitions	13	4	11
Business start-ups	10	3	10
Shorter-Term Experiences			
Significant other people	40	12	32
Special projects, consulting roles, and staff advisory jobs	27	8	24
Developmental and educational experiences	29	9	23
Negotiations	10	3	8
Stint at headquarters	7	2	7
Perspective-Changing Experiences			
Culture shock	29	9	27
Career shifts	25	8	21
Confrontations with reality	21	6	18
Changes in scope or scale	21	6	17
Mistakes and errors in judgment	12	4	10
Family and personal challenges	8	2	8
Crises	7	2	7

Note: Experiences in italics are the five described by the largest percentage of the executives.

developing global executives is different and, we might add, more difficult and unpredictable is the added factor of culture shock. We consider the developmental experience of culture shock one of the perspective-changing experiences (table 5-1). Adding the element of crossing cultures, in fact, changes all the other experiences. The global context adds the element of challenge that can turn ordinary experience into the teachers of global development. Tim Hall, Gurong Zhu, and Amin Yan put it well:

> Being suddenly immersed in a foreign context, where just getting through the mundane activities of everyday life (having a telephone

installed, hiring a new employee, getting directions while driving) is a struggle, a powerful personal and professional role transition, requiring communicating across language and culture boundaries. There are constant surprises, where the person is rudely brought up short and told that his or her usual programs for behavior no longer apply. These daily challenges and "routine busting" upending experiences provide compelling personal feedback and force a person to become aware of new choices, explore situations and his or her own identity in a new way, and to try out new behaviors.[5]

But we are getting ahead of ourselves. In this chapter, we will explore each of these eighteen experiences in some detail, describing what they are and how they act as teachers of essential lessons. These experiences are the ones that shaped our sample of global executives. Clearly, they are not the *only* experiences that will teach lessons of global leadership; as broad as is our sample of 101 executives, other companies with other strategies will offer other developmental experiences. Understanding these in depth, however, will serve as a basis for organizations to implement development programs that are based on experience.

As we begin our description of the eighteen experiences, there are some considerations to keep in mind. First, the experiences are often quite complex. In spite of our best efforts to classify a specific experience into only one of the eighteen categories, many of them obstinately defied simple categorization and ended up in two categories. For example, many turnaround experiences were accompanied by powerful culture shocks. We will note these interactions in the overview that follows and try to sort out the implications of compounded experience at the end of the chapter.

Second, the compound nature of many experiences results in the confused patterns in the lessons taught by them. It was not always possible to separate out the lessons that were unique to a single category of experience from those resulting from the interaction of several categories. The result is that it is harder in an international context to predict what a particular experience might teach.

Undaunted by this complexity, we will summarize the various experiences and the lessons they typically offer, not just for understanding these specific experiences, but also to illustrate how to think about the relationships between any experience and its developmental potential.

Tables C-1 through C-4 in appendix C contain detailed descriptions with examples of the executives' actual experiences and the lessons learned.

Foundation Assignments

Foundation assignments provide experience on which later experiences are built. We categorize two types of experience as foundation assignments. The numbers in the parentheses below represent the percentage of executives who listed one of these events as among the top three experiences that shaped their global careers:

- Early work experiences (12 percent)
- First managerial responsibility (7 percent)

As a general rule in executive development, more recent experiences supersede earlier ones in perceived significance. This makes sense; experiences occurring later in a successful career typically involve greater challenges, and those occurring more recently are fresher in memory. So when senior executives list an early experience as among their three most powerful events, they are listing something significant indeed.

One executive provided a good example of the lasting impact of early work. At the time of the interview, he was fifty-nine and back in the United Kingdom after numerous assignments abroad. He impressed us as a "tough old bird," clearly a survivor in the survival-of-the-fittest school of development. From a modest family background and the first in his family to go to college, he became an engineer and was forged as a leader by difficult turnarounds in some very difficult parts of the world. His total commitment to his work and the hardships it created led to a breakup of his family—and that experience also shaped his character. But his education began early, and even all these years later, he remembered:

> I was born in an industrial town. My parents were old when I was born, and neither of them was educated. They always wanted me to do more than they had done. I was the first member of my family to go to a university, and I chose engineering (typical of our area) and

was sponsored by the company. I had summer jobs working on projects for the company, so I knew it and its structure.

Within twelve months of graduating, I was into foreign assignments. By age twenty-seven, I had been to South America, Canada,
the Middle East, and Czechoslovakia. I developed an oil field in Abu
Dhabi. I was sent to the Balkans to restore services after an earth-
quake, where for six months I dealt with people during the greatest
of tragedies. I had been overseas, as you can see, many times as a
young man; I learned very young that working on a construction site
involves working with people, governments, contractors. I learned a
helluva lot in those early experiences.

Early work experiences like these became the foundation for later
development. They usually were functional or technical jobs with
unusual developmental power because they exposed the executive-to-
be to the "ways of organizations," to significant cultural differences, or
to both. Indeed, early work experience was frequently so confounded
with culture shock that our coders could not separate the two components. Through these early experiences, some executives said, they
learned the value of listening and seeing the world through other people's eyes. Because the jobs were often in another culture, these people
were forced, early on, to learn to do business in another culture, frequently in a language other than their native tongue.

The second foundation assignment was the first managerial job.
Again, because of the powerful events that occurred later in careers, a
first managerial job had to be extraordinary in some way to retain
developmental prominence so much later—only 7 percent of our executives told us about their first managerial job. Those who did so told of
numerous challenges over and above the normal trials of first-time
supervision. Often, these future executives had to navigate difficult
relationships with bosses or had to cope with a foreign culture. They
might find themselves promoted over, or having to supervise, older or
more experienced employees or, in some other way, having to establish
credibility in the face of a doubting constituency. To add a little spice to
an already tasty experience, many of these first managerial jobs were
confounded by a huge increase in the scope of responsibility.

But there was often good news, too. In many of these jobs, another
person (usually a boss) appeared at the crucial time to provide support,

help, a sounding board, or advice. These significant people were often key to the learning from the experience, and the whole thing resembles the hero myth, in which "the first encounter of the hero-journey is with a protective figure (often a little old crone or old man) who provides the adventurer with amulets against the dragon forces he is about to pass."[6] Overwhelmingly, the lessons of powerful first managerial experiences were belief in oneself and learning to take responsibility for one's actions. When in another culture (and most were), the experiences added lessons about working effectively in that culture and often forced the incumbent to learn to speak for the company as well as for himself or herself, sometimes even representing the company in the media.

Although foundation assignments make up relatively few (only 6 percent) of all the events in our study, we can't overemphasize the importance of early experiences in shaping executives, especially international executives. Early exposure to challenging assignments, whether technical or managerial, in another culture with a competent boss (or adviser) can have a lasting and highly significant impact on a talented person. They provide a basis for learning absolutely critical skills in an international career: listening, seeing the world as others see it, and the confidence to act.

Major Line Assignments

What we have labeled major line assignments involved executives in significant business situations in which they were in charge or played important roles. Our executives described the following major line experiences:

- Business turnarounds (30 percent)
- Building or evolving a business (16 percent)
- Joint ventures, alliances, mergers, or acquisitions (11 percent)
- Business start-ups (10 percent)

Major line assignments as a group make up almost a quarter of our events, and turnarounds are the second most frequently reported of the eighteen individual categories.

In many ways the story below tells it all: A third-country national is sent to save a business in trouble and finds himself on his own, far from help, and responsible for aspects of the operation that in the home country would be handled by various staff and support groups. Not to mention that he was under intense scrutiny by the press, was dealing with economic and political factors beyond his control, and had inherited a legacy of distrust from a predecessor who was still there. And as was the case in many international turnarounds we heard about, not only did he consider it "the toughest experience I ever had," but he also believed that "at our headquarters, they don't realize what I know."

There was a huge mess in Venezuela. Everyone was going to the U.S. headquarters to complain about it, but I was in Australia looking at Venezuela from the outside. I got a call to help—to be president of our operation there. With my previous experience, I thought I was ready; it would be a challenge. So, I moved my family there.

I remember vividly the exact date I arrived. You can't imagine what it was like. It was a huge mess. Customers were saying that the company was corrupt, and some of them were politicians also and were speaking to the newspapers. My predecessor was still there, and on paper, I reported to him.

I was in the middle of trying to sort this out when the currency collapsed. Now I really had a plate full of everything. The market vanished. We had one-million-dollar-a-day losses. I reorganized, and fifty percent of the people had to be let go. A major newsmagazine came in to interview people, and I was made to look heartless.

I had to change the attitudes of the customers—they are different from customers in other countries; they express their views in different ways and I had to dig to find answers. I had to make individuals understand what we were trying to do. I listened and heard what they cared about. I told them we could find a way out. They began to trust and believe me, to understand that we were on the same team.

It was the toughest experience I ever had, and there was a lot of learning. I learned to be passionate but cool—emotional while keeping my cool at the same time. I learned to turn around a major business in a foreign country, not just drive sales as I had before. I learned to deal with morale, dollars, distributors, customers, the government—so many things at the same time. I learned that you can't wait to rebuild and hope it will all straighten out; you have to get rid of the wrong people and processes.

I am extremely proud of what we did. The company doesn't say thanks, but I consider this thanks enough: One day I received a call from the CEO of one of the world's most admired companies; he interviewed me about how I did it. But at our headquarters, they don't realize what I know—you have such a deep understanding if you have managed internationally.

Business turnarounds were important both for the number of executives who had experienced them (a top-five event) and for the number of lessons that turnarounds taught—it was the single event that produced the most lessons in our entire study. Turnarounds also seemed to be the most difficult, challenging, and powerful learning opportunities. Almost all of them involved an expatriate or a foreign national sent to another country to fix a business in trouble. Because of that, the challenge of the job was often compounded by culture shock. Taking on a turnaround frequently meant a career shift as well, as the protagonist moved from a functional or product-manager role to a general management role. And perhaps because of all these factors, the range of lessons that might be learned was among the widest of all the experiences.

From turnarounds, the executives took away a heavy dose of self-confidence, as well as lessons about running a business, dealing with a variety of relationships, staying focused, building a team, making tough calls on people, and, ultimately, managing their own careers. And, of course, there were lessons about crossing cultures. Indeed, turnarounds offered the opportunity for an executive to learn something from each of the six lesson themes discussed in chapter 4.

The second major line assignment is *building or evolving a business* that is already in place and performing at least adequately. In many cases this event is best described as leading transformation, because it requires fundamental changes in how the business is structured and the basic processes involved. Like a turnaround, this experience is frequently accompanied by a career shift into a general management job and a huge shift in scope for the manager coming in.

The lessons taken from building or evolving a business, like those of other major assignments, include increases in self-confidence. They also include learning about both the broad strategy of the business and the details of running it (the processes, structure, etc.). People with this experience also report learning how to stay focused on a few significant objectives and how to encourage change among people who are comfortable with the status quo. Almost all these assignments took place in another culture and offered those lessons as well.

Joint ventures, alliances, mergers, or acquisitions, whether the executive is working alone or in partnership, provide our third major line assignment. The challenge in these assignments, frequently start-ups, was working with an organization, individual, or group from another culture and with differing goals or perspectives. There were, needless to say, substantial conflicts and misunderstandings to be resolved.

Given these characteristics, the lessons most frequently taken from these experiences involved learning about the specific culture in which they took place, negotiating with other parties, and running a business under extenuating circumstances. Other lessons might involve dealing with the government or other relationships crucial to making the venture work in that environment.

Business start-ups included a range of start-up situations, such as starting a department, setting up an office, starting a business, and establishing a subsidiary. Sometimes these were personal entrepreneurial ventures rather than activities carried out under a corporate umbrella, and they typically took place in another culture (with its accompanying culture shock). As in first managerial jobs (which the start-ups sometimes were), another person was frequently central to the experience, but not always in a positive way.

We were surprised at the relatively few start-ups that were reported (only 3 percent of the events, experienced by 10 percent of our executives) and the relatively narrow range of lessons learned, usually lessons about the specific culture in which the start-up took place and about the importance of being open to and respecting others. Perhaps start-ups are relatively rare as pure events because many global start-ups are done in a joint venture or alliance, or through a merger or an acquisition. When this is the case, the challenge of the relationship itself or of integrating the organizations appears to have more influence on the executive's learning than the start-up itself.

From a developmental perspective, the major line assignments offer a great variety of lessons, some of which can also be learned in shorter assignments, but some of which seem largely the domain of these kinds of immersion experiences. Most specifically, the line assignments require learning to set a clear direction (focusing on what is really important), to build an organization that can achieve those goals, and to motivate people and teams to carry it out. All these experiences are enormous confidence builders and produce *true global learning:* "a 'real' job, with a long time frame, with accountability for results, and other people (who one sees as different from oneself) with whom one is interdependent."[7]

Shorter-Term Experiences

For the experiences described as shorter-term, not only are they on average considerably shorter than the major line assignments, but the executive is not necessarily in a significant leadership role. As a group, this category included over one third of the events (35 percent), and it included three of the top five experiences in terms of the number of executives who experienced them.

- Significant other people (32 percent)
- Special projects, consulting roles, and staff advisory jobs (24 percent)
- Developmental and educational experiences (23 percent)
- Negotiations (8 percent)
- Stint at headquarters (7 percent)

Exposure to *significant other people* was the experience described by the largest proportion of our executives (32 percent). When another person was described as a key developmental experience, that person was usually (but not always) a boss or a superior and may have been either a positive or a negative influence. These people were almost always encountered as part of the ongoing work, but the relationship with the person was what made the experience developmental, with the job per se very much in the background. When the appearance of a significant other person occurred in conjunction with early work assignments, the experiences were usually good. When other people figured prominently in clashes with organizational reality, the experience was usually unpleasant, though it might be a powerful teacher.

The learning gained from exposure to other people was most frequently a better understanding of oneself—one's own strengths and weaknesses, likes and dislikes. Or, because of the encouragement and support of these other people, there might be an increase in confidence. From *effective* bosses, executives learned what it took to develop people; from *difficult* bosses, executives might learn how to handle their superiors and how *not* to treat people.

But to focus on the most frequent lessons, particularly when it comes to what can be learned from other people, is to lose the true flavor of this kind of experience. Other people provide role models for almost any aspect of human endeavor, so the lessons taken from working with them or observing them can be about almost anything. In the international sphere, the lessons are often directly related to handling the cultural issues around work and relationships. When the contact with another person occurs early in a career, the learning is often about the basics of managing people. Such learning, of course, may be a matter of watching rather than doing, but it is no less valuable.

There is a large gap between seeing what someone else does well or badly and actually incorporating the lessons into one's own behavior. Nonetheless, the importance of other people—the largest single category in our study—in developing global executives cannot be overemphasized. We asked additional questions about these kinds of relationships, and they will be explored more thoroughly in the next chapter.

Special projects, consulting roles, and staff advisory jobs represented another of our top five experiences. While these experiences usually involved working as part of a team, giving advice, or doing a study rather than taking on bottom-line responsibility, they can be efficient teachers and are usually less risky than the major line assignments. Their well-defined tasks and time-limited nature allow for considerable flexibility, making this type of experience accessible to junior managers and technical people, and making it relatively easy to include a cross-cultural component in the event. When sufficiently challenging, these experiences bolster belief in oneself; when they provide exposure to serious business issues, they can teach lessons in business strategy and running a business. Although this sounds similar to some of the lessons from major line experiences, these less dramatic experiences are not so powerful as teachers. Nonetheless, a corporation's larger strategies and structural issues are sometimes more apparent to staff and consultants than to people out on the firing line, so the learning can be quite valuable.

Frankly, we were surprised at how frequently *developmental and educational experiences* was mentioned as a key event in these executives' lives. Relatively short-term and clearly defined, these experiences covered a broad territory, from undergraduate programs in another country to M.B.A. programs to executive programs run inside the company or externally, and from development programs featuring action learning projects to rotational programs. Most of these experiences gained their power from taking place in a culture other than one's native country—ironic in light of recent trends toward making education local through the use of the Internet or the establishment of university extensions in key countries. In fact, the most frequent lesson from these experiences was learning about other cultures, either by actually living in the culture while attending the program, through exposure to people from multiple countries who were in the program, or both. Other lessons included learning how to run a business (it was nice to see that content could play a part in education!) and learning to be flexible and adaptable. The flexibility and adaptability presumably came from the demands that attending the program added to an existing job, or from cultural immersion created by where the program was held or who was in it. In programs such as action learning that involved work projects, the executives learned about putting together an effective team (much like the lesson from negotiations). In the more academic programs, the executives learned about how to develop people (one wonders what this was about—and whether the learning was purely theoretical or if there was something more personal about it).

A *stint at headquarters,* although a low-frequency event, could leave lasting impressions. These events might involve a foreign national's coming to the corporate headquarters—usually intended as a developmental move—or an expatriate's return to the home country. In either case, the experience was usually memorable more for its unpleasantness than for its opportunities. Consider this example:

At age thirty-two, after managing a large subsidiary in my home country, Brazil, I was sent to the headquarters in Europe. I had been with the company for ten years, and I was sent to the parent company to learn from it.

This was a very difficult challenge. At headquarters they were not used to expats, so they weren't organized to handle them. They received me as a lower-level manager, even though my job was supposed to be at a higher level than I had held. They were very arrogant—they acted as if they were doing me and my company a favor by letting me come.

I almost gave it up after a few months. I had been successful in South America with our most important product, and now I was given a lower job with a product that was a low priority. Because of the language difference, I had difficulty expressing myself. The product was a political issue because the president wanted it to be successful, but my immediate boss didn't care about it. Why did I deserve this?

Once I committed to "playing their game," I learned an enormous amount. They were very good at what they did, and I learned the sophisticated tools of marketing. I learned that with so many bright young people around, you can't just sit quietly—you have to challenge and disagree. You don't have to win all the time, but you have to be prepared by doing an in-depth analysis. I learned to be humble. What matters is what you think of yourself; never give up your ethics, your core values. Setbacks teach you how to cope with tough times, give you perspective.

I provided the evidence the president needed to justify going to market, and I eventually built a relationship with him. He recognized that I could do a lot more than this job demanded. The second year, they gave me the most important product to manage, with assistants and a secretary.

My family situation at the time was significant. We had three young kids, and my wife didn't speak the language. I had to go to take the boys to the schools; in South America there had been maids for all that. She had to cook, take care of the baby. I changed diapers, fed the baby bottles. The kids adapted after six months, but, for my wife, it was a difficult two years. But because of this, we became a closer family, we supported each other. This strength served us well later on.

This story is not unusual. A well-intended effort by the company to develop a foreign national almost backfires, but ends up as a powerful learning event. Unfortunately not all the learning was positive, but in this case, it came out all right and the executive built some important relationships. In this example, "building a relationship with the president" might indeed be critically important for an executive from outside the home culture of the company.

Clearly, interacting with corporate office executives provides valuable lessons in managing the interface with headquarters. From being treated in a condescending manner, or through an act of kindness, many of these executives learned the importance of treating other people with fairness and respect—especially people from other countries. By watching and being a part of the top-level decision-making process, they learned about the hows and whys of running the business. From the relocation, they learned a lot about the culture they found themselves in. And finally, from surviving all of it, they learned to believe in themselves.

Our final short-term assignment was involvement in the *negotiations* that global organizations have in abundance. The developmental negotiations described to us were usually short-term, specific, and formal and usually involved a customer, a union, a government, or a partner. The outside party, often from another country, was reluctant if not hostile, and the goal of the negotiation was to arrive at a price, a contract, or an agreement. The executive was usually part of a team representing the company, and the stakes and the visibility could be enormous. As one might expect, the primary lesson from these intense experiences was negotiation skill, including the more generic but central skills in listening carefully to the other person's perspective and persevering through adversity and setback. Less obvious were the lessons learned from building and motivating the negotiating team itself.

Perspective-Changing Experiences

The perspective-changing experiences reported by our executives included the following:

- Culture shock (27 percent)
- Career shifts (21 percent)

- Confrontations with reality (18 percent)
- Changes in scope or scale (17 percent)
- Mistakes and errors in judgment (10 percent)
- Family and personal challenges (8 percent)
- Crises (7 percent)

For lack of a better label, we called the last seven experiences perspective-changing because that is what they did. All seven were ancillary to the executive's job assignment in the sense that they came along with it, even though, as teachers, the experiences may have been far more important than the job per se. From the perspective of an assignment-based approach to developing executives, it is important to note the pervasive influence of this type of experience. These perspective-changing experiences plus the events coded as *significant other people* (part of a job only in the sense that a boss usually comes with the territory), all of which were not job assignments per se, accounted for half of all the 332 events described, and they were a significant component of many of the other half.

Culture shock was about the impact of being in a culture dramatically different from one's own. Among the eighteen developmental experiences, culture shock is the single experience that by itself is unique to global work. It was important not only because it was among the top five developmental experiences described by the executives, but also because it was a *powerful* experience, bested only by business turnarounds in terms of the sheer number of lessons taught.

Not surprisingly, the learning from culture shock is all about understanding and dealing with a new culture and with one's reactions to it. All three of our cultural lessons—lessons about foreign language, about specific cultures, and about changing cultures—are focused on this event. The experience of culture shock also teaches the important underpinnings for effectiveness in foreign environments: learning to listen and ask questions, seeing the world through other people's eyes, learning the value (indeed the necessity) of being open and genuine, learning to be flexible, and learning to adapt to the differences. An outsider or a foreigner could also learn about the importance of establishing credibility in the local environment—of bringing something of value to the situation. Culture shock is such an important transformational experience that we will deal with it in greater detail in the next chapter.

In some cases, taking on a new assignment required the manager to change career direction dramatically, experience we have labeled *career shifts*. The nature of the shifts varied widely and included some of the following experiences:

- Leaving a domestic career for an international one
- Changing from one function or product line to a different one
- Shifting from staff to line, or vice versa
- Leaving school to take a job
- Leaving one company to join another in a different industry
- Leaving an organization to start one's own business

Along with the career shift, the person often had to deal with a new country, family issues, changes in scope, or a joint venture—just to make things interesting.

The lessons of career shifts could be as varied as the shifts themselves. Most frequently, people reported learning something about running a different kind of business or about working in a different culture, and they also gained self-confidence from getting through all the change. Depending on the magnitude of the change, a career shift could involve considerable personal risk, in which case it offered lessons in risk taking. Sometimes, the career shift involved major disruption for the family, or the family's security, offering perspective on the importance of family and family support. In still other cases, the executive learned to recognize the developmental value of the shift and translated that into how to develop others.

Another kind of shock that resulted in lessons learned was about the realities of organizational life. We called these *confrontations with reality*. Unpleasant surprises were common in careers. These surprises included entanglements in corporate politics; being the victim of the arbitrary actions of others; feeling betrayed, exiled, or unfairly treated; and having one's ethics and values tested by circumstances. The events sometimes involved foreign bosses or cultural biases, but one needn't be in a foreign country to stumble into the dark side of organizations and human relationships. Almost always surprises, the experiences often caused frustration and disillusionment. The lessons they taught were invaluable, however. From such dark moments, executives learned to

persevere through adversity and, correspondingly, that they could succeed in the long run. They learned about organizational politics and
sometimes how to cope with it. They learned from being badly treated
how important it is to treat people fairly and to be open and genuine
with others. And they learned about themselves—what they liked and
didn't and what was important to them.

Other perspective-changing events were *changes in scope or scale* that
accompanied a new assignment. The changes could be from small and
simple to large and complex, from domestic to global, or from tactical
to strategic—a variety of possibilities. The shifts, though, were almost
uniformly sudden and large, and often came along as part of a turnaround or of building a business. Having access to a significant other
person to help was often an important part of a successful change in
scope. The primary challenge here was to learn how to run a business
on a much larger scale, so most of the lessons were about that. They
included the importance of listening to other people (how else could
you learn to deal with the complexity?) and the need to build credibility (others could also see the dramatic shift and wondered if the executive would be able to do it). Increased scale in an international setting
usually brought with it many new relationships, including at times the
need to learn how to deal with foreign governments. And, as is the case
with almost all demanding experiences and particularly perspective-
changing ones, getting through it added to a person's self-confidence.

Although confrontations with reality usually reflected on the organization or other people's actions, *mistakes and errors in judgment* were
clearly of the manager's own doing. Mistakes and errors in judgment
have long been recognized as great teachers, and these global executives had made many of them. In these experiences, a person's own
actions or misjudgment caused things to go wrong, either with the
business aspect at hand or with key relationships. The learning
occurred when responsibility for the mistake was accepted, though it
may have come at the time of the mistake or sometime afterward. Most
of these mistakes involved cultural differences, so among the most frequent lessons were realizations about the culture the manager was in.
From these mistakes, managers tended to learn the importance of
listening to other people and understanding their perspectives, as well
as the importance of their openness and genuineness in dealing with

others. When the event involved a mistake they made as a leader, they also reported learning some important lessons in what motivates people—particularly people unlike themselves. And, as in most of the perspective-changing events, the executives experienced an increased belief in themselves, especially from successfully recovering and getting past the mistake.

As has been well documented in previous research, most expatriates don't go to the new country by themselves; the executives thus face numerous *personal and family challenges*. The obvious issues stem directly from being in a foreign culture, from finding a house to finding a dentist. But some are subtler, for instance, when an international career demands extensive travel. Many people learned to ignore their families' experiences at their own peril. Expect a foreign assignment to repair a relationship, and you'll most likely be in for an unpleasant surprise. Of course, this was the major lesson when family stress became a key event—how to manage the family under stress and what support you need from others to survive the stress yourself. Our executives learned many lessons about the specific culture they were in, as well as about the importance of perseverance, both for the executive and for the family. We will discuss this more in the next chapter.

Crises can occur in any job, domestic or international, and handling a crisis is often remembered as a developmental experience. The poisoning of Tylenol, for example, that rocked Johnson & Johnson and became legendary as a result of CEO James Burke's handling of it, had all the elements of a crisis: unexpected and largely out of the control of the executives, intense media pressure, novelty, deadlines for action, and high stakes. The Tylenol scare was no doubt a crisis of the highest magnitude, occupying the full attention of the senior officers and testing their values. No one involved in it or watching it unfold firsthand could ever be quite the same again.

Not all the crises we heard about were so dramatic, but dealing with terrorists or attempted sabotage are by most people's standards demanding events. Most crises took place in another country, where the executive on the spot had to handle the situation. In other words, the lessons of international crises, such as learning to handle the media and to take responsibility, are forced on the on-the-spot executives. Often far from the support available at home, these executives had to take care of things themselves and do so immediately. A European exec-utive described his experience with a crisis as a young and new general manager in an Asian country. Faced with accusations of bribery and a hostile press during holiday time in his headquarters' country, he finally reached a senior executive by cell phone, who replied, "You handle it, Mats. We trust you." From dealing with crises, the executives learned something about themselves and what they stood for, as well as about developing a business that could cope with a crisis and its aftermath. Fortunately, large-magnitude crises were relatively rare.

Perspectives on International Experience

Providing thumbnail descriptions of so many kinds of experiences has two serious disadvantages. First, it in no way captures the richness of individual experience so evident in the personal stories such as those in chapter 3. Second, in looking at the details of many experiences, we are in danger of losing sight of the larger significance of the results. In the next chapter, we try to get back up on the balcony to survey the larger landscape. We will do this by looking more closely at some experiences that are particularly salient in the context of international executive development. These experiences include culture shock, the role of other people (the most frequent experience cited), formal programs, and the impact on the family.

Making Sense of Culture

It has become commonplace to speak of the discomfort that occurs on meeting members of another culture as "culture shock." . . . True culture shock occurs when differences run deep and immersion is complete, so much so that ordinary assumptions are overthrown, when panic overcomes irritation. In severe culture shock, one may feel that one is going insane.

—*Mary Catherine Bateson*,
Peripheral Visions: Learning along the Way

We described the experiences that develop global executives in chapter 5. Of the eighteen types of experiences, seventeen are superficially similar to those experienced by any executive. They seemed to take on new meaning, however, when accompanied by the remaining type of experience: culture shock. Mary Catherine Bateson, herself an anthropologist, describes the experience of culture shock well; as she implies, the term is hardly new with her, and it isn't with us either.[1] More than forty years old and usually attributed to anthropologist Kalvero Oberg's 1960 article, the term *culture shock* has come to mean the surprise and anxiety that we experience as a result of a loss of identity when we are immersed in a different culture.[2] Not only is the term hardly new, but culture shock has been studied extensively by cross-cultural scholars.

In this chapter, we will discuss at some length the way culture shock, as we use the term, combines with business experiences to develop the global mind-set. Culture shock, in one form or another, drives learning across cultures. Our study clearly supports the conclusion that cross-cultural work experience is essential for developing the global mind-set.

. . . . .

But when people learn about culture, they are not doing it by them-selves, and not always in results-oriented business assignments. As it turns out, significant other people in an executive's life are major con-tributors to global executive development, to an extent and in ways that far exceed their impact in developing domestic executives. The same is true of developmental and educational experiences, a type of experi-ence that we found to be, at its best, an efficient teacher of global les-sons. For each of these developmental experiences, we provide in this chapter additional discussion and new findings.

Finally, we add some perspective on family issues, an area well known for its impact on global executive success, and one that our executives brought to the fore also. Family issues, like it or not, may well be different if the executive is a man or a woman. Although our sample included only nine women and we did not set out to address the issues of women and family in global work, we discuss some of the issues, even if our results are tentative, at best.

Culture Shock

. . . . .

Our use of the term *culture shock* is slightly different than the standard usage described above. We use *culture shock* to classify a particular type of developmental event—one in which development is driven by the fact that the experience takes place in a different culture, rather than by the business experience itself. This follows our definition of global work in chapter 2 as some mix of crossing business and country cul-tures. Cross-cultural research—focusing as it does on crossing cultures rather than on doing business—has only limited applicability. Indeed, we might have used the term *opportunities to learn about other cultures,* but we used *culture shock* to reinforce the essential cultural nature of the learning and the transformational nature of this experience for the global executive. Here are examples that, brief as they are, just touch the surface of what culture shock can be:

> They offered me a job in Singapore, and I took it even though I was unfamiliar with the culture. I started looking for help and took a "basic culture course" for expats, and I thought I was prepared. How

wrong I was. When I got there, I found that my subordinates answered the way they thought I wanted; it took me some time to figure out the sign they gave me that something wasn't true. Finally I figured out that the company that looked good on paper was, in reality, a bleeding hole. I was too young to be there (thirty-three years old) and too Swedish, managing Indians, Malays, Chinese, Indonesians. I made many mistakes, and ten thousand miles from headquarters, I had to manage on my own. I had a good boss who understood the culture, and he helped me with that part of it. (A Swede in Singapore)

I was sent to Thailand as a computer instructor, teaching in the sales school. I was not in Bangkok, but in a rural area where people didn't speak English—I had to learn Thai to eat! We ate with flies all over the place. . . . They would fly into your mouth as you ate. It was a real culture shock. I was teaching salespeople from all over Asia, all with different backgrounds. They were not all alike, but I had assumed they were. They were so different—the Malaysians hated the Singaporeans, for example. I made stupid assumptions and up-set people with my insensitivity. It is different today. Countries ac-cept multinational presence, and expats are more knowledgeable. (A Hong Kong Chinese in Thailand)

It is easy to imagine the anxiety and discomfort caused by these experiences, and without diminishing the importance of the amount of learning about business, it is not hard to see why the cultural differ-ences overshadowed the business learning. Learning about business in a different cultural context is fundamentally different from learning about business in one's own culture.

Despite our examples, as the saying goes, "an example is not an argument." Perhaps, considering all the experiences across all the cate-gories, they are not really all that different from what domestic execu-tives experience. Some additional evidence shows that they are quite different indeed.

As mentioned previously, our study uses basically the same method-ology as did an earlier study conducted in the United States with U.S. executives.[3] As a result, we could compare the experiences of our global executives with the experiences described by U.S. executives, albeit

* * * * *

fifteen years earlier. For the research-oriented reader, table C-5 in appendix C presents a detailed comparison of the experiences.

The experiences from the two studies show striking similarities. Indeed, the kinds of experiences that executives, whether global or in the United States, say shaped them are still turnarounds, start-ups, changes in scope and scale, special projects, significant other people, and the like. To be sure, there are differences in the specifics (for instance, a stint at headquarters and joint ventures are separate categories in the global study) and in the percentages, but we were initially surprised (or perhaps relieved) at just how similar the experiences were. The one experience that is obviously distinct for the global sample, culture shock, is no surprise at all, given that the U.S. group was domestic. We might conclude from these results and from the similarities among the lessons learned, described in chapter 4, that for all practical purposes, developing global and domestic executives is the same.

But before we accept that conclusion too readily, let's take a deeper look at the experiences of our global executives. In both the experiences themselves and in the lessons they learned, *culture* stands out as the differentiating factor. So even if that were the *only* difference between the two studies, we would still have to deal with its implications. But it is not the only difference.

Although the types of experiences are similar, *where* the experiences took place was not. To explore this further, we divided the 332 experiences according to whether they took place while the executives were living and working in their home countries *(domestic)*, living in the home country but working across country borders *(international)*, or living and working in another culture *(expatriate)*. We set up an index, albeit rough, of the degree of cultural challenge in an experience, from domestic through international to expatriate. We could then apply our index to the experiences of global executives, asking what types of experiences produce the lessons of the study.

The results are clear-cut. For our global executives, whatever the type of developmental experience, the experiences were far more likely to take place in cultures other than their own, either in expatriate assignments or in international ones. Whatever the lessons of international experience, the *experiences* that teach them take place overwhelmingly when the executive is working in another culture. As a result, for global executives, events that may seem similar on the surface

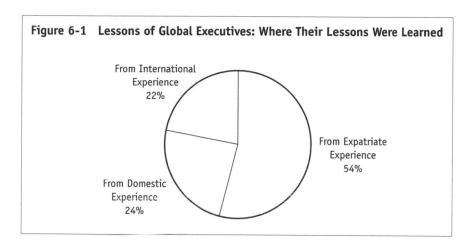

Figure 6-1   Lessons of Global Executives: Where Their Lessons Were Learned

From International
Experience
22%

From Expatriate
Experience
54%

From Domestic
Experience
24%

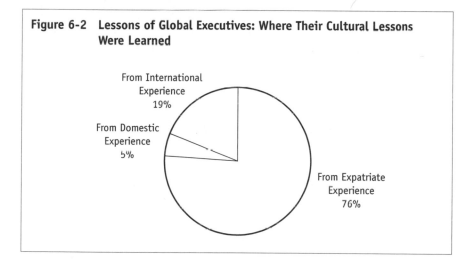

Figure 6-2   Lessons of Global Executives: Where Their Cultural Lessons Were Learned

From International
Experience
19%

From Domestic
Experience
5%

From Expatriate
Experience
76%

(e.g., a business turnaround) take place in culturally challenging, more complex, and more difficult settings.

We did the same analysis for the lessons discussed in chapter 4, with essentially the same result since the lessons flow from the experiences (figure 6-1): *The lessons learned by global executives are learned in global work.*

Although this is true for all lessons taken as a whole, this is even more dramatic for lessons about dealing with other cultures. Nearly all (95 percent) lessons of culture are learned outside of the domestic setting (figure 6-2). Clearly, the lessons of culture simply aren't learned by sitting at home.

For the unconvinced, one final question remains: Are the lessons of experience taught by crossing cultures truly important in developing global executives? Are they simply lessons of culture, or are they closely linked to learning about business? We explored this question by examining the extent to which culture shock took place concurrently with the line assignments, such as turnarounds and start-ups. Our analysis (the process of assigning double codes to experiences, as described in appendix B) showed that experiences that might be primarily a business turnaround, for example, also usually included culture shock and taught culture lessons as well.

An additional observation from comparing the two samples has very practical implications for companies designing global development programs: Relative to the U.S. study, *the links between an experience and the lessons it taught were not nearly so systematic in the global study.* This means that predicting what an executive will learn from a specific experience, uncertain at best even in domestic settings, becomes even less certain in the global sphere.

What Makes a Culture Shock Developmental?

The term *culture shock* and our examples belie the variety in the stories we were told. True, in its broadest sense, the experience is one of going into a culture different from one's own. But virtually all these executives had gone into countries other than their own, often into many different countries, and yet not every cultural encounter was dramatic or even memorable. Nor were the potent cultural experiences limited to assignments with the additional stress of being in countries torn by war, poverty, or disease. Culture-shock stories occurred just as often in the United States, England, Norway, France, Argentina, Sweden, and other countries with living conditions more similar to where most of our executives came from.

As diverse as the specific incidents were, culture shocks that were developmental usually had the following common characteristics:

- There was some kind of disconnect between the person's prior experience and expectations and what happened in the new country.

- The person was surprised by the disconnect.
- It was usually the first time such a disconnect had been experienced.
- What was confronted was broader than differences in business practices and included deeper cultural issues.
- The executive had a strong sense of being an outsider.

The surprise took various forms. At times it was driven by the executive's incorrect assumptions about other people's values, motivation, willingness to be candid, or lifestyles. Because the assumption was incorrect, the executive ended up surprised or shocked when things didn't go as expected. Other times it was driven by the executive's own style or behavior: being aggressive, passive, autocratic, or consensus-oriented in a culture that valued the opposite and where those actions had little effect or even backfired.

In both cases, expectations were not met. Some of the most frequent examples included Western executives in Eastern countries who found out the hard way that candid feedback and confrontation are not always the norm; and Eastern executives in the West who discovered that if they sat quietly they were left out.

Acquiring the Global Mind-Set

If learning from experience is substantially different in a cross-cultural context, it throws us back into the ongoing debate about transformational experiences and the development of a global mind-set. As suggested in chapter 4, cultural immersion leads to a personal transformation. The exact nature of the transformation is harder to elucidate, as it contains elements of a changed perspective about other people as well as about oneself. Joyce Osland described this as both "letting go" and "taking on": the letting go of "cultural certainty, unquestioned acceptance of basic assumptions, personal frames of reference, the unexamined life, accustomed role and status, knowledge of social reinforcement, accustomed habits and activities, and known routines," and the taking on of "positive changes in self, changed attitudes, improved work skills, increased knowledge, and closer family relationships."[4] Craig Storti describes it as *either* positive or negative, but transformational either way:

. . . . .

> The experience of living abroad profoundly transforms all who
> undergo it, whether they adjust to the culture or not. Such is the
> impact of the experience, at so many levels—physical, intellectual,
> emotional—there is not the possibility of a moderate, much less
> neutral, reaction. We either open ourselves to the experience and are
> greatly enriched by it. Or we turn away and are greatly diminished.[5]

But as profound as personal transformation may be, including psychological changes as well as changes in perspectives and skills, its
value in the executive job or in organizational life can be difficult to
translate into concrete business terms. Perhaps only the business-
related components of the transformation—a narrower view of what
constitutes a global mind-set—are directly, or at least visibly, transfer-
able to other business settings. Stewart Black and his associates, for
example, said that "leaders with global mind-sets view the world—not
just the home country—as the arena for value creation."[6] Christopher
Bartlett and Sumantra Ghoshal describe it in purely business terms:
"Managers with a global mentality, in contrast, focused on creating
products for a world market and manufacturing them on a global
scale in a few highly efficient central plants. They assumed that
national tastes and preferences were more similar than different, or
that they could be made so."[7] But we believe that developing such
a business mind-set is much more easily achieved than the other kinds
of changes suggested by transformation. Indeed, international experience, not necessarily expatriate experience, may be sufficient to create
such a limited mind-set. Perhaps this narrow view of what it means to
be global explains why expatriates so often feel frustrated and under-
used when they arrive home filled with personal as well as business
learning.

The point here is that expatriates may be transformed and, according to the chapter 2 definition of the global executive, they may be the
most global of executives. But others may develop the global mind-set,
even if in a more limited form. Group Senior Vice President, Group
Function Human Resources, Arne Olsson, of ABB Ltd., described to us
the need for such a mind-set throughout the global organization:

> A "local" leader can be a "global" leader, sometimes even more
> global than colleagues who are working or have been working in a

country other than their own. . . . A global organization . . . will not function well as a global organization unless a lot of local people in that organization, wherever they are, think global, seeing the big picture beyond the local picture. It could be a secretary or it could be a person dealing with production scheduling. These are people who make things work across national border lines, providing an "organizational glue" which helps to keep the pieces together behind the global heroes who make statements publicly on behalf of the company or sign an important contract with a customer.

As our discussion indicates, we have come away strong believers that learning to work across cultures is done by doing so. Before we summarize the implications of chapters 5 and 6, we will look at three additional experiences in more detail: significant other people, developmental and educational experiences, and family and personal challenges, all of which have special significance in developing global executives.

Significant Other People

"Significant other people" was the most frequent of the eighteen experiences described by the global executives, and it assumed even greater importance in our study than in the earlier domestic studies.

Perhaps not surprisingly, the lessons taught by significant other people are most often lessons of leadership—how to lead and what it takes to be a leader. Leadership is a relational activity; it takes place between leaders and followers. Even when we attempt to teach leadership in books and classes, the cases are about leaders, not abstract concepts. The open, listening, flexible, optimistic style that works so well in the global context appears in the two lesson themes that involve leadership (see chapter 4): learning about the personal qualities of a leader, and learning to lead and manage others.

By a wide margin, the most common significant other person was the executive's boss. Asked who they learned the most from, the executives replied that 77 percent of those listed were bosses, and 8 percent were their boss's boss. Sometimes our executives learned by *watching* their bosses lead—for good or ill, but usually for good—and sometimes they were intentionally taught, but learn they did. This learning was often expressed in rules of thumb or maxims that were remembered years later:

- "It is not just what results you get, but what you are doing to grow people."
- "Select the best people in the world."
- "If you know more about something than anyone else, you don't need to be nervous."
- "You can give away little things (in negotiations) that don't matter at all to you, but matter a lot to the other side."
- "Don't lose patience with the locals."
- "You have to understand the facts."
- "Know how the customer benefits."

As we examined our data, we found that although we had wonderful examples of significant other people as teachers in expatriate assignments, in fact such people were more likely to be encountered when the executive was in a *domestic* assignment. In a sense, the importance of other people as teachers was diminished when an executive was on an overseas assignment. In those cases, the culture and the business situation (e.g., a turnaround or start-up), rather than a significant other person, constituted the largest part of an executive's development. This is important news for organizations—they can take advantage of opportunities to provide good teachers in a simpler environment.

The influence of significant other people, as an experience, can teach as many kinds of lessons as there are teachers and situations and learners who are open to the lessons. One executive had learned a fundamental lesson of life at an early age by observing the most impressive person he knew—his girlfriend's father, a rich and famous physician—lose his power and influence through arrogance and pride. Another considered himself lucky to learn from a customer that he needed to do an about-face in his management style if he was to succeed in that country. On his first trip abroad, one executive learned the basic rules of entrepreneurship from a wise old businessman in Singapore. When one man watched his boss—the wrong person in the wrong job at the wrong time—fail, he learned "to think very hard about who you put into a job" and the key role that culture can play. Another leader learned from her boss, "a good teacher," a total grasp of the business, the politics, and how to get things done. She also learned how important it is to provide a safe environment for giving feedback to the boss. Finally, one woman gave us an example of the possibilities for learning from a global boss while in a domestic job:

> When he came in as my boss, I was suddenly reporting to someone at a much higher level, and I was now dealing with people several levels above me. This made me very uncomfortable, but he was extremely supportive, gave me tips, opened doors for me, and got people to sit down and talk with me. And I traveled with him once a quarter, and he would give me tips on how to get my points across. He is very different in managing people and has a kind of command-and-control style that is effective in Latin America, where he is "God," but not in the U.S. He relies on me to moderate his style. I know what will be foreign to him.

Experiences offer us many people as teachers, whether they intend to teach us or not, and people differ in how much they make use of them. Some people find the teachers and learn from them; some don't. Andrew and Jean, of chapter 3, represent perhaps the two extremes. Jean seemed to learn from significant other people in every experience he had. Andrew never told us of learning from others in any of his experiences, and when we asked whom he learned the most from, he replied, "There is not one person I can say, because the truth is I did not have very good teachers." Some executives, like Jean, characteristically seek out other people as teachers; Andrew seems to try it on his own and, as we saw in his story, has a bent for drawing strategic lessons from the experiences he has.

Even if people have the same teachers, however, we are never quite sure what students will learn. Three executives listed Percy Barnevik, the larger-than-life former CEO of Asea Brown Boveri (ABB), as the person they learned the most from, but the lessons they took away were different. One learned "the business basics: Customers and competitors are the heart of it. He taught me simplicity. And he taught me it's not just you, it's what you are doing to grow other people." Another learned

. . . . .

"to think about the importance of motivating people, making people want/like to do what you want. Now I try to present things in ways that create that enthusiasm." The third executive learned that "in any transaction, you have to understand the facts. . . . [Barnevik] would never react without understanding the facts. But once he did, and he could analyze them in seconds, he would act fast, do things immediately. With these simple principles, I can do this job well."

Our examples provide several thinking points:

1. Other people are a very significant source of global leadership development.
2. Although the lessons that can and will be learned are legion, the lessons of leadership are the natural curriculum.
3. For the great majority of people, bosses are the most significant teachers.
4. Some people characteristically learn from other people; others do not.
5. What an executive learns will very much depend on who he or she is and what the situation is, even when the teacher is the same.
6. With so many opportunities to provide significant other people to learn from, even in domestic settings, organizations can add global dimensions to domestic work by using global bosses as teachers.

Developmental and Educational Experiences

. . . . .

In our emphasis on *job* experiences, we sometimes forget that education is experience also, with important lessons to be learned that are probably more predictable than the lessons learned from other kinds of experiences. For our study executives, the category "Developmental and Educational Experiences" was third among the eighteen categories of experiences in terms of frequency. It was cited more often by our global executives than by the domestic executives of the earlier study.

Unlike job assignments, the primary purpose of developmental and educational experiences is development rather than immediate business results. Even action learning programs, which make the solution of some business problem a part of the program, usually begin with a development purpose. Without a direct business purpose, whether the education takes place inside the company or outside in a setting such as MIT or INSEAD, organizations are continuously asking, "Are these programs worth the cost?" The answer is, of course, "It depends."

Of the experiences we coded as developmental and educational, more than a third took place in high school, college, or graduate school, during the preparatory stage of people's careers. The lessons learned at those early stages of the executives' lives often involved self-confidence and the knowledge of where one fits in the world, as well as a maturing worldview. An executive growing up in Singapore told us of how a student-exchange program to Australia opened up his eyes to another world and caused him to see himself as a citizen of the world, not just of Singapore. A Swedish executive who went to New York City for post-doctoral work was surprised at how different Sweden and the United States were; he learned how Americans do things, and he came away understanding a fundamental fact of culture. "There is more than one way to skin a cat," he said, using the American idiom.

Although these early experiences represent opportunities for the organization to "cherry pick" applicants who have profited from those early experiences, perhaps of more interest are the educational experiences *after* they come to work. The internship programs that have characterized entry into large, global companies provided experiences for several of our executives and were recruiting enticements as well. They provided useful lessons in two areas: first, foundation knowledge of the business across a broad spectrum and, second, a core set of colleagues who would be helpful throughout their careers. An executive at Johnson & Johnson explained the importance of his participation in an early program. As an Indian coming to work in India for a U.S. company, he had much to learn:

> They sent me to the U.S. for training. First of all, I thought it was incredible that they would send an Indian to do that. But they made sure that everyone in the company gets a common experience. Seeing

&J in the U.S. made me think about world-class benchmarks, and it gave me a new goal, to be world-class rather than local. It also taught me the level and type of management skills among people there. It was a team approach, a new way for me. I learned that things can be done differently than the traditional Indian way. I also learned values—to ask, What is the best thing to do for the company? How does it fit the Credo? And, [I learned] that they trust me to make those decisions.

An ABB executive told us of the importance of an internship program just after he had joined the company nearly twenty years earlier in Brazil:

> When I joined Asea we had a big project and needed to double the size of the company to do it. We copied a Swedish program to train engineers quickly by rotating them across businesses. I was one of fifteen engineers rotated across departments to observe and give suggestions on how to improve. We very quickly learned who people were and made friends; they began to use us to help and as a channel to the president. Our challenge was not to be seen as a threat. In this one year, I learned to analyze all the processes . . . quality, contracts, production. I learned to respect people, to see their side, to go into a new situation and make new friends. Now when I go into a new job, I take the time to know the people and learn the processes. Then they sent us to Sweden for a year, so all fifteen of us knew almost everyone in the company.

The program described above might well have been at Ericsson, which has a long history of using an internship program with new hires. Here is an example:

> I was twenty-five when I started in the trainee program. I quickly got to learn about my colleagues, the company, the product, et cetera. I learned about the "Ericsson" experience. After a year and a half, I was asked to go start up a production facility in southeast Asia. I saw an early learning from my training course—that culture is about managing through people.

What made these programs stand out twenty or more years later? The elements are easily identified, even in these diverse examples: First, they provide the opportunity to learn something useful—what the business is about. Second, they expose the trainees to the culture of the company—how it does business. And finally, the elements introduced them to a network of people who they could work with in coming years. Especially for the Brazilian and Indian executives cited, it is not too far-fetched to imagine that they would never have made it into corporate management without close-up understanding of the "foreign" company they had gone to work for.

External executive educational and developmental programs provided another source of key experience. In a sense, these programs, typically attended by executives, not trainees, provide opposite opportunities: They teach about general business, not one company; they teach about other cultures, not the company culture; one gets to network and learn from executives from other companies, not one's own; they are a time for reflection, not action. Not surprisingly, the lessons are different:

> I attended INSEAD. Why? I wanted to reflect . . . and I wanted to go into international. Much more important than the textbook learning were the thirty to forty different nationalities. This forces you to act and react culturally and socially—in the U.S. you have a total absence of knowledge of the world outside. When you work and live with these groups, you can't escape. But it is learning without being in a fishbowl—you don't pay the consequences you would inside the company. There is less risk. We had to learn French, German, and English, and working in a different language forces you to see things differently.

Another executive, a scientist, went to a management program at Henley. Although he was from the United Kingdom, it was a different world from the one he was used to:

> This was my best training experience. I'd had exposure to business, but not to this extent. We were a multicultural group, as well as a mixture of functional specialties. Everything we did, every case, would be argued out and decided by your project team. First you'd

study on your own, and then be faced with the team's view and have to deal with it. Then you would adapt your view as the discussion flowed until we as a team settled on a strategy, a decision, a course of action. I learned the power of teamwork, of technology, of planning—the importance of singing from the same hymn sheet, the need to understand people. It shaped me in a way and style that helped me reach where I am now—open, communicative, with a participative style. I learned to live and work in a different environment.

These executives' reactions are not very different from those typically found in executives who have attended university-based executive programs. The safe environment, the comparisons with other executives of every stripe—especially from other cultures—encourages them to broaden their perspective and learn new behavior and leadership styles. New concepts and ways of thinking (e.g., Brian's experience in systems thinking at MIT, described in chapter 3) can make for powerful and useful experiences.

Action learning programs, typically done in-house with a group of high-potential executives addressing a significant corporate issue, are designed to combine the advantages of inside programs, outside programs, and work assignments. Although the programs sometimes do accomplish these goals, organizations are finding that they are time-consuming, expensive, and difficult to keep going. The programs lack the advantages of trainee/internship programs that are a part of the fabric of the organization, or of university-based programs that require little effort or involvement by the organization, other than paying the bills. But when effectively carried out, action learning has benefits to offset those disadvantages. Here is an example from one executive:

This was an internal program on leading change—high potentials in teams were given problems to work on that were serious business problems. My team included people from Germany [and] the U.S. and was very diverse. The whole thing was very intense, with lots of travel. It exposed me to our company perspective at a very senior level, and it taught me to deal with top companies from around the world. We eventually brought in top executives to meet with our top management, and I could see how other companies look at issues. I learned what individuals bring to the party, including myself, and I learned about how high-performance teams work and how to do it.

From a more general standpoint, what makes these more formal developmental and educational programs work? What turns training programs into key events for developing global executives? We start with intent: The organization and the executive must take the experiences seriously, see them as serious sources of learning, and have high expectations for the participants. And the programs must be global. The participants and the content must reflect the global nature of the organization, across cultures and across businesses. What's more, like the other development processes of the organization, the programs must be integral parts of the business strategy of the corporation.

Family Challenges

The family's importance in global success is hardly a new idea.[8] Most discussions of global work, especially expatriation, stress the importance of successful family adjustment; failure to adjust on the part of the family is often cited as the reason that executives return home early from overseas assignments. Nor is family adjustment a uniquely U.S. issue. Not only did we find it mentioned by our largely non-U.S. sample of executives, but authors from other countries also consider family adjustments a serious issue. For example, Monica Rabe, herself a Swede, has published a whole series of books that are devoted to family adjustment overseas and written for a broad audience (and published in Singapore!).[9]

Family issues came in two types: direct and indirect. The direct factor is the adjustment of the family itself; for example, we heard of one family that arrived in a particularly difficult country one day, only to depart the next, leaving the executive behind. A more indirect factor is simply the greater demands of global work on the executive, including extensive travel. Those demands produce greater stress, which in turn places greater demands on the resources of both the executives and their families. Some of those families survived, some didn't. Without asking, we heard of examples of both, but in both cases, the executives learned lessons about themselves and their families:

For the most part, the lesson learned was the importance of their family:

- "It took all my time—there was no time for family, my children. It was a very difficult period, personally. Now I can separate personal life from business life; I can switch it off."

- "I spend a hundred and fifty days per year traveling. My family is a key. I have a very brave wife, and I learned to respect the fact that all spouses can't take this. It's like an enterprise of its own. . . . After a long day, it is so important that she understands and supports me. Without her support, I'd be in Finland doing something else."

- "I had let my work become too dominant—my wife's decision to leave surprised me. I had been caught up and excited about work. As a result, I learned to keep some perspective."

- "Because of my family, we decided to live in Stockholm, where there were English-speaking schools, rather than two hours away, where the facility was. One of my key lessons was how to balance work and family life. I would work all week, but on weekends I was one hundred percent devoted to my family."

- "We were in London as third-country nationals when I was assigned to Paris. My family stayed in London, and we had a new baby. I brought the family over, but then I had to travel for six months. I should have left them in London, where they were settled in. . . . It would have been much easier for them. . . . I would think more about that in the future."

One doesn't have to move to another country to find that a global assignment produces family stress, notably, extensive travel and time away from the family. Regional assignments in a foreign country with responsibilities throughout a geographic region (e.g., Asia Pacific) seem designed to include the worst of both worlds—extensive travel, *and* a family adrift in a new location. Compounding the difficulty for the family is that the difference (if they come from a different culture) will be greater for them than for the executive. The executive will move into an office with a familiar company culture and procedures and everyone (at least at senior levels) speaking English. As one of our executives in Asia pointed out, the role of nonworking spouse in Asia may be more difficult for a husband than for a wife because most Asian societies are simply not accustomed to husbands staying at home. Despite the admonition, we know of cases in which "trailing" husbands worked out just fine.

The solution to family issues would seem to be the placement of those without families into global jobs. Even if there were enough single executives to fill the jobs, our executives pointed out that such a solution is not without problems of its own. People without families have their own particular sets of difficulties. Another solution might be to use dual-career couples, but that solution is not without its problems too. As global as the world may be, in many countries, spouses—either husbands or wives—cannot be employed. Where both can work, child care becomes a special problem. One executive, half of a dual-career couple, explained that neither her job nor her husband's could be done without extensive travel, and that even with live-in help, she and her husband must schedule their trips months ahead in order to keep one parent at home.

Families fashion a variety of solutions to these issues as diverse as their situations. Our executives seemed perhaps too bound by their own experience to see what could be done, leaving us with many seeming contradictions born of their experience. The wife of an Australian executive in Japan spent most of her time back in Australia with their family, but another executive said that he would never send people who didn't have their family with them. One executive said that he would never again send single people—they couldn't adapt—but another had great success in sending a physically striking, six-foot-tall, single, black woman to Italy as an expatriate.

The executives and their families managed, however well or badly. Many had been divorced—it was difficult to tell how many; we didn't ask. But what was clear was that, in their eyes, at least, their organizations had done little to help them deal with family issues. This came as a surprise to us, given that most organizations were well aware of the family issues related to being a global executive and believed that they provided extensive support.

. . . . .

The Experiences of Women Executives

. . . . .

Our sample of 101 global executives included nine women. Although we have included many of their comments in the quotations throughout these chapters, nine is too few to offer generalizations with any confidence. Still, nine global women executives is too many to resist the temptation of at least offering observations. We arrived at our observations by both reading over the nine interview protocols and by comparing the coded key events and lessons.

In terms of background, the women were as diverse as our men. Their origins were Africa, Australia, France, Holland, Indonesia, the United Kingdom, and the United States. We interviewed them in their offices in New York, New Jersey, Hong Kong, London, The Hague, Jakarta, and Paris. Their positions included business head, worldwide sales and marketing vice president, company general manager, regional human resources manager, and country director—finance and administration.

We were struck by the lack of differences in key events and lessons learned between the men and women executives. We had reviewed all the individual key events in our analysis, but without any gender identifier. Reading them again, however, this time grouping them by gender, we seldom found anything that would suggest gender differences. "Leaving a large company to run a smaller software company," "a first international assignment in Africa in a department that was in total disarray," "starting my own business in Singapore," "deciding to leave a Ph.D. program in biology and go to work for a business," "became the R&D director for Asia-Pacific"—all these sound as typical of men as of women. Of the twenty-five-odd key events from these interviews, only two specifically related to gender—one, the experience of being the only women engineer in a chemical plant, and the other, the experience of being one of only two women in a largely male external program. From both of these, a major lesson was learning to get along in a "man's" world. While this lesson is unique to women, it was common for international executives to be the only one of their kind—nationality, function, age, or the like. For them, the lesson was to learn how to get along in someone else's world.

Another area where we noticed a difference was in the background factors that contributed to going into or being effective in global work. Only one of our women could identify *no* important influences: "My dad was a policeman, and my mom was a housewife. They were horrified when I went to Brazil." More typical were these responses:

- "I grew up in two cultures, traveled a lot, was in school with people from all over the world."

- "Even as a child, I had the urge to travel."

- "I was brought up in a politically unstable environment (South Africa), where I was very much aware of being an exile, and in a very multicultural environment."

- "My grandmother took me all over the world when I was thirteen or fourteen and taught me to value other cultures, and my father was in the Air Force and we traveled a lot."

- "My father was Indonesian, my mother Chinese. We lived in Singapore, then Australia. . . . I was always interested in new things and developed cultural sensitivity early in my life."

Our interviews suggested that fewer women "happen onto" international careers and that, to get into global work, they very much have to be interested and pursue it. This would be consistent with the general tendency of companies to show reluctance in sending women overseas.

Although the *descriptions* of events by men or women were so similar as to be indistinguishable, our statistical analysis indicated that there is a difference between men and women in the overall *number* of events listed across categories, but not in the lessons learned. Women were over-represented in the event categories that we labeled career shifts, culture shock, and developmental and educational experiences, and under-represented in the events involving business turnarounds, building a business, and joint ventures.

Without overinterpreting the data from our very small group of women global executives, our results at least suggest that women learn the same lessons from the same kinds of global experiences as do men. They also suggest, however, that the women executives were not experiencing as often some of the key events that men found most valuable, especially the very difficult experiences like business turnarounds.

Now What?

In chapters 5 and 6, we described eighteen kinds of experiences that global executives said were important to them. The data have perhaps raised more issues than they have resolved, and our conclusions include what some will take as unhappy news. Specifically, if using experience to develop *domestic* executives is imprecise, then using experience to develop *global* executives is even more so. At a minimum, the latter requires considering simultaneously the person, the assignment, the context, and the culture, all of which muddy the waters considerably when it comes to what will be learned from an experience. What is clear, however, is that you don't learn about other cultures and about running a business in other cultures by staying home—even though those who do stay home may think that they have learned these lessons. As Craig Storti put it, "How can we learn and grow from our experiences if we don't have any?"[10]

The good news is that organizations directly control some of the developmental experiences, at least in terms of giving specific people the opportunity to have these experiences. These include assignments that require evolving a business, starting from scratch, turning a business or part of one around, negotiations, joint ventures, special projects, and a stint at headquarters. Organizations also control exposure to exemplary bosses and access to globally meaningful educational opportunities. Organizations can influence early work and first managerial experiences as well, if they attract talented people early enough in their careers. They also have control over whether a person has an expatriate opportunity, and if so, where, and whether a given job has an international component, whether or not it involves expatriation. But what actually happens in those experiences is less amenable to organizational control, especially when the uncertain impact of exposure to other people and foreign cultures is added in.

Other kinds of experiences are largely beyond the organization's control, except in how the organization reacts when they happen or what an organization does to prepare people for them. These include experiences that executives bring with them to the organization, those that occur unpredictably (such as confrontations with reality, mistakes, and crises), and those that are highly personal (such as culture shock, career shifts, and family and personal events).

Although a person can't learn more from an experience than is in it, "what is in it" very much depends on a person's background, prior experience, and growth. And, as Barbara Tuchman so effectively documented in *The March of Folly,* just because the lessons of experience are readily available doesn't mean that anyone will learn from them.[11] For these reasons, formulas for using experience for development are exceedingly dangerous in a global context. The good news is that many of the critical lessons needed by global executives can be learned (and need not be "born") and that organizations do indeed have considerable latitude in making the learning opportunities available and helping people actually learn from these. However, as the stories of Andrew, Jean, and Brian illustrated in chapter 3, in the final analysis the individual is the one who must do the learning.

Sometimes individuals do not learn because of their own inattention, ineptitude, or bad luck. Other times, they don't learn because the organization has not given them experiences that can teach, or has not provided the support for them to learn the critical lessons. But whatever the cause, when executives do not learn, they often derail. We take up that issue in the next chapter.

When Things Go Wrong

We are all flawed, and creatures of our times.

—*Carl Sagan*, The Demon-Haunted World

Global work is a risky proposition. Given the wrong set of circumstances, even the most talented people can derail. Consider the following descriptions of five capable people:

> Cheong had a very strong and shrewd understanding of people and financial processes. He was honest and stuck to his guns. He was able to look for opportunities. He knew the politics and the technical content that he needed to know. He was a good teacher.

> Lars was very likable, he was inspirational, people were warm and affectionate toward him.

> Paul was analytical, he cared about people, and he was imaginative. He seemed to have everything.

> Jorge had great interpersonal skills, was a very hard worker, was a great salesman, and went the extra step to learn cultures.

> Johanne listened, understood things, and could get right to the core issues and make a decision. He was personable and promoted an open environment. He made it key to be honest, even if you didn't know the answers. He was a good role model and made good decisions.

No doubt about it: All five of these international executives were talented people. Most companies would be delighted to have any of them, and it is no surprise that they reached very high levels of global responsibility. They were, however, among the 121 talented people described to us who had derailed in international assignments.

No matter whom you ask, developing global executives is an expensive proposition, especially when expatriate assignments are involved (as is usually the case, at one time or another). But the expense can be viewed as an investment with a significant expected return—provided that the knowledge and expertise gained from the experience can be used effectively by the corporation. When things go wrong, not only is the investment sacrificed, but so is a person previously judged by intelligent people to be quite talented. In other words, global executive derailments are doubly expensive. The executives in our study, with their average of nine years' expatriate experience, were in a unique position to observe other global executives come and go, and the five tales that started this chapter are revealing. What became of these five?

> A huge change was going on in the organization, and Cheong had a different point of view on a couple of key business issues. Even though he delegates, he gets too involved in detail. He may have swamped himself in the details, which takes time out from the strategic view. He failed to see the strategy. He is also a very volatile person, and he finds it hard when his loyalty is not returned.

> Lars was too inspirational, and he lost touch with realities. He was so inspirational his boss adopted his idea and took it and explained it to other people, but unfortunately the story crumbled. The boss was quite angry. Eventually he was fired; his flaw was that he was so inspirational that he would convince people of things without realizing the implications of them. He took his great communication skills too far.

> The company started to change and became more results-oriented and performance-driven. Paul was totally unable to change from the old way to the new. His intelligence stopped being an asset and became a hindrance—he used it to find reasons why things should not be done a new way. He was shunted aside.

Jorge paid too little attention to detail; he never wanted to get into it. Occasionally you have to get underneath the surface, and he got caught once or twice way off track because he didn't pay attention. When he got more on his own, his vision wasn't covered by others who could implement.

Johanne was a relatively quiet person who wasn't comfortable giving talks. He didn't have a strong leadership image. He didn't appear to be aggressive enough. He got caught up in change, and he wasn't getting visible results fast enough. He was replaced by a more dynamic person.

These stories do not tell the whole tale, but they do highlight some themes. The obvious one, of course, is that great talent does not prevent weaknesses from having an impact and may even hide the weaknesses when a person is away from home. Other themes also stand out. The world changes. Cultures change, people in key positions change, strategies change, corporations restructure and realign—all of these require executives to adapt. It's easy to say you should adapt, but when you are some distance away from home, struggling with running a business in another culture, you can just as easily miss the changes afoot and, even sensing them, underestimate or mishandle them.

Another theme is to deliver on your promises. Especially if a person is charismatic or even just defending his or her turf by making enticing promises, the assessment back home may be performance against an inflated expectation.

Still another theme, made especially poignant by all the emphasis placed on having a global perspective, is that in foreign cultures things may not always be as they appear on the surface. Sometimes an executive has to know the details, go beneath the surface, to see what is really going on. Many derailments we were told about involved executives who were too hands off—too removed—from what was happening in their backyard.

Finally, it is clear that image (or at least appearances) matters. In international work, an executive must take into account many perspectives, not the least of which is back at headquarters. But there are also many other audiences—subordinates, peers, customers, partners, governments—all of whom may have particular cultural lenses through which they interpret the actions of an executive.

The Dynamics of Derailment

The concept of derailment came from work done with U.S. executives in U.S. corporations, so in doing this study we wondered if the process would be the same in the international context. Derailments occurred when talented and erstwhile successful people failed to live up to corporate expectations. A derailment does not necessarily mean failure in larger terms; rather, it simply means that career progress "jumped the tracks" for some reason. At a later time, in another context, or in terms of personal aspirations, a person who derails might still be a success.[1]

Four dynamics describe what happened to primarily U.S. executives who derailed.[2] In many cases, the early strengths that propelled a person to success became the weakness that did him or her in. Most often this took the form of technical, functional, or market expertise that led to early successes and promotions. Later, the narrowness of that expertise, combined with a reliance on the strengths that had served the executive well, served as blinders that prevented him or her from seeing the bigger picture or acquiring new skills essential in a higher-level job.

A second dynamic involved flaws that usually had existed for some time but became salient in a new situation. Some leaders, for example, had *always* been abrasive and arrogant, but, getting great business results, were never really hurt by their flaws. When the results weren't as good as expected or when the situation changed so that relationships became critical to success, the flaws "suddenly" became paramount and the executive derailed.

The third dynamic involved the consequences of continued success. Some executives simply began to believe that they were as good as they seemed, and like the Greek tragic heroes, they suffered an eventual demise as a result of their hubris.

Finally, some executives just appeared to be unlucky, ending up in the wrong place at the wrong time or running afoul of the wrong person. Sometimes circumstances were described as being things that "might not have derailed someone else." Though bad luck was clearly a part of it, other ongoing factors usually contributed to the fall.

As we examined the global derailment cases, we feared being overly influenced by McCall's earlier domestic studies—so much so that we bent over backward trying not to find patterns that we suspected might be there. No matter how we cut it, however, the four dynamics were still apparent in the international derailments. Early strengths still became weaknesses:

> He was excellent in manufacturing but not in operating the business. As a general manager, he spent too much time on manufacturing and he trusted other people to handle the other areas. He failed.

> He was smart and tended to overcomplicate things. He would design things that weren't executable. Smart people mess up simple ideas. If your strategy is too complex, you can't align the variables, which leads to inaction. Thinking through every angle slows things down.

> He was a brilliant person. He was revolutionary, he fought like hell, he took different approaches, and his thinking was outside the box. He made one big mistake—he thought he was brilliant and that other people were stupid. This guy was brilliant, but he showed it too much.

> This was an American who came to work in Asia. He was highly regarded in the U.S. and held a senior position in Asia, dealing with many cultures. He was a typical American, very well qualified and very conscientious. However, he had an acute lack of cultural sensitivity. He was very focused on getting the job done and that was his strong point—but it was also his weakness. He had no hidden agendas, and he failed miserably because he was unable to adapt to different modes of operation.

Long-standing flaws still mattered in new situations:

> He was a rising star, on a fast track his whole career. He was personable and very smart. He seemed political, but that was important

in the company. As I got to know him, it became apparent that you couldn't trust a word he said. Eventually he lost the support of his people. The lower you are in the organization, the less you need the support of the people below you. The higher you go, the more you need that support.

He was a very intelligent person who was very good managing upwards with the CEO and the board. He had a good vision of where the organization was going. The problem was that he was not very good at managing down. He always maintained distance between himself and his management team. He generated fear in them and often set unreasonable targets. People would not tell him the truth. He was not only bad with his people, he was also very bad with customers. Eventually he did not deliver the results that he promised. He had no respect from his people, he was a poor motivator, and when he did not deliver the results, he was taken out of the job.

Arrogance still led to a fall:

He was decisive, a strategic thinker, could pay attention to detail, had a gift for language, and had good client relationships. But he was arrogant, he stopped being perceptive to signals around him. He stopped listening and did not notice signs of difficulty with some of his stakeholders of the future, namely, his peers. Or, he noticed but didn't care. When he made a couple of mistakes that would not ordinarily derail a person, he had so little in his emotional bank account with others that he started to collapse rapidly.

He rose quickly as a shining star, but he got so obsessed with his own dealings that he started to be self-centered around the business. It was hard for him to take a broader view. In the end he became an "over-promiser." He created people who were fed up with him. Things always had to be on his terms, and then people didn't stand behind him. Finally, through his way of dealing with them, customers got put off. He was demoted.

He was intelligent, hard-working, with tremendous energy and drive, working from five A.M. to nine P.M. every day. He was very out-

spoken and had a great many ideas, but he stepped on lots of people on the way up. He was too ambitious. He had no second
thoughts about not caring for people. He had a very high opinion of
himself. He eventually fell quite hard. He could have even survived
this, but he had so many enemies that there was no safety net.

I sent a guy over I thought would be great. He was sensitive and tolerant. He wasn't a "fair-haired boy," and he had the perspective of
the little guy. Unfortunately, he didn't turn out like I expected. He
saw this as his chance to be the "fair-haired boy," the big man, and
he failed.

And there was still a modicum of bad luck:

The company changed what it rewarded and valued, and he got left
behind.

He got into a conflict where he had very strong convictions and
he and his boss saw the business situation differently. He was involved in an investment that was going poorly, and he was used as
a scapegoat.

He was the wrong person in the wrong role in the wrong country at
the wrong time, and the deal cratered. It was a disaster, although it
was not totally his fault. In fact, the managing director was blamed.
They put in a new managing director, and it's still not working.

Sometimes, overseas assignments are outside of the mainstream. If
a person stays too long in those jobs, he will no longer be on the cutting edge and he may be working on old technology or the organization may have passed him by.

If you are in a growing business with the right boss, you will move
forward. However, when the business stops growing, there is no
place for you to go.

But even though the basic dynamics were much the same, in a global
context there were also some striking differences. Considering the

number and magnitude of the strengths that led to success before their derailment, the international executives were probably much more talented to begin with than their domestic U.S. counterparts. For example, global international executives were commonly described with multiple strengths such as brilliant *and* interpersonally skilled, technically skilled *and* shrewd about people, *and* people- and results-oriented.

In addition, their flaws were more enigmatic than those of domestic executives. Not only were there *more* flaws described, but also many flaws seemed paradoxical in the sense that the opposite of the flaw could be equally lethal. For every "too ruthless," there was a "not tough enough." Those mired in detail were offset by those described as too visionary but unable to bring a vision into reality. The imperious autocrats were balanced by executives who delegated too much.

While numerous flaws were uniformly problematic, whether or not they played out in an international setting (e.g., failing to adapt to changed situations and an "appalling lack of people skills"), many more flaws were anchored in context. Losing touch with the home country was a major one that often appeared when the time came for repatriation; building an empire and undermining or ignoring the company's global strategy was another.

And the contexts in which the derailments took place were far more complex than those we usually saw in the domestic U.S. studies. The degree of challenge and complexity in some global jobs made us wonder if anyone could have succeeded. Take, for example, the European who had been successful in a focused job on the continent. As an executive who was familiar with the situation described it, "He moved to a ten-times more complex job in Asia—a joint venture with lots of initiations, cost cutting, different products to deal with, et cetera. Within a simple environment, he had been clear on his purpose. Suddenly all that changed. It was overwhelming. . . . He had too little support and too little control before he realized it."

Finally, it was clear that the organizations for which the derailed executives worked made numerous mistakes. Whereas the organizations were found to be complicit in the earlier studies, they were sometimes the culprits in the global arena. The saga of one executive was described this way: "The company contributed [to the derailment] when they led him to believe they would back him up no matter what, but they didn't. They backed him when things went right, but they

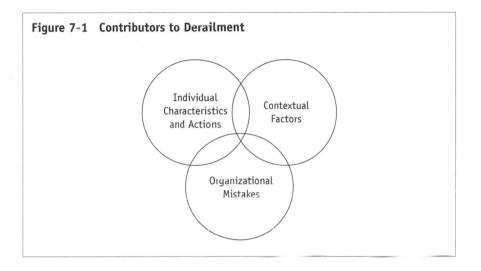

Figure 7-1   **Contributors to Derailment**

deserted him when things went wrong." Absence of honest feedback was pervasive, as were mixed messages or unclear expectations from "back home." Companies picked obviously wrong people, promoted people too fast (they were "untested"), or kept them out too long. Frequently, expatriate executives did not have access to the kinds of technical or other support that domestic executives could call upon.

Derailment cases clearly involved talented but flawed individuals who relished the independence of global assignments. Working in complex, usually foreign (to them), and largely unforgiving environments, they were usually at some distance from headquarters and support. Their distant bosses frequently did not understand the local situation, maybe didn't really care about it, and often did not stay in close contact unless problems arose. In short, a potentially lethal combination of individual flaws, contextual factors, and organizational mistakes fuels the derailment dynamics already at work (figure 7-1).

The Individual's Contribution: Fatal and Not-So-Fatal Flaws

• • • • •

Roughly 300 flaws were described to us, depending on how you cut up the pie. Seven categories of these flaws stood out as clear, if predictable, troublemakers (box 7-1). The first category was the failure to adapt to

. . . . .

Box 7-1   Universal Fatal Flaws

- Failure to learn or to adapt to change
- Bungled relationships with key people
- Failure to take needed actions or to deliver on promises,
  and failure to ask for help
- Narrow or parochial perspective
- Lack of people skills
- Loss of contact with the rest of the company
- Select ineffective people

---

change. What had changed varied considerably—markets, bosses, business strategy, leadership philosophy, technology—but it was clear from the stories that the executives in question remained rooted in the past, sometimes even defying attempts to get them on board. One is left wondering if all the changes were for the better, or whether some of the derailed leaders might have been right in resisting. Nonetheless, the "northbound train" left them behind.

Often the inability or unwillingness to change had its origins in too narrow or parochial a viewpoint—a common result of a career in a "silo," or a single function. Unable to see the big picture or unwilling to accept the value in another point of view, some narrow executives (unaware of their flaw) either refused to accept change or could not put their energy behind it. Still others, at least partly as a function of their blinders, chose people who later failed or did not provide the needed support or expertise.

Other flaws in the "clearly lethal" category included bungling relationships with key others (such as customers, partners, senior management, or peers), a pattern noted by Jack Gabarro in his 1987 study of new (presumably U.S.) general managers who failed.[3] Often the bungling occurred in conjunction with a decline in performance or some other significant mistake, which made it all the more toxic. And this was related to a broader category, an "appalling lack of people skills," which sometimes caught up with people over time. In a global context, quality relationships are crucial in some countries and in some business situations (such as sensitive negotiations, joint ventures, and cross-cultural alliances). So although a lack of people skills can be annoying in any context, in the international context, the flaw more often becomes fatal.

Another clear mistake in global work combined the failure to take needed action or to deliver on promises with the failure to ask for (or accept) help when things went wrong. Perhaps because of the heavy investment in these executives or because they inevitably are somewhat removed from the home country, organizations are reluctant to derail an executive without first trying to fix the situation. The executive in trouble, however, may try to deal with matters on his or her own, without interference from the outside. This can be a fatal mistake, made all the more likely whenever, as an expat, the executive has lost contact with the rest of the company.

But It Is Seldom So Straightforward

While some global derailments were straightforward, and the flaws obvious, many others were not. In fact the results of our first analysis of the data were downright baffling—this one derailed because of "insufferable arrogance," but that one derailed for being too humble. "Too Swedish," one executive said of a derailed colleague. This one was so mired in detail as to miss the possibilities, while that one was too visionary to get anything done. One was an imperious autocrat; the other delegated too much. One was overly analytical, but the next one was unfocused and not analytical enough. Didn't keep promises; didn't let go of promises that didn't work out. Couldn't achieve consensus, or achieved consensus by surrounding himself with yes-men. Didn't "suck up" to his boss, or did and was derailed for being too political. Couldn't lead others, or led others but in the wrong direction.

That the world is filled with apparent paradox is not a new observation: It was the Greeks who observed *areté hamartia,* translated as "your unique excellence becomes your fatal flaw." But in case after case, whether a flaw was fatal or even whether an action was a flaw depended on the context. This was not unlike the findings of the earlier study of domestic U.S. derailments, except that in the global arena the context was ever so much more complex. By far the greatest number of derailments could be understood only by examining the context in

. . . . .

which they occurred. It was rarely sufficient to say that an executive's traits or flaws "caused" him or her to derail—most of these executives were extraordinarily talented individuals—unless one could place that trait or action in a larger context.

A Complex Context for Derailment

. . . . .

Behavior always has a context. To derail because of a bungled relationship, there must be a setting in which the quality of relationships is important. To derail because of a narrow perspective requires that there be a bigger picture and that the bigger picture makes a difference to the actions of the executive; otherwise, a narrow perspective might be seen as "focus." But beyond the obvious, the global context creates a whole new layer of demands and potential pitfalls.

First, the context is significantly enriched in international settings by the added stress of a foreign environment and by differences in language, culture, and belief systems that make inappropriate behavior and misunderstandings more likely. The increased stresses of global work include isolation; family pressures; and broader job responsibilities, which may involve dealing with politics, government, corruption, and so forth, without the help that would be available in the home country. Contributing to the stress, but demanding in their own right, are the difficulties of understanding and being understood in one or more foreign languages and the (often subtle) differences in values, norms, beliefs, religions, economic systems, and group and community identities.

All the above and related dimensions can contribute directly to derailment dynamics. In one particularly poignant derailment, an Asian executive who had run highly profitable operations in Asia was moved to corporate headquarters in a non-Asian country. Described as "great" by his fellow Asians, at headquarters his social skills were found wanting. "He simply did not fit in, because of the rough side of his social skills," we were told, but "he thought it was funny . . . and did not realize the importance of it. He did not act as officers should." He was passed over for promotion and eventually retired embittered. Apparently no one ever told him what was wrong, because, as the story was told, "he could have changed quite easily."

The natural reluctance of people in organizations to be candid with each other can be magnified by cultural norms, as well as by the inability of outsiders to read the subtle cues. One executive, quite successful in a series of functional assignments, was promoted to a general manager job outside of his own country. He did well initially, probably because of his functional expertise, but "when things started to go wrong, he did not realize it; when he realized it, he didn't have the ability or business knowledge to diagnose the problem and figure out what was wrong." One can't help but wonder if, had this happened in his home country, he would have seen it sooner and been able to draw on the expertise of others.

The business setting can compound the complexity of the cultural situation. Here complexity again takes several forms, including the potentially lethal—or at least convoluted—web of relationships and the potential presence of different business models and practices. As we interviewed executives, we saw how the web of relationships can grow more and more complex: from subordinates from a different culture who don't speak the executive's first language, to subordinates from multiple cultures speaking multiple languages in one region, to subordinates from multiple cultures speaking multiple languages and physically dispersed around the globe. To thicken the roux, add a boss from a different country who speaks a different language or multiple bosses from different countries in a matrix structure, and so on, through suppliers, customers, partners, shareholders, peers, consultants, and others. As if that weren't complicated enough, different countries may have different business models, different definitions of ethical behavior, and different business approaches and systems.

Different economic, religious, government, and social systems in some countries have direct effects on how business is carried out. An outstanding example is the experience of the European executive in Malaysia described in chapter 4. The executive laid off a Muslim chef who, unbeknownst to the executive, was the only chef who could prepare the meals required by the many Muslim employees of the company.

All these complexities and others, too numerous to recount, impact derailment. The more relationships an executive has to cultivate, and the more varied they are, the greater the chances that some of them will go wrong. The greater the differences in how business operates in the countries involved, the greater the likelihood that an executive will make erroneous assumptions or commit errors without even knowing that anything is amiss. The more diverse and culturally different the countries, the greater the likelihood that seemingly extraneous factors—or what would be extraneous factors in the home country—will affect business results, the outcomes of deals and negotiations, and other activities for which the executive is accountable. In other words, not only are the executive's actions more likely to be ineffective or even counterproductive, but circumstances beyond the executive's control are both more prevalent and more likely to affect outcomes, regardless of the executive's actions. And for all the reasons we pointed out above, the executive may not get timely feedback and may not pick up the clues that anything is wrong in time to do anything about it.

Although cultural and business differences create a complex and sometimes treacherous context for executive action, international assignments also offer seductions that can lure executives onto the path to derailment. Being on their own, often far from direct supervision and with tremendous authority over local operations, global executives can come to believe that they are all-powerful, even above the law. We heard stories of sexual peccadilloes, larceny, and locally illegal acts, as well as a holier-than-thou arrogance that sometimes emerged. Feeding self-aggrandizement were the perks of foreign duty, which might include servants, cars and drivers, luxurious homes, impressive expense accounts, invitations to galas and state affairs, and other special treatments that, over time, some executives began to view as entitlements. Lacking the beeswax of some outside force (such as headquarters' scrutiny) to protect their ears, executives may find the Sirens' alluring songs irresistible. Perquisites aside, the stress of the assignment could lead down an equally destructive path—including alcohol, drugs, illicit sex, and the like.

Even if an executive successfully completes an expatriate assignment, he or she still faces a final risk that may cause derailment: repatriation. Though it is tempting to view coming home as an easy transition, it turns out to be anything but. Most commonly viewed from a Western perspective—a U.S. or European executive returning home after an assignment in a "less developed" nation—the potentially negative impact of repatriation has been well documented.[4] Executives may return to find that they have lost their business networks and their

*"Just tell me about the new continent. I don't give a damn
what you've discovered about yourself."*

friends, that their home country is not the same as it was when they
left, and—perhaps the unkindest cut of all—that no one cares. Their
living conditions may actually be worse, with no servants, drivers, luxurious homes, access to exciting events, or relationships with top business and government leaders. They may come back to lesser jobs and
reduced responsibility, they may find themselves outside the mainstream, and they may feel that their organization does not take advantage of or appreciate what they have learned. In such circumstances,
the skids are greased for derailment.

Our interviews also generated stories of another kind of repatriation
problem: third-country nationals returning home, especially those returning to a country that is less developed than the country they just
left. Having attended prestigious schools, held important positions in
prestigious global companies, experienced the amenities and the abundance of these other countries, and enjoyed greater civil liberties or
wealth, they may return home arrogant or resentful, or both. This

quickly undermines the executives with their local constituencies, again setting the stage for derailment. One such successful returning executive apparently believed that he had risen above his home country colleagues and customers, as he told them, "Don't call me Juan anymore; call me John." What had taken him a long time to build before he left was destroyed very quickly.

Organizational Mistakes

The complexity of the global context increases the odds that the organization will make various mistakes that contribute to derailments. Few mistakes that we heard about appeared to be deliberate, but most were avoidable. Our executives described the absence of feedback, little monitoring, the tolerance of existing flaws, and a lack of support. Because the organization can control these factors, which are particularly important in global settings, we fault the organizations for being lazy, or worse, negligent. Although we don't absolve executives from taking responsibility for their actions and the impact they have, certainly the organizations' lapses increase the probability that flaws and inappropriate or ineffective behavior will go unnoticed.

Our global derailment cases also resulted from poor selection decisions. Organizations sometimes chose people who obviously would not fit in the environment, failed to prepare them properly for the challenges ahead, and/or failed to communicate expectations or *changes* in expectations. In still other cases, organizations made decisions that directly affected the executive's operation without considering the situation "on the ground." At times, an organization made strategy or design changes without consulting, or even informing, the local executive.

As mentioned earlier, derailment risk is also high for foreign nationals coming to headquarters (e.g., Jean's coming to Boston from Paris, as described in chapter 3) and for other executives returning home. Organizations seem consistently to botch both events, contributing their share to an already difficult situation for the executive.

Finally, we were told of derailments in which an executive's career was exploited for short-term gain. In these circumstances, the organization knew that the situation was not viable—the executive was assigned an impossible job, or one that would almost certainly create an intolerable aftermath for the executive.

This combination of personal, contextual, and organizational forces makes international derailments much harder to codify than their simpler domestic counterparts, and makes it much harder to identify a single cause. Because most executives who derailed were quite talented to begin with, the cost of these derailments is also disproportionate.

The Importance of Understanding Derailments

Events as complex as global derailments will not be prevented by a single intervention or by a miscellaneous smattering of human resource programs directed at international executives. Like global executive development itself, preventing derailment requires an integrated approach that connects strategic intent with the systems and practices that affect the selection, development, and movement of global executives.

To begin with, solutions must address all three culprits in derailment: the executives' strengths and weaknesses, the global context in which the executives are placed, and the organizational practices that surround the whole process. All three depend on the fundamental strategic issues facing a global business: What kind of global company is it and what kinds of leaders does it need? Only the strategy can determine how many and what kinds of global executive jobs are required, and how many and what kinds of executives are needed to fill them. Only the strategy can determine how many truly global executives are needed (if any), how many foreign nationals are necessary, how the international jobs will be structured and positioned, the extent and nature of alliances, how business will be done internationally, and so on.

The implications of these strategic decisions will be explored more fully in chapter 8, but we must point out that there are important differences in the development of local nationals, host-country nationals, and third-country nationals. Further, global executive jobs, whatever the home country of the executive, are fraught with dangers, not the least of which is the increased derailment probability associated with poorly designed and poorly managed assignments. Because derailment involves so many factors outside the control of the executive, development efforts aimed exclusively at the global or international executives themselves will not solve derailment problems. Organizational strategies that deal with derailment must include the domestic workforce (both in the headquarters country sense and in the local nationals sense) as well as those destined for expatriate assignments or global responsibilities. The broader the understanding of the demands and challenges of the international scene, the better the chances that people and organizations will avoid making the contextual and organizational mistakes that make derailment so treacherous.

8

Developing Global Executives: The Organization's Role

> When Linnaeus sought to classify all of life in 1758, he called his great work the *Systema Natura,* the "System of Nature." Biologists of all subsequent generations have flooded the scientific literature with alternative, but equally comprehensive, systems. The content changes, but the passion for building systems remains. Our urge to make sense of the complexity that surrounds us, to put it *all* together, overwhelms our natural caution before such a daunting task.
>
> —*Stephen Jay Gould,*
> Hen's Teeth and Horse's Toes

It is a continuing message of this book that development involves both the individual learner and a context from which the individual can learn. That context can be both positive and negative: positive when it provides an opportunity to learn important new things, negative when it contributes to derailment. Some aspects of context, for example, what the local culture provides, are not under the control of an organization. Other aspects, such as organizational mistakes that lead to derailments or timely feedback, which leads to learning, are well within the organization's purview.

In this chapter, we first will put the findings from our study into a framework for understanding the development issues. We will draw the development implications that follow, and suggest actions that organizations can take if they truly want to develop global executives.

. . . . .

A Framework for Developing Global Executives

. . . . .

In chapter 1, we reviewed a general model of executive development, the high-flyer model, which has been described in detail elsewhere.[1] The message of the model is that if you can identify talented people, give them appropriate experiences, and provide the necessary support, they may learn the lessons needed to achieve the business strategy. These elements are portrayed in figure 8-1. According to the model, the "business strategy" produces the leadership challenges which, in turn, determine what "experiences" are needed for developing executive talent. Those experiences potentially yield relevant lessons (called "the right stuff" in the figure). Key organizational issues revolve around identifying those with potential ("talent"), the "mechanisms" (or processes as they might also be called) used to get talented people into needed experiences, and providing "catalysts" to facilitate learning from those experiences. As we have shown in earlier chapters, "context" (usually culturally related) plays a major role in shaping experience, so it is indicated by the outer circle surrounding "experience" in the figure.

One of the "good news" conclusions from our study is that this basic process of development is the same for all executives, regardless of the countries they come from or whether the development is for global, expatriate, or local executive work. All our interviews, lessons, experiences, and derailment examples support the conclusion that the model in figure 8-1 is as relevant for global as it is for domestic executive development. But while the basic elements identified in the model are useful as an organizing principle, the specifics applied to developing global executives are different in very significant ways.

Global executive development is much more complex and unpredictable and requires greater focus, effort, and resources concentrated over a longer period. To an even greater extent, the "right stuff lessons" are contingent on the global business strategy, which determines a wider range of more difficult experiences that develop more talented executives. The global environment in which this all plays out (the "context" in figure 8-1) adds layers of complexity to the process. The interactions of a more complex business strategy, multiple cultures, and the widely varying backgrounds of the executives impact the entire

Figure 8-1   **A General Model for Developing Global Executives**

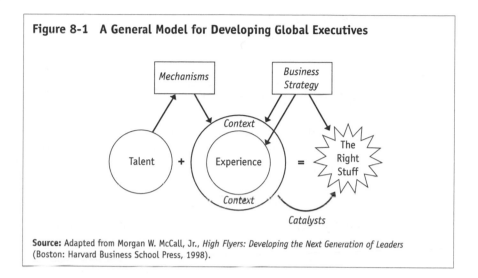

Source: Adapted from Morgan W. McCall, Jr., *High Flyers: Developing the Next Generation of Leaders* (Boston: Harvard Business School Press, 1998).

process. The mechanisms to make development happen and to maximize development opportunities reflect the greater complexity—they too are more complicated themselves, more difficult to administer, and more expensive to maintain. Global executives *can* be developed—they learn the lessons of experience much as domestic executives do—but the process requires far more organizational commitment, focus, and resources than a similar domestic development process does.

Clearly, an organization cannot make someone develop. The ultimate responsibility for development lies unequivocally with the individual. Indeed, the notion of developing executives raises the question of an organization's right to manipulate developmental experiences, even if doing so is in the presumed best interest of the person. Nevertheless, the organization is a major partner with the executive in the joint venture of development, and it plays a critical role in creating a context that supports or inhibits that development. When asked what help they had received from their companies, the executives we interviewed all too frequently said that they had received none. "Sink or swim" was the dominant paradigm; a few even said, "Fine, that is the way it should be." Throw-them-in-and-see-who-floats may have been considered a good development strategy in the past, but with the cost of executives and development today, we doubt that many organizations can afford to endorse it now. Although executives often develop, whether or not anyone intends for them to, intentional partnering on the part of the organization can make a significant difference in the process. Organizations often are important sources of development by chance, but this is a costly and inefficient way to operate.

We prefer to think about the implications of this research for an organization in terms of a partnership, where the organization enables development to take place. The question then becomes, How can an organization create a context in which the possibility of development is maximized, while at the same time respecting the individuals' responsibility to participate in managing their own careers? With this perspective, we will discuss each of the elements of our global executive development model growing out of figure 8-1, highlighting the role that each plays. We believe that it all starts with clarity about the strategy of the business.

Business Strategy: The Strategic Imperative

The major differences between developing global and domestic executives are determined by the business strategy and structure of a global corporation. These two factors directly affect how many and what kinds of international jobs will exist; how many executives of what kinds and of what mix of nationalities will be needed; what lessons these executives will need to learn; and what kinds of experiences are available to teach those lessons. The mechanisms for assuring that talented executives get those experiences will follow, and the factors that assist in the learning will take shape, depending on the strategy and structure.

Global strategy has long preoccupied scholars, and there is no shortage of literature suggesting that it is central to effectiveness and is far more difficult than domestic strategies once were.[2] Discussions of global strategy usually end up in issues of the design of a global organization, which again emphasizes the increased complexity of such designs and of the alliances and joint ventures that often accompany global expansion.[3] The implications of these strategic and design choices for executive development are a less frequently trod pathway.

Christopher Bartlett and Sumantra Ghoshal, for example, describe four kinds of organizations that do business on a worldwide basis: multinational (strong local presence), global (centralized global-scale operations), international (parent-company knowledge diffused world-wide), and transnational (dispersed, interdependent, and specialized). Each of these forms, the authors argue, requires a different set of management skills.[4] In a similar vein, Lynn Isabella and Robert Spekman look at different types of global alliances and identify the unique leadership skills required for effective performance in those organizational arrangements.[5] They take the argument one step further, suggesting that effective alliance leaders possess the skills needed to lead global organizations of the future. Both Laree Kiely and Alison Eyring explore in some depth the implications of managing across time and space, pointing out the different skills required to lead when people are located far away, widely dispersed, and in different time zones.[6]

Our point is not that we should create some huge matrix that dictates the executive development implications of all possible global forms. Rather, it is that strategic intent and organizational design are critical in determining the foundations of an executive development process. These factors dictate how many global executives of one type or another are needed and what roles they play (e.g., country managers versus global business managers versus functional managers versus alliance managers), what kinds of assignments are available for development and where they are located, and what cultures need to be understood. An organization that is confused about its global business strategy will be hard pressed to design a coherent strategy for developing its executives. Even those that are clear on their strategy face formidable challenges, in part because of inherent integration problems across the world and in part because strategy and structure must remain flexible and must change with changing business needs. Figure 8-2 shows some of the ways business strategy affects experiences needed and the relevant lessons to be learned in global executive development.

One of the biggest development challenges facing any organization is preventing the narrow specialization of its talented leaders. In a domestic context, we worry about "silos"—be they technical, product, functional, or business segments. In the global context, these are still issues, but the problems are magnified enormously by nationality, geography, distance, and language, to mention only a few. It is easier to imagine developing people to be country managers or alliance managers or worldwide functional managers than it is to imagine developing executives by moving them across those domains. But, to develop

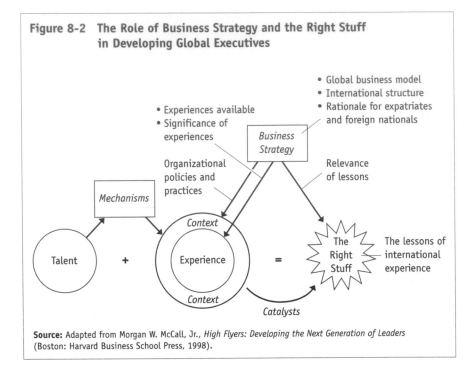

Figure 8-2   The Role of Business Strategy and the Right Stuff in Developing Global Executives

- Global business model
- International structure
- Rationale for expatriates and foreign nationals

- Experiences available
- Significance of experiences

Business Strategy

Organizational policies and practices

Relevance of lessons

Mechanisms

Context

Talent   +   Experience   =   The Right Stuff   The lessons of international experience

Context

Catalysts

Source: Adapted from Morgan W. McCall, Jr., *High Flyers: Developing the Next Generation of Leaders* (Boston: Harvard Business School Press, 1998).

global executives, an organization must indeed move them. Keeping them within narrowly defined areas simply perpetuates at the global level the same issues of parochialism already present in domestic organizations. Of course, whether moving people out of silos is worth the cost remains a strategic issue—how many cross-boundary individuals are needed to fill the pipeline?

It is tempting to say that the rationale for choices in development rests on strategy, and leave it at that because there are so many permutations. However, the strategy and structure decisions seem particularly important in development because they affect the following specific areas.

Where a business locates its headquarters can have profound effects. If it resides in a country with a very large domestic market, such as the United States, then its approach to the worldwide marketplace is likely to be very different than if it had a small domestic market such as Belgium, Norway, Switzerland, or the Netherlands. In order to grow, companies with small domestic markets have been forced to develop global strategies and structures and to learn how to work with different cultures. They have had little choice but to send out expatriates to establish their businesses worldwide, and a high percentage of their executives have responsibility for global businesses. Royal Dutch/Shell, for example, reports that 95 percent of its senior executives have lived in a country other than their own. That means that many senior people have had the opportunity to develop from nondomestic experience, and that they understand the importance of that experience and how to help others through it.

On the other hand, companies with large domestic markets may have a relatively short history with the global market and have the luxury of only incrementally increasing their out-of-country involvement. Fewer of their executives have been forced to take on international responsibilities or expatriate assignments. In these companies, such experience may not be valued as highly or used as wisely or necessary for advancement in the ranks. While history rather than volition may determine where a company is based, some companies, notably, Asea Brown Boveri (ABB), have deliberately located their headquarters so that there is a small domestic market, have kept headquarters very small so that it is not the only focus, or have made sure that various business segments or functions are centered outside of the home country.

Another significant factor in strategy-determined development is the number of and use of foreign nationals. If an organization intends to manage its businesses locally with local nationals, but not to increase the presence of foreign nationals in its senior ranks, then the development issue involves how to get local nationals connected with the global strategy and the workings of headquarters. If the organization chooses to manage the local operations with expatriates, the strategic issue involves developing talent for expatriation and running a business in another culture or, more importantly, how to use expatriates to develop local talent. A truly global strategy, however, might involve increasing the cultural diversity of the senior management ranks. In this case the challenge is to help local nationals develop expatriate skills, or at least to develop global perspective. And the developmental challenge presented by this strategy would differ, depending on the home countries of the local nationals. Individuals from developing nations may need different experiences than would executives from more developed nations.

. . . . .

Another kind of strategic choice concerns the design of the organization itself. Matrix, product, functional, business segment, geographical—the varieties and hybrids are limitless, and each different form has direct implications for the kinds of experiences available for developmental purposes. Geographical structures, for example, often emphasize autonomous country managers, and these positions can be useful for helping expatriates learn to run a business in another culture. An organization built on global functional lines may not have experiences like that to offer. Add in decisions to gain worldwide position through alliances, mergers, acquisitions, or joint ventures, and the developmental implications multiply rapidly. There are now "on-boarding" issues (integrating people from outside the company), different kinds of leadership challenges, and perhaps even conflicting philosophies and values to resolve.

In spite of the complexity, the impact of strategic decisions on the development of international executives is primarily in a few areas: the cultural mix and size of the talent pool, the nature of the work to be done by the executives, where the work is to be done, the numbers of types of executives required to do the work, the types of transitions talented people must go through if they are to develop outside of their "silos," the availability of the different kinds of experiences needed to develop the talent pool, and the organizational policies and practices that encourage or discourage developmental choices.

The Right Stuff

"Right stuff" thinking in business, especially in global business, has meant that leadership and executive ability are presumably born, not made. We disagree. Naturally, organizations should select the most capable people they can find, wherever those capabilities come from. Nevertheless, much of the "right stuff"—what executives need to implement business strategy—is learned (see chapter 4), and learned primarily in the crucible of global experience (see chapter 5).

We can take three progressively sophisticated perspectives to view the lessons learned. First, there are things that any executive needs to know, whether his or her job is domestic or global. These include a wide variety of essential skills, from learning to run a business to managing people to understanding the technology. Second, while these same kinds of lessons are certainly relevant and necessary in an international context, the demands of a global context increase their difficulty and subtlety. Executives still must learn to run a business, for example, but now they may be running it in a foreign country with a different business model and a host of cultural contingencies. Finally, some of the lessons are uniquely related to international work and are largely determined by cultural differences and the added complexities of expatriation.

Our eighteen lessons of international experience, because of the limitations of our study, do not define all the lessons that any executive in a particular business must learn, and they undoubtedly include some that are not universal competencies. They do, however, illustrate the kinds of lessons that can be learned from experience, experience driven by the business needs. And it is this third kind of lesson, which is uniquely related to global work, that we believe is essential for global executives. This category of learning includes lessons such as the three lessons of culture: when and how to use a language, lessons of specific cultures, and general lessons of culture. Recognizing that there are as many global executives as there are global jobs, at some level, global executives must become "culture comfortable." And they do that while living and working in other cultures and countries, not by staying at home.

The implications for organizations may be obvious, if unwelcome. Global executive development is expensive, time-consuming, and uncertain. In times of scarce resources, more organizations may be trying to *limit* the expensive experiences that teach global lessons than are trying to *expand* them. The lessons, however, must be learned.

Experience

In the same way that many lessons that executives must learn are the same, whether the executive's job is domestic or international, the experiences that shape global executives are basically the same as those that shape any executive. However, when the experiences are embedded in an international as opposed to a domestic context, they take on a decidedly different tone, are clearly more complex, and teach different lessons.

Our executives overwhelmingly advocated experiences involving real work in a cross-cultural setting. There is no substitute for actually working in another country, even though what is learned from transformational experiences may or may not be relevant to the corporation. And if business and global acuity are important, a person usually requires at least two expatriate assignments to achieve it. Furthermore, the international context is multifaceted and includes many things beyond the obvious cultural differences. The family is a more central issue than it is for the domestic executive, the organization makes more mistakes, and support and monitoring are harder to provide. Figure 8-3 highlights some of these elements for experience and talent.

The kinds of experiences that our international executives thought were important, along with what they learned from them, were described in chapters 4, 5, and 6 (see tables C-1 to C-4 in appendix C for a summary). Many of these experiences (if they exist at all) are directly or indirectly accessible to the organization for developmental purposes. As we noted at the end of chapter 6, those that are directly accessible include all the major line assignments (business turnaround, business start-up, evolving a business, joint ventures, alliances, mergers, and acquisitions), most of the shorter-term experiences (special projects, consulting roles, staff advisory jobs, stint at headquarters, negotiations, developmental and educational experiences, and some significant other people), and both of the foundation assignments (early work experience, first managerial responsibility), although many people being developed may have spent their early years elsewhere.

The category "significant other people" deserves special attention because most of our executives felt it was so important, even if the organization has only limited control over an executive's exposure to other people or what happens in a relationship. Especially in global work, opportunities to work in parallel with a predecessor, on-site learning (intentional or not) from a local national, and exposure to others with global careers had important influences and offered important learning opportunities.

Organizations can also have significant effects on other potentially developmental experiences not under their direct control. By creating an environment that encourages reasonable risks, mistakes and errors in judgment can become learning opportunities when they occur. By providing timely support, organizations can help talented people suc-

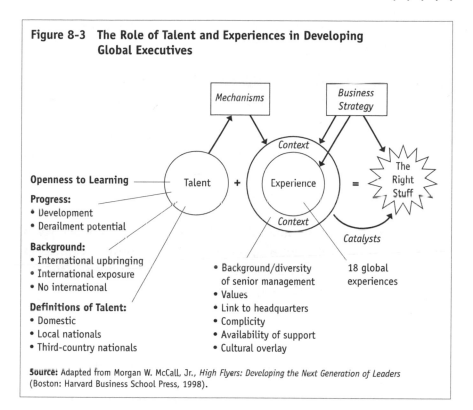

Figure 8-3   The Role of Talent and Experiences in Developing Global Executives

Mechanisms

Business Strategy

Context

Openness to Learning —— Talent + Experience = The Right Stuff

Progress:
• Development
• Derailment potential

Context

Catalysts

Background:
• International upbringing
• International exposure
• No international

Definitions of Talent:
• Domestic
• Local nationals
• Third-country nationals

• Background/diversity of senior management
• Values
• Link to headquarters
• Complicity
• Availability of support
• Cultural overlay

18 global experiences

Source: Adapted from Morgan W. McCall, Jr., *High Flyers: Developing the Next Generation of Leaders* (Boston: Harvard Business School Press, 1998).

cessfully work through and grow from family and personal challenges, career shifts, crises, changes in scope and scale, and culture shock. (These last two, incidentally, are under an organization's control to the extent that increases in scope and exposure to different cultures can be achieved through assignments.) Only one category, confrontations with reality, is difficult to position from an organizational perspective.

That organizations have varying degrees of control over these experiences does not guarantee that the experiences, when they occur, will be developmental. But organizations can design assignments to maximize developmental potential by thinking through the kinds of support and intervention that enhance learning, and by providing them at appropriate times. Only by following the incumbent's progress can an organization know what help is needed and when.

Clearly, the factor that determines which experiences are most important for developing international executives—at least from the corporate perspective—is the business strategy. There is no substitute for knowing what the future holds and the kinds of experiences that talented people need to prepare for it.

The Illusion of Control over the Lessons of Experience
While organizations can influence the context in which development takes place and do have some control over who gets what experience, it would be a mistake to overestimate the extent to which development can be programmed. There are good reasons that fixed career paths and rotational assignments have limited effectiveness. Two major sources of variance exist: people and experiences.

First, each person is a unique individual, which means that each person has a different background, is at a different stage in his or her development, learns in a different way, is more or less receptive to experience at any given point in time, and so forth. When the individuals in the talent pool come from different cultures, the differences are magnified.

Second, experiences are affected by context, especially in an international setting. A turnaround in the Sudan is not the same experience as a turnaround in the United States. Additionally, experiences change over time—what is powerful one year could be mediocre the next.

Obviously, there are strong interactions between the person and the situation. A Brit starting up a business in Indonesia will not have the same experience as a Japanese starting an operation in Japan. An experienced expatriate working a joint venture in China has a different learning experience than a novice in the same job.

What this means is that global executive development, even more so than domestic efforts, must be individually tailored. Broad principles clearly guide the process, but when it comes down to highly valued, talented individuals who have the potential to grow into senior international executives, rigid programs will not suffice. Nor will it work if the people running the process are not themselves international and sufficiently experienced to understand the complexities of the people, the jobs, and the cultures. As a result, line input, if not direct line control of the process, is almost always a prerequisite. The companies participating in our study alerted us to how difficult meaningful line participation is—normally, the human resources functions are handling transfers from a contract and administrative point of view. We have no easy answers; it is always tempting to let "staff" handle the details. Nevertheless, the same information systems (e.g., company worldwide intranets) that permit individually tailored development will also permit line management input, if not control. That input/control, of course, begins in the staffing sessions that determine who gets what job.

Logical Sequence, Lots of Flexibility

When it comes to developing global executives, the tangled web of possibilities is at once daunting and liberating. On the one hand, all the complexities and interactions make overly programmed developmental efforts seem futile, which argues perhaps for a selection approach, in which an organization merely selects people who it believes are already qualified for global executive positions (as if there were no such complexities involved!). On the other hand, complexity opens up possibilities, allowing for multiple pathways and creative options. Development need not be rigid, perhaps things don't have to unfold in sequence, not all skills are progressive, and not everyone has to have the same skills—or at least not acquire them at the same stage—to be effective. Indeed, maybe there need not be a career "path" so much as a trek, a meandering journey from here to there with considerable ambiguity at either end.

It seems clear, however, that the trek will be less convoluted if it begins with early exposure to international work and cultural differences. The importance of starting early was the almost unanimous opinion of the veterans we interviewed, and an early start is particularly important for people from relatively homogenous countries or with parochial backgrounds. Early work experiences can be designed with broadening in mind, for example, by sending people to other countries to do technical or functional work or putting them on teams or in situations in which they work closely with people from other cultures. Nonmanagerial jobs can be designed to include at least some international elements (e.g., customers, vendors, and geography). First-level supervisory jobs can be designed with similar elements or expanded to include responsibility for subordinates from a different culture or working for a boss from a different culture. Involvement with special projects, task forces, negotiations, joint ventures, and the like, can come early in a career and can provide numerous opportunities to work in other countries and with people from other countries. Activities such as these do not guarantee that specific lessons will be learned or that people thus exposed will grow into international executives, but they provide the opportunity to lay a foundation for future learning and, more importantly, for the discovery of a passion for international work.

So one bit of good news is that, though the outcomes may not be pre-ordained, organizations have numerous ways to get development started early. But there is more good news. Subsequent development does not have to be lock-step either. If our sample of executives is at all representative, development can take multiple pathways and often follows the opportunistic choices that organizations are almost always forced to make. Rather than rigid rules, there are some general guidelines for using experience for development:

1. **Avoid the trap of repetition.** As tempting as it may be to keep an effective person in the same country doing the same kinds of things, or to move effective people to different countries while having them do the same thing, development is more likely when things are different.

2. **Avoid pushing people too hard.** The line between challenging and overwhelming can be hard to see and occurs in different places for different people. Considering what we know from our studies of derailments, we must be sure that people have some anchor in their experience and some source of credibility to draw on when sent into a vortex.

3. **Be careful not to assume what has been learned.** Although the first expatriate assignment (when in a country quite different from one's own) is a powerful learning experience, clearly, a whole new field of learning opens up with the second such assignment. It is not safe to assume that a person is "international" simply because of success in an expatriate job. Further, an executive can hide within his or her expertise, even as an expatriate. The authority of being "from headquarters," distance from scrutiny, a good local business situation, and many other forces can shield a manager from the developmental demands of the new environment. Just being there is no guarantee of growth. This effect can be compounded if an organization moves people too fast, before they are required to master new skills or have an opportunity to do so, or if it leaves them in a comfortable situation too long.

4. **Consider background.** As we demonstrated with the stories of Andrew, Jean, and Brian in chapter 3, the kind of experience that will lead to growth is directly related to where a person has been. People who grow up speaking multiple languages or having lived in several different cultures have different developmental needs and learn different things from similar experiences than do people with less exposure. As an obvious example, an expatriate who speaks the local language will have a very different experience leading a turnaround than will an expatriate who does not speak the language. Although both executives may learn some of the same things, the former is more likely to be learning a great deal about turnarounds in that country while the latter is learning more about the importance of clear communication and establishing credibility.

Talent

Assessing talent (potential) for global work is far more difficult than assessment for domestic executive jobs. Not only does openness to learning vary, as it does for domestic executives, but individuals from different countries bring with them a very wide variety of background and experience factors that may help or hinder development. Because different countries can vary dramatically in their development and promotion processes, it can be extremely difficult to find a common standard across candidates.

But there are additional difficulties. For one, as we argued in chapter 2, no unitary concept defines what a global executive is—international executives and international executive jobs come in many shapes and sizes. As a result, there is no specific target at which selection and development can be aimed. This is true for domestic executive jobs as well, but the playing field is infinitely larger in global work.

Second, background and experience, while important in assessing any executive, are even more significant when the work is global. Because different countries have different mechanisms for assessing, promoting, and developing managers, comparison across multiple cultures is difficult if not problematic.

Another complicating factor is the interaction of the organization's home country with the nationalities of the executives in the talent pool. The definition of potential and of developmental needs may vary considerably, depending on whether a person is from the home country, a local national, or a third-country national, and on what kind of career moves are envisioned (expatriate, domestic, nomadic). Such factors are directly related to the probability of eventual derailment as well (see chapter 7) because movement across cultures creates unique dynamics.

As with the use of experience for development, the difficulty of assessing potential does not mean that nothing can be done. On the contrary, the very richness and variety of the candidate pool are essential to an organization that aspires to global success, even though they make it more difficult. To take advantage of that variety, additional considerations must be taken into account.

1. **Interpretation of career history.** We were told that, in Japan, promotion is sometimes determined on the basis of one's school or one's relationship with a boss. Several times, we heard of European companies that would only promote people of home-country nationality to senior ranks. These and other examples of non-merit-based career progress simply highlight what we already know—that different countries do things differently. But those differences have many implications for the management of a worldwide talent pool, especially when people in the pool have been hired from outside the company or brought in through merger and acquisition.

2. **Analysis of preexisting assets.** Choosing who gets what experience is a selection exercise that should be based on an assessment of where a person is now, where he or she could go, and what the next experience might contribute to his or her career path. The richness of a global pool means that there is tremendous variety and that many people bring relevant characteristics to the table— some speak multiple languages, some have lived in multiple cultures, some have been expatriates, some have been educated in a country other than their own.

3. **Ability to learn from experience.** The very core of using experience for development is the expectation that the person getting

the experience will learn from it. Therefore, *the* key selection factor for who gets an experience should be the person's ability to learn from that experience. Fortunately, Gretchen Spreitzer, Morgan McCall, and Jay Mahoney's empirical work on an international sample shows that the ability to learn from experience is positively related to a variety of relevant outcomes.[7] They identified the underlying dimensions of the construct, which one of us (McCall) subsequently interpreted in a developmental context.[8] The two primary conclusions from that work were that international executives rated highest in potential were (1) more likely to get, take, or make opportunities to learn and (2) more likely to create a context for learning from the opportunities by remaining open to criticism, soliciting feedback, and leading in a way that develops trust and openness.

4. **Potential to derail.** Assessing potential is not just about assessing what growth may take place, but also about anticipating what could go wrong. Our discussion of the dynamics of global executive derailment offers convincing evidence that even talented people are not immune to allowing their strengths to become weaknesses, to getting blindsided, or to growing complacent or even arrogant in the glow of their success. Because the traps are more numerous and deadlier in the international context, it is imperative that organizations consider the possibility of derailment when assessing talent.

Taken together, these issues simply reinforce the essential need for development processes to be run by, or at least depend heavily on involvement of, experienced international executives. Just as people who lack global experience cannot effectively make judgments about experiences that are relevant for global development, so must people who understand the demands of international work make the judgments about potential. International experience does not automatically make the assessors' judgments valid, of course. Organizations need a process that systematically applies those judgments to the issues highlighted above.

In addition, we believe it is critical that development be tracked over time. If anything, tracking is more important for people with global careers than it is with domestic executives, and it is harder to do for all the reasons we have discussed. With all the different directions a career might take, what should be tracked? Over time, perhaps the best index of growth and maturation is the group of lessons discussed in chapter 4—the lessons of international experience. Some subset of these, we suggest, makes up the skills on which long-term success in international work is based.

And a final thought: It would seem that monitoring and working with the talent pool must start early if talented people are to get international experience early in their careers. This means that the involvement of globally experienced executives must not be restricted to the top levels, but must include those at lower levels as well.

Mechanisms: Getting People the Experiences They Need

"Getting the right people into the right experiences" can be added to our list of factors that are more complicated in a global context. In part because the backgrounds of the international candidates vary so widely and in part because a love for international work is not always apparent. Organizations need a blend of strategies that select for some things, provide an opportunity to discover other things, and provide tailored development opportunities for still others. All this, on top of the business need to put proven, capable people into the important global jobs!

Many forces operate to keep talented people doing what they do well rather than allowing them to develop new skills. This has even become one of the latest management panaceas—use people's strengths and don't waste time on weaknesses. It is certainly easier in the short run to use people to their proven strengths than to deal with losses in efficiency from the learning curve or with the risk of failure when a person is stretched too far. The forces pushing for the short term are magnified in global work because a talented executive may not just be a technical or functional or business segment expert; he or she may also now be a cultural, language, or national politics expert as well.

Sometimes, however, a shortage of experienced global executives leads organizations to work the other way. Instead of keeping people where they have proven themselves, an organization throws them willy-nilly into new assignments precisely because they have some

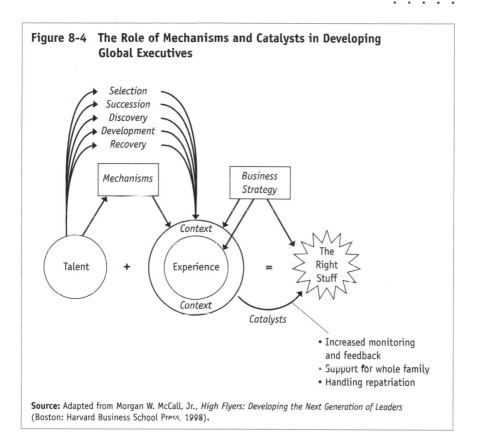

Figure 8-4   The Role of Mechanisms and Catalysts in Developing Global Executives

Source: Adapted from Morgan W. McCall, Jr., *High Flyers: Developing the Next Generation of Leaders* (Boston: Harvard Business School Press, 1998).

international experience—without regard to the developmental value or even the relevance of the previous experience. Leaving the disposition of the talent pool up to the ebb and flow of short-term needs almost certainly leaves to chance the development of one of an organization's most important resources. As we see it, an organization needs to set up and maintain five parallel processes, not just for development but for the short-term business needs as well: selection, succession, discovery, development, and recovery (figure 8-4).

Selection and Succession

Because of the dynamic nature of global business, it is folly not to have in place "ready-now" candidates for key positions around the world. One aspect of that ready-now approach is to develop a process for selecting candidates when critical jobs come open unexpectedly.

Replacement planning is one such process, in which an organization maintains a list of several candidates with (or soon to have) the required skills for key positions. Should a runaway bus hit the incumbent, one or more qualified replacements have been identified in advance. By considering likely vacancies ahead of time, an organization can deal with the tendency of various sectors to horde talent, to look narrowly within their own spheres when considering successors, and to end up homogeneous in spite of diversity goals.

Two aspects of selection and succession strategies distinguish them from the other three processes. First, they focus on critical jobs or simply on the top jobs, rather than on the aspects of jobs, assignments, and people that might make them developmental. While one might expect overlap between critical jobs and developmental jobs, there are many experiences, especially at lower levels and outside of the mainstream jobs, that could serve as developmental grounds for the future.

Second, when the objective is to match the most qualified person with the job rather than to develop a person in the job, selection and succession processes focus on existing skills rather than on developing new skills. Ironically, the most qualified person—the one who is ready now—is also the one who will develop the least from doing the job.

Selection and succession are the basic mechanisms for getting people into developmental jobs. Other than emphasizing their importance, we leave to others the details of describing effective systems. We will mention, however, a common organizational failing to which global organizations seem especially vulnerable. Global assignments offer unusually good opportunities for organizations to try to solve personnel problems by exporting the problem. "Out of sight, out of mind" can become the easy answer for dealing with an individual of limited capability. Unfortunately, exporting the problem too often has the expected consequences: It taints the whole process of using global assignments for development, and it may make repatriation of the "problem" executive nearly impossible.

Discovery and Development
Without denying the importance of contingency planning, it is also essential to have in place processes that focus directly on developing talent for the future. When considering the global talent pools that grow out of the succession process, an organization probably needs two

approaches. For many in the pool, their passion, background, and basic skills already identify them as having high potential for global work. Someone who wants an international career, speaks several languages, and grew up in different parts of the world is an obvious candidate. For people like this, processes of development can begin early and continue throughout a career. The emphasis for these folks may be on business-related skills rather than cultural ones.

But our study also revealed that a significant number of people eventually turn out to be successful international executives, but never "had a clue" when they started what their futures would be. They came from parochial backgrounds or showed little interest in travel or in some other way would not have discovered their interest without an intervention or accident. For people like this, it is important to have processes that allow them to discover their interest early in their careers. Early experiences that involve international people or businesses can serve this purpose at the same time that they identify those who show neither interest nor aptitude for global work.

Recovery

The term *expatriation* originally referred to banishment from one's native land. Although modern usage simply refers to an expatriate as a person in residence in a foreign country, the difficulties that our executives experienced in returning home come close to the earlier meaning. Repatriation has become one of the standing problems in international organizations. But although it has long been identified as a key transition, awareness of its problematic nature has not led to effective practice. Repatriation takes several forms: foreign nationals returning to their home countries after time in the headquarters country, home-country expatriates returning, and third-country nationals returning to their home country. While the dynamics for each group may be somewhat different, the need for processes to help the integration is universal. Often, neither the returning executive nor the organization realizes the potential trauma of the return for the executive and his or her family. As paltry as most preparation for expatriation appears, preparation for the return is nonexistent by comparison. Nevertheless, the actions recommended by executives to ease repatriation are widely known. Such things as frequent home visits during expatriation, maintaining contact and networks, assistance with the family's relocation, providing meaningful work when he or she returns home, and the like, are all widely recognized if not widely implemented actions.

Catalysts: Helping People Learn from Experience

Even getting high-potential people into strategically valuable experiences may not be enough. While one hopes that a talented person in a challenging assignment will learn everything there is to learn, it does not always happen. A catalyst is something that is added to a mixture and that causes a reaction to take place. Developmental catalysts help executives learn. Although the same catalysts may enhance the learning from any experience, global or not, the physical and psychological distance that characterizes global jobs makes it much harder to provide feedback, monitoring, support, and resources to the executives. Expatriates, especially, are particularly vulnerable to weak linkages to the headquarters and to family pressures.

An organization can take many steps to facilitate learning, whether the assignment is domestic, international, or expatriate. Some of them are listed in table 8-1.

Expatriate assignments require some additional considerations. Because of the distance from the home office, special attention must be paid to staying in contact. Monitoring what is going on and providing useful feedback are helpful to learning, but both are considerably more difficult across time and space. In addition, what feedback is useful, and from whom, may not be obvious, as the local scene may be quite different from the home-country environment. Indeed, a multicultural workforce can present many unexpected reactions to typical human resource interventions involving performance assessment, feedback, coaching, and the like.

Perhaps because of the uniqueness of expatriate assignments, one of the most significant potential catalysts and one mentioned quite frequently by our executives is a boss who understands international work and is willing to spend time working with the person. A second special condition of expatriate assignments that influences learning is the reaction of the family. We conclude perhaps the obvious, that families play a critical role in the effectiveness of expatriates. The difficulties faced by the family can affect executive performance, contribute to derailment,

Table 8-1 Examples of Catalysts for Development

Improving Information	Providing Incentives and Resources	Supporting Change
• Provide specific feedback • Provide lots of examples • Provide feedback on important criteria, possibly on identified competencies • Provide feedback on development as well as on performance and outcomes • Expect supervisors to confront problems • Use credible (to the recipient) sources • Don't dance around the issues • Give needed feedback even if the person is performing well • When messages are mixed, provide perspective • Interpret feedback in terms of the future as well as the present • Provide a context for feedback that reflects the organization's future strategy • Give feedback in a form acceptable to the recipient • When possible, enrich feedback from the job, customers, and other "natural" sources	• Set specific and measurable developmental goals • Put development in context of business strategy • Find ways to assess progress on developmental goals • Hold people accountable for achieving developmental objectives • Involve the person in setting goals and measures • Make development a real priority • Make part of pay contingent on development as well as performance • Promote or move people for developmental reasons • Promote people who model desired developmental behavior • Provide as many rewards and as much recognition as possible for growth • Involve multiple sources in setting developmental agendas • Above all, be sure existing reward system is not contradictory to development • Provide access to role models • Make it safe to practice, try new things • Coach and train people how to acquire new skills	• Provide emotional support • View change in a systems context; consider how the desired change will affect other people, the nature of the work, etc. • Change the context as necessary • Create an environment in which change is supported and encouraged

Source: Adapted from Morgan W. McCall, Jr., *High Flyers: Developing the Next Generation of Leaders* (Boston: Harvard Business School Press, 1998).

and, most likely, distract from potential learning (although dealing with family issues in itself is a fertile ground for learning). While perhaps an *indirect* catalyst, support for the whole family turns out to be important from a learning perspective.

Another special issue of expatriation is repatriation. As mentioned earlier in this chapter under mechanisms, the recovery of expatriate executives warranted special processes because repatriation is when talented people often grow frustrated and even leave the organization.

• • • • •

The challenges of repatriation also present a learning opportunity. Some of the executives we spoke to described reentry as just as much a cultural shock as their expatriate assignments had been. This implies that with proper support, repatriation can be of developmental value as well.

Some Closing Thoughts

• • • • •

This chapter has developed a framework for understanding the critical processes that go into developing international executives, and expanded the elements of the framework with implications for organizations. We have avoided the temptation to present a list of global development imperatives that should be followed by any organization. We do not believe that bits and pieces, no matter how sensible they may appear, will solve the development conundrum. Only by viewing development as a strategic imperative and with strategic perspective can an organization combine the pieces synergistically to create a coherent whole. Although for clarity we have examined the elements of our model individually, we do not want to lose sight of the bigger picture of what it takes to develop people. When these elements are put together, as we have done in figure 8-5, one cannot help but get a sense of the complexity of it all. We are tempted to throw up our hands in discouragement, not knowing where to start.

In closing, then, we return to the initial premise. The first order of business is to get the organization's strategic act together. Knowing what kind of global presence is desired, an organization can then link organizational design with the development of its leadership assets. Since the driving force in a development effort is experience, the design decisions determine what experiences will be available—and just how many international and global jobs, projects, task forces, and other opportunities there will be.

But in practice, organizations don't always have their strategic acts together; it is not always possible to start with the strategic imperative. What then? Organizational practitioners know that sometimes one must start where the energy is, rather than at the beginning. In fact, we can enter the global development process at any of the elements. The

Figure 8-5 In Detail: A Model for Developing Global Executives

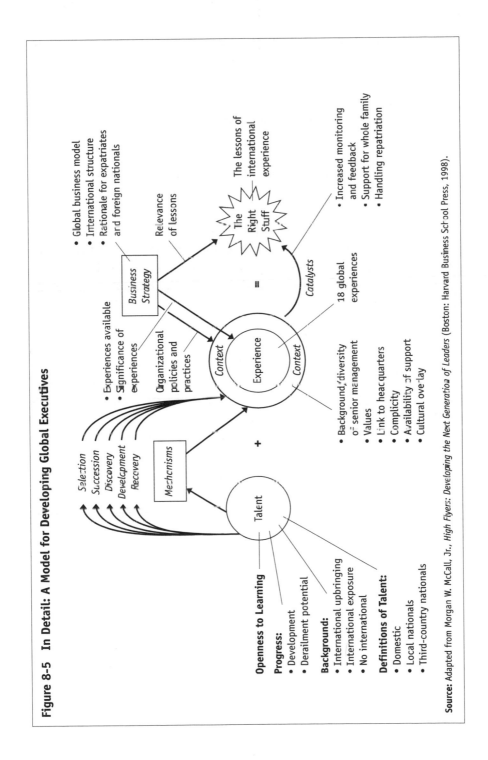

Source: Adapted from Morgan W. McCall, Jr., *High Flyers: Developing the Next Generation of Leaders* (Boston: Harvard Business School Press, 1998).

complexity of our model reflects the complexity of development. Sometimes we have to start where we can. With so much to be done, any start is better than none at all.

Our goal in this chapter has been to examine the organization's role in creating a context in which development can thrive. It helps in that regard to consider that the word *develop* is derived from the Old French *des*, meaning "undo," and *voloper*, meaning "to wrap up, or to envelope." Literally, then, to develop is to undo the wrapping. While common usage includes the idea of evolving and growing as well as the idea of bringing out what already exists (as in "developing a photograph"), to develop clearly has more to do with releasing and enhancing what is already there than in installing something new. To suggest that someone develop a new skill is to suggest that the root of that skill is there, waiting to be unwrapped. This idea is also at the root of the word *education*, derived from the Latin *educare*, "to bring out." Which, of course, was the Socratic method. Creating a context for others to grow is not a new idea.

In creating a context for growth, however, the organization can only do so much. The ultimate responsibility for taking advantage of opportunities to grow lies with the individual, and that is the topic of the next chapter.

9

Building a Global Career: The Individual's Part

Common sense does not ask
an impossible chessboard, but takes
the one before it and plays the game.

—Wendell Phillips (1811–1884)

We began this book with the premise that globalization is upon us, like it or not. Within that framework, the individual considering a twenty-first-century career in business, like it or not, is considering a career in *global* business. The career question becomes not *if*, but *how much* one's career should involve international components: "How global should I be, do I want to be, could I be? How can I manage that?"

Careers, like lives, never quite have the predictability that we try to impose on them. They never unfold quite as planned, so we don't presume here to prescribe how a career should be sculpted. In this chapter, we bring together the findings from our study, the wisdom of our executives, and the current thinking about career development in a fashion that will help individuals considering global careers think through the issues. Our goal is to offer advice and counsel that will prove helpful in making career decisions. Our advice is, in a sense, the flip side of chapter 8, what companies should do.

The State of the Career

• • • • •

Careers are not what they used to be. The rules have changed, as have the rewards. The old career model, with lifetime employment in a single company, an ever-upward-spiraling career path planned by the company, unswerving loyalty throughout one's working life, and retirement with a comfortable company- or state-provided pension at a certain age (be it at 55, 60, or 65), looks surprisingly outdated. If not "dead," the old model is changing to a new, more flexible paradigm that fits a global world.[1]

Although these changes are most salient from a U.S. perspective, it would be a mistake to believe that they are not happening worldwide. As responses to globalization and a global business model, they seem as inevitable as the newspaper headlines. In "Japan's Long Decline Makes One Thing Rise: Individualism," Yumiko Ono and Bill Spindle describe the changes taking place in perhaps one of the most career-structured countries.[2] Countries may have different employment requirements and customs, but the themes are the same—plans for restructuring, outsourcing, and downsizing are global, not domestic.

The developing consensus is that the new career will be a "sequence of work-related experiences over a lifespan."[3] The best companies will provide experiences that reward and develop their executives; when the experiences end, the new executive will move on to new experiences, either within that organization or in a new one. A description of this new career contract appeared on the bulletin board of a U.S. company (box 9-1).[4]

In such a career environment, individuals no longer depend on companies to manage their careers; they do it themselves. They don't look to the company to provide a career; instead they look to it to provide challenging, interesting, and rewarding opportunities, and the information to take advantage of them. Up is no longer the only way (to paraphrase a book title). Assignment choices, both by the individual and by the company, may be made with an eye toward development opportunities and broadening experience (as one executive put it, "increasing the value of my brand") rather than simply moving up the hierarchy, if there is one. The new career model calls for considerably more flexibility. Some career theorists predict that career beginners will, in fact, have multiple—as many as four or five—different careers over the course of a life span. And the whole notion of a working life span is changing. During the twentieth century, the average life expectancy increased by thirty years; to "quit working" at any age may become an anomaly for healthy executives.

Clearly, the new career model requires that people managing their careers have a different perspective and different skills. Recognizing that the new career model may have been adopted unevenly around the world and among companies, our task is to raise awareness that the

> **Box 9-1   The New Employment Contract**
>
> - We can't promise you how long we'll be in business.
> - We can't promise you that we won't be bought by another company.
> - We can't promise that there'll be room for promotion.
> - We can't promise that your job will exist until you reach retirement age.
> - We can't promise that the money will be available for your pension.
> - We can't expect your undying loyalty—and we aren't sure we want it.
>
> **Source:** From a company bulletin board.

new model, 100 percent adopted or not, will form the basis for new careers, and to look at what we have learned and how that would apply to a global career.

Especially Relevant Findings

In the same way that the new career model requires a different perspective, the global experiences of the future are unlikely to mirror the experiences of our global study executives. At average age forty-eight, these executives look back on more than twenty years of experience that inevitably will be significantly different from those beginning careers today. Can the lessons of our study possibly provide any insight into future careers?

We think they can. There is a timelessness in the lessons, experiences, and insights that we believe is well worth the consideration of those just starting the journey. The hows may change, but the *themes* are unlikely to become obsolete. In addition, the advice from these veterans to those who would follow in their footsteps may well be the best advice available. Their careers, with their emphasis on autonomy and self-reliance, have embodied elements of the "new career" far more than have the careers of domestic executives.

We begin with themes that seem especially relevant to global careers. We continue by applying those themes to six essential career processes, which we then relate to the advice from our study executives (summarized in box 9-2):

. . . . .

Box 9-2   Career Relevant Findings

- There are many paths to a global career.
- Global leaders develop in the global arena.
- Culture shock is the unique global experience.
- Lessons of culture are the unique global lessons.
- Line experiences are the crucibles of development but other experiences assume more importance in global than in domestic.
- There are more hazards and traps in a global career than in a domestic one.

---

1. **There are many paths to global leadership.** In the same way that there is no one type of global executive, there is no one global executive career. Many paths can be taken, from many starting points. Half of our executives could identify specific factors in their backgrounds that contributed to their interests in global careers, but half could not. Some executives came to their jobs with a yearning for adventure or travel, but many simply "rolled into it." Asked about their first international assignment, as many were sent by their companies as asked for that assignment.

   The new career model in companies that are changing rapidly to adapt to external changes is likely to offer even more and more diverse routes to global leadership. Already a world of complexity, global business will get even more complex as the number of players, suppliers, and entrants into the global economy increases. The career implication is that on the one hand, executives must increasingly be in charge of their careers, finding pathways that suit their needs and talents. On the other, a person needn't worry too much if not born to global leadership. Many routes can lead there. Layer upon layer of complexity can also be seen as layer upon layer of opportunity.

2. **Global leadership development happens in the global arena.** Although close-to-home, domestic experiences can teach important lessons (the foundation lessons that all executives must learn, such as how to manage), the critical lessons of global leadership are learned in global work. Whether a leader is living domestically and working internationally, or working and living as an expatriate, the combination of business and culture is essential. The implication? Get that experience!

3. **Culture shock is the unique global experience.** Working *and* living in another culture is different from domestic experience, or from working *or* living (but not both at the same time) cross-culturally.[5] The magnitude and type of changes experienced as an expatriate force people to develop new perspectives, attitudes, and skills. For many, the experience transforms them in important ways—ways that they value—and teaches them generalizable lessons of culture. Global careers require experience outside one's own country . . . prepare for it.

4. **Lessons of culture are the unique global lessons.** Many lessons required for success as an executive appear to be much the same, whether the context is domestic or global. Executives in either arena must learn to establish credibility, build an effective team, and handle bosses and superiors. Even lessons like learning to listen, so much more important in a global context, must be learned by domestic executives also. It is the *lessons of culture* that truly differentiate the global context.

5. **Line experiences are the crucibles of development, but other experiences assume more importance in global careers than they do in domestic.** The nature of shorter-term experiences in an international setting, experiences like those that fall in the "significant other people" and "developmental and educational experiences" categories, makes them fruitful sources of global lessons. That is good news for future careers; the opportunities for learning the crucial lessons aren't limited to long-term assignments.

6. **There are more hazards and traps in a global career than in a domestic one.** Derailment takes place in global work in much the same way that it does in domestic, but the global arena presents a wider array of hazards, traps, and temptations. Typically operating at a greater distance with great freedom, global work is often exhilarating, sometimes dangerous, and once in a while downright scary. Expecting a different world is a significant part of the battle in overcoming obstacles. The new careerist should know what to expect.

All these findings have broad implications for global leadership careers. The implications, like the careers themselves, will depend upon the individual and the context.

. . . . .

Essentials for a Global Career

. . . . .

The frequent flyer model for global executive development presented in chapter 8 for helping organize an organization's perspective can also help individuals look at careers. Specifically, we will develop a slightly different perspective based on the mechanisms described in chapter 8, examining their implications for individual careers. In this context, the mechanisms used by an organization to manage the movement of talent can be translated into a set of essential tasks for an individual to manage his or her own global career. Our discussion will include the implications of our study findings and the advice from the global executives we interviewed. Underlying our discussion is a prescription for the new career—your development is your responsibility. We can give the advice, but you are the agent of change, you must make it happen, you must take the risk, and you will reap the rewards.

The five essentials, discussed below, form the basis for a new global career contract (box 9-3) designed for your benefit.

Discovery

Few, if any, of our study executives knew the full extent of their journeys when they began their careers. Tempted though we all may be to plan our thirty-year personal strategies, we can say with confidence that none will work out as planned. Half our executives could identify no particular influence that got them started on a global career.

In the same way that early careers require a person to develop foundation skills and reputation (David Thomas and John Gabarro call this developing competence, credibility, and confidence), it helps early on to set yourself up with opportunities to discover how global you want to be.[6] This is especially true if you are one of those who "has no clue." Seek out opportunities for travel, for working with those from other cultures—at the next desk, in teams, in task forces. Individuals (as well as organizations) make a mistake when they settle too soon on their likes, dreams, and goals, and in what context. There are many paths to a global career; don't assume too early that such a career is not for you. Discover!

> **Box 9-3   Global Career Esssentials**
>
> **Discovery:** Initiate and take advantage of opportunities to discover how global you want to be. There are many paths to global leadership—find yours.
>
> **Selection:** Select yourself, your company, the people you work for, the assignments you get. The career is your responsibility. You be the agent; don't wait for others to do it for you. Selecting wisely depends on a good assessment of yourself. Be brutally honest: Do you have the energy, adventure, curiosity, health, and stress tolerance?
>
> **Development:** Learning from experience, rather than going through the motions, will determine whether you develop the right stuff. How do you do it? Reflect, talk, listen, examine. What have you learned, and how can you use it?
>
> **Recovery:** You will have successes *and* failures.The difference for your career will be your capacity to experience failure, to learn from it, and to bounce back to learn another day.
>
> **Relearning:** New careers require lifelong learning. Learning must be 24/7/365. In a fast-track world, business never stops, and the opportunities to learn (and the requirements for learning) never stop either. Find sanctuaries, but keep learning, again and again.

Selection

Selection here means *self-selection*. With you in charge of your career, it is essential that you make choices that consistently lead you toward global leadership. The ambiguity and complexity of the global context lends itself to self-selection rather than to waiting for someone else to do it. A recent article in the *Houston Chronicle* reported that fewer women than men were asked to go on expatriate assignments, but the article misses the point.[7] Whatever their personal characteristics, people interested in global careers don't wait to be asked. They select themselves and let it be known in the organization. Only about a quarter of our executives said that they had been sent by their companies on their first international assignment. Most others took an active role. You can take the initiative in participating in anything international—travel, task forces, training programs, receptions—whatever it takes to give you exposure and experience in the global arena.

Self-selection begins with finding an organization that fits your values and temperament. Organizations differ widely in their need for global leaders and their views of global leadership, depending on their strategy and their history. If you want a global career, find a global organization. We found Royal Dutch/Shell executives who specifically chose Shell because it promised (even demanded) international assignments. An executive at Hewlett-Packard (HP), already aware of his own interest in international from his days as an exchange student and leading overseas study programs, sought an interview at HP because he learned that more than half its revenues came from outside the United States.

Another selection point is jobs and bosses. With significant other people such an important source of learning, self-selection means finding and choosing bosses who can teach you about culture and international business.

Selection depends on assessment, and in *self-selection*, the key is *self-assessment*. You must seek out and be receptive to feedback on which to base that assessment. As you have an opportunity to experience global business, at whatever level, you must be brutally honest in assessing your likes and dislikes, strengths and weaknesses, and whether or not your own interests and abilities fit the requirements.

Development

Global careers are built upon experiences that provide opportunities for learning, but those opportunities may be expensive and difficult to obtain. Our executives advised us on the importance of first developing technical, functional, or business expertise for a reason: expertise enables you to add value in a global assignment. International assignments, by virtue of their being outside one's home country, are inevitably more expensive than domestic assignments. An expatriate in China can cost fifty to eighty times as much as a Chinese national, so someone from the outside taking that assignment *must* have value added.

Not all experiences are of equal value for development, and companies will differ in the experiences and lessons that are available and those that are most important. In your company you must experience the assignments that develop, and develop from the experiences.

In high-performance organizations, leaders are tempted to pursue results at the expense of their own development. Certainly, performance counts and is the ticket of entry into the next round of the tournament, but *success* in the next round will depend on one's accumulated learning, and that depends on development. The real key then is not just the ability to produce results, but the ability to learn from experience *while* producing results. A single-minded focus on performance can shutter one's eyes to the lessons in the experiences. We found example after example of executives who had derailed when they were unable to keep learning and growing. Our study amply demonstrates that the essential lessons of global leadership can be learned in a wide variety of experiences. Overwhelmingly, however, the lessons are learned in international work. Our executives reflect that in their admonition to "go early." Get involved early on in work that enables you to discover, select, and develop.

There is, of course, no secret to learning from experience. It begins with openness to learning and to rethinking one's characteristic ways of thinking and viewing. If there is an essential lesson of global leadership, it a perspective that recognizes the constancy of the *what* and the variability of the *how*.

Recovery

Our discussion of derailed executives pointed out that the difference between derailed and successful executives is not that the successful executive has never experienced failure, but that successful executives are able to recover, to learn from the experience, and to move ahead. The cardinal sin at high-performance organizations like Asea Brown Boveri (ABB) is not a project's failure to meet its numbers, but an attempt to hide the failure, to deny one's role, and to learn no lessons. Especially in global work, where the ambiguity and uncertainty inevitably result in the unexpected, you must develop resilience and the ability to learn from bad experiences as well as good ones. Anger, defensiveness, hostility, and rigidity are the hallmarks of an inability to recover.

Relearning

Viewing careers as a series of work-related experiences over a life span dictates the need for continually learning new skills, new attitudes, new ways of thinking. Most discussions of the "competencies of the future" emphasize the need for lifelong learning to adapt to a changing world.[8] The greater the change, the greater the need for relearning. The complexity, uncertainty, and rapid change that come with working across countries, cultures, and businesses present new challenges at every turn. While those challenges are, in fact, the excitement of global careers, they also increase the demand for continuing to learn.

Advice from Those Who Have Done It

We doubt that any of our study executives, from the youngest (age thirty-five) to the oldest (sixty-two), think that future careers will be the same as theirs. Nevertheless, they had no difficulty drawing upon their experiences for common themes likely to impact future careers as global leaders (box 9-4). Their advice reinforces the essential points developed above.

Develop Your Expertise

There is no substitute for value-added skills. Assignments with global requirements are expensive to fill, and the cost of failure is high. One attains these assignments not just by expressing interest; the price of entry is a demonstrated ability to contribute to the work of the organization. Especially early in a career, that expertise is likely to be relevant technical, function, or specific business skills. An early focus on expertise provides opportunities to discover, to self-select, and to develop credibility.

Go Early

Global work inevitably involves travel, relocation, intense time commitments, and the physical and family stresses that go with all that. Our study executives emphasized that getting an early start not only provided early opportunities to discover, to self-assess, and to develop,

. . . . .

Box 9-4   Advice from Those Who Have Done It

1. Develop your expertise.   5. Focus on business results.
2. Go early.   6. Don't confine yourself to business.
3. Just do it—take a risk.   7. Maintain your networks.
4. Be open to learning.   8. Take care of your family.

---

but also takes advantage of the optimism and flexibility of youth, the psychic and physical energy and tolerance for discomfort, and the relative freedom from constraining social and family relationships.

How early? Task forces, business travel, and international developmental and education experiences can offer early opportunities while one is establishing a foundation, but most would say that, if possible, don't wait ten years.

At the same time, we found exceptions to the rule. Our study included executives whose first international assignments came after age forty or even fifty, with twenty-five years in the company. One executive even pointed out advantages from going late. An older executive can command a higher-level job, with working and living conditions that more closely approximate what he or she leaves behind. We concluded that, for the executive eager for the experience and willing to sacrifice, it is never too late to "go global."

Just Do It—Take a Risk

Going global, that is, getting involved in global work, inevitably involves taking a risk as a person moves from the comfortable to the uncomfortable, from the familiar to the strange. Our executives warned against the temptation to settle for the safety of home rather than the excitement of adventure. No matter how much one has traveled or participated in global activities from the comforts of a domestic job, a decision time comes. Sometimes the decision is driven by an offer (26 percent of our executives were sent on their first international assignment), but more often it is driven by the executives themselves, and the executive must decide to step across the line. Our study executives, looking back on their experiences, advise, "If you want to do it, just do it; you may never get a chance again." As one executive put it: "Forty years from now, I would hate to think I hadn't tried it."

Be Open to Learning

If there is a single theme that runs through all these pages, it is that success in global work depends on an openness to learning. "My way or the highway" was the road to failure; as we have noted numerous times, the *what* may stay the same, but the *how* will be different. This basic rule for adaptability and openness to learning applies equally to personal as well as business life. Several times we heard the advice that satisfaction can be achieved anywhere in the world, but with different things. One executive saw it this way: "Wherever you go, your satisfaction index will be one hundred. But in different places, the mix will be different that gets you there. If you insist on replicating life back home, you will always be unhappy." Told to us in the context of personal satisfaction, this advice can be applied equally well to business.

We found that the experience of culture shock tests one's openness to learning, but is also a great teacher of a wide range of lessons. Stepping across cultural boundaries inevitably challenges one's view of the world. People respond differently, some by withdrawing, and some by expanding their views. The more one does it, the easier it gets, so the career challenge becomes never losing the openness.[9]

Focus on Business Results

Working across cultures, perhaps across businesses, sometimes a long way from a watching eye, global executives are tempted to forget that performance matters. Our executives warned against the tendency to use "cultural excuses" to explain business failures. Only at his or her peril should an executive forget that the purpose of the trip is to accomplish business results. Performance indeed matters. As one executive said, "Your career is the most important asset you have. Focus on results."

Don't Confine Yourself to Business

At the same time, although getting results is the main business purpose, understanding the context in which those results are obtained is essential. A single-minded focus on results may keep you from that broader understanding. To understand another culture, you must first get into it. Never leaving the office, always eating at the "American Club," staying in the expatriate compound—these are sure routes to isolation. Our executives pointed out that not only must one understand the context in order to get business results, but not experiencing the cultural variety provided by global work deprives a person of one of the greatest personal rewards: the excitement and exhilaration of experiencing people and cultures different from one's own.

Maintain Your Networks

The sine qua non of career management for the global executive is developing and keeping up networks of colleagues within, but also outside of, one's organization. Doing business in a global context typically involves a complicated array of suppliers, support, and controls, and maintaining career momentum depends on connection with "organization central." Not only are networks required to get business results, but they are the implements of learning and career movement. Who you know is never enough by itself, but neither are business results alone.

The physical and psychological distance associated with global assignments puts special strains on the bonds of networks. "Out of sight, out of mind" is the rule, rather than exception, and the longer "out of sight," the further "out of mind." One executive described his networks as a depreciating asset in his current assignment. Another described how easy it is to lose touch when outside the headquarters location, either because of extensive travel or because of expatriation.

Well-maintained networks provide the global executive with a kind of safety net against the increased risks of a global career. Business setbacks are inevitable in volatile and changing environments; currencies devalue, governments change, customer goodwill ebbs and flows. One executive described the two-to-one vote at headquarters to keep

. . . . .

him in his job when he was caught in a regional economic crisis with (admittedly) inadequate controls: "It could have gone either way. The only thing that saved me was that I had maintained my contacts."

Those contacts are also the key to repatriation. Try as they may, organizations cannot guarantee a successful repatriation—business situations are too volatile; no one knows just what will be happening three or five or seven years ahead, when it is time to come back. Organizational memories are short, executives come and go, they rise and fall. Promises are made, but organizations do not keep promises, people do. Global executives cannot afford to leave the management of careers to others, much less strangers who may be miles away.

Take Care of Your Family

A truism of international careers is the importance of the family. In a changing world with the term *family* taking on a range of meanings, perhaps we should change the category to "the importance of support relationships." But the point is the same: Global career success depends on more than the executive alone. The farther one is from one's natural home base, the more important is that support. "Happy families" are important in two ways. First, they can provide a base of support from a sometimes foreign and harsh world and can enrich one's life. Second, unhappy families distract and sap energy at the very time one is most likely to need focus and drive.

Our executives described the excitement and intensity of global work as too often driving out concern for others. An executive who moved to Hong Kong with regional responsibilities considered himself fortunate that his boss forced that concern upon him: "You must be concerned about your family," the boss told him. "I know," the executive replied. "No, I mean it, really concerned," the boss said. "Anyone who travels two hundred days during the year and has a family living in a new world must take this seriously." Our executives time and again expressed a similar admonishment. They recognized how difficult it was to get the message across, and many of them spoke from bitter experience, but they couldn't help saying it. Families are different, as are cultural expectations of families, but without successfully managing one's support relationships, one puts both personal and business success at risk.

Is It Worth the Price?

. . . . .

Given our descriptions of the difficulty and complexity of global work, the ambiguity and uncertainty of success, the dependence on external factors, the effort and stress that accompany it, and the dangers and opportunities for career derailment, why would anyone intentionally pursue such a career? Where are the rewards, and what are the benefits?

Our first argument dodges the question. Like it or not, globalization is upon us. As we said at the beginning of this chapter, the question is not whether careers will be global; the question is, Within that framework, how global do you want to be, and in what ways? As we look back over our discussion of global work, global development, and the careers of our executives, the thing that impresses us the most is how many choices global careers offer. The answer then becomes finding the rewards within the choices you make and the ones thrust upon you— the rewards that global careers offer.

Global work is different from domestic work, and the more global, the greater the differences. Our executives found those differences exciting, stimulating, exhilarating at times; the differences demanded high levels of energy, resilience, ingenuity, and adaptability. But our study executives, having lived the global life, couldn't imagine living and working in less challenging contexts.

There is, of course, another side of the coin. Although we heard examples of executive failure, they were secondhand—we didn't talk to the executives who opted out of international work. What is challenging about international work can also be dangerous and debilitating. Achieving their success required our executives to make many sacrifices: relationships were disrupted, a sense of country or culture was lost, being separated from family and friends was a hardship.

Without doubt, global careers will offer the financial rewards that place executives in the top tier, wherever they may live. From all appearances, our study executives lived well—they were well housed, well fed, well dressed, and well entertained, and their children well schooled. Many felt that, financially, they had profited from global careers, but few, if any, felt that money alone was a sufficient reason to put up with the hardships of global work.[10]

- - - - -

> **Box 9-5   Changes over the Course of a Global Career**
>
> | | | |
> |---|---|---|
> | • More cosmopolitan | • Value other people | • More focused |
> | • Broader perspective | • More sociable | • Wiser |
> | • More balanced | • More knowledgeable | • More self-confident |
> | • More tolerant | • Tougher | • Know more who I am |

In evaluating their careers, the executives valued highly the changes that had taken place within themselves. They are different people now as a result of the challenges they encountered in their global careers (box 9-5).

And although global careers will no doubt be different in the future, the personal changes described by our executives will be similar. The characteristics of global work that produce these kinds of changes are likely to be as common to work in the future as they are today. As a result, then, future global careers will offer the same types of opportunities for people to develop.

Globalization makes it unlikely that future senior executives, whatever their organization, can reach senior ranks without global experience. But such careers provide wonderful opportunities to explore the richness of the world and to grow in ways that many of us can hardly imagine.

10

Epilogue

> So the journey is over and I am back again
> where I started, richer by much experience
> and poorer by many exploded convictions,
> many perished certainties. For convictions
> and certainties are too often the concomi-
> tants of ignorance.
>
> —*Aldous Huxley,* Jesting Pilate

The executives whom we studied cautioned us that the world has changed, that those beginning global careers today are different from what they themselves were (today's youth are more accustomed to living well, among other things) and would face different challenges. That leaves us with some questions: In a globalizing world, will organizations need global executives anyway? Will domestic and global be synonymous? Will the same principles apply?

We cannot close without addressing those issues. They boil down to one question: Are our prescriptions and descriptions for global executive development only nostrums of the past, or do they apply as well for future executives as they do for today's? We believe that the changing world makes the need for global executives even greater, that the same basic processes govern—and sometimes retard—development, and that the real danger in the new world is not wasting resources for development that no one needs, but rather underestimating the significance of cultural differences.

. . . . .

The Changing World

. . . . .

Arriving at the ultramodern Changi Airport in Singapore on a nonstop twelve-hour flight from London, we had no difficulty imagining what it might have been like to arrive in Singapore ninety or a hundred years ago, to stay at Raffles, and to end the day at the Long Bar fanned by punkahs and sipping a cooling Singapore Sling. It is harder, somehow, to realize that fifty years later the journey still took three days and required nine stops along the way. Even twenty-five or thirty years ago, after touching down in Teheran and Calcutta, we arrived to find only intermittent, voice-delayed telephone service, no fax, no e-mail, no computer, and probably no air conditioning.[1] Some might say that Singapore is a special case, having undergone enormous development over these years, but the case is hardly unique.

Yes, the world has changed, but it has also become much more homogeneous in many respects. Especially for the business traveler, the world has evened out significantly. With a common business language almost anywhere we go, with the Singapore Regency essentially the same as the Inter-Continental London or the Hyatt Regency Jeddah, with a luxury sedan to meet our plane at any airport, the faraway places of the world are indeed becoming much more alike. We have nearly worldwide access to CNN day or night; there is a McDonald's in many, if not most, of the places we are likely to go; our cell phones will now work almost anywhere; throughout the world, we meet with M.B.A.s who have studied the same books and cases, sometimes in the same schools with the same professors. With all this convergence, it is tempting to conclude that business is business wherever we go, that differences don't matter much now, and that in only a few years they won't matter at all.

There is another argument, of course, that cataclysmic changes of climate or society will fundamentally alter the world. We won't speculate on those possibilities, real or imagined; we can neither predict nor prescribe for such a world. We will instead accept that in many ways global business takes place with many similarities, wherever it is, and that homogenization is likely to continue. Within that context, however, what are the implications of our study for the future of executive development, both domestic and global?

Plus ça change . . .

·   ·   ·   ·   ·

We come away from our research convinced that the same processes that have worked to develop the domestic and global executives of today will be the processes that work in the future. The expatriate housed at Raffles in 1900, the executive of the 1970s, and an executive today—all learned (or failed to learn) from experience. The same will be true in the times ahead. Those who get the important experiences will learn the important lessons (or at least have the opportunity to learn them); those who do not, won't. Executives of the past may have had longer to learn the lessons that an experience offers; hiding their failures may have been easier in a less connected world; their experiences and lessons may have been less complex and may have come in a slower stream. Nevertheless, the basic processes of development (and many of the lessons) we conclude, are the same.[2]

Perhaps the greatest danger is that organizations may assume that they no longer need executives with deep cultural understanding, that the homogenizing world no longer demands that the lessons of culture be learned at all, much less away from home. We think that assumption is wrong, for many reasons; four of them follow.

First, as Thomas Friedman so convincingly argues in *The Lexus and the Olive Tree,* and as we see in the international news every day, globalization involves both homogenization *and* particularization.[3] The same information technology that enables globalization also allows people around the world to reinforce the old borders of "who they are" and even to form new ones. Globalization does not mean the end of differences.

Second, the twenty-first century is shaping up as the century of crossing cultural borders. Pascal Zachary, for example, argues in *The Global Me* that success will go to the hybrid nations and corporations rather than to monocultures like Germany and Japan. In a world of cultural diversity and crossing borders, the ability to deal with differences will be more important, not less, and will be a competitive advantage for the organization that takes them seriously. In a company and country of hybrids, even managing domestically becomes a "global" experience.[4]

Third, our research has convinced us that the personal transformation that accompanies doing business across cultures is indeed a transformation, one that can fundamentally alter a person's perspective and teach the skills and attitudes that global executives require. Managing a diverse work force at home is important, and we have demonstrated many lessons of business that can be learned in the domestic setting. There is no substitute, however, for living *and* working outside one's own culture. And that includes learning another language, if one doesn't already know one.

Why not simply select for high-potential global talent, and failing that, why not hire all the globals we need? We found in our study that selecting the right people is important—more important, we judged, than in a domestic organization—but that many global executives (in our study, half) were unlikely prospects until they found that their interests and abilities were a good fit. An entry-level selection strategy is probably not enough; it will exclude the other half.

Failing an entry-level selection strategy, why don't we hire all the global executives we need from among those who have already developed? After all, in the war for talent, the free agent is the "hero of the new economy."[5] However, as a review in the *Economist* insightfully pointed out, these free agents are not easy to control. Get too many, and you risk losing the concept of corporation. What's more, the notion of a hard core of executives who manage a fluid pool of free agents breaks down upon analysis: "Much as do-no-wrong Jack Welch might want General Electric to be like that . . . the giant American corporation still has 340,000 full-time employees."[6]

Our fourth point is that in a world of hypercompetition, there will be little room for error. Decisions not only must be made quicker, but must be better. And that is exactly where deep cultural understanding comes in. As one executive told us, echoing an idea sometimes attributed to Percy Barnevik, "culture makes no difference ninety-five percent of the time; it is the other five percent that is critical." Developing the executives who can tell the cultural difference will be an essential ingredient of the route to success.

So much for the view that organizations will not need executives who understand culture. To the extent that organizations, in the interest of saving developmental dollars and developing local nationals, limit the opportunities for cross-cultural learning, they also limit the cultural developmental opportunities and, in turn, the executive bench strength that they will almost certainly need to carry out global strategies. Organizations will need *more* executives with that understanding, not *fewer,* if they intend to compete on the global stage—and with rare exceptions, organizations of any size will have little choice.

In Closing

. . . . .

We end our journey, as did Aldous Huxley, back where we started. We long ago gave up the notion that there is one type of global executive or that there is a simple answer for how to develop international executive talent. Our own experiences, however, and those of our executives, tell us that our model still holds: Strategy must drive development, select talented people but leave room for discovery, start them early and make sure they are able to get the global experiences that matter, and give them support and help in the learning, and "the right stuff" will emerge.

Returning to Heraclitus one last time, yes, it appears that the true nature of things likes to be hidden. But the philosopher also said that the hidden harmony is better than the obvious. The truths of global work are often difficult to discern, but this makes them all the more valuable once found.

Appendix A

Interview Questions

We hope you will take some time prior to the interview to think about the following questions. Please pay particular attention to the first two, as they require some reflection and are the heart of the interview. We are including the other questions that we will cover as time permits, so you may want to review them as well.

Primary Questions
(Please think carefully about these prior to the interview)

1. When you think about your career as a manager, certain events or episodes stand out in your mind—things that changed you in some way and have ultimately shaped you as an executive. Please choose three of these experiences that have had a lasting impact on you as a manager or executive in international work. When we meet with you, we will ask you about each of these "key events" in your career: What happened? What did you learn from it (for better or worse)?

2. Now think about someone else—someone whose career you have seen rise and fall. This should be a person who initially was very successful as a manager or executive in international work and who was expected to continue to be successful—but who failed to live up to those expectations. This previously successful person may have reached a plateau, been passed over or demoted, or even fired. Without revealing the identity of the person, please be

prepared to discuss with us your views of: (a) why this individual had been so successful prior to the derailment; (b) the flaws that eventually were his or her undoing; and (c) the circumstances that led to the derailment.

Additional Questions
(Please look over these questions)

3. If it wasn't one of the three events you described in the first question, tell me about your first international assignment. Why did you take the job? What were the biggest surprises? What were the biggest challenges? Did you make any mistakes? Did you get any help?

4. Are there any other experiences that you think helped prepare you for international management?

5. Who was the person from whom you learned the most about managing in an international setting? What did you learn from him/her?

6. What are the special challenges of having a boss who is from a different culture than yours? What about having subordinates from different cultures?

7. What are the most important differences between managing in international work and in domestic assignments? What special qualities would you look for in choosing a person for an international assignment? What traps would you avoid?

8. What kinds of preparation or support did you get from your company or from some other source that helped you succeed as an international manager? In retrospect, what could your company have done that would have been helpful? What do you recommend that they do in the future to help talented younger managers who want an international career?

9. Was there anything special in the way you grew up or in your early life that caused you to seek out or to be especially effective in

an international context? Something special about you (for example, special interests or special abilities such as speaking several languages)?

10. In what ways have you changed over the course of your career? If you ran into someone who hadn't seen you in many years, how would they say you are different?

11. Looking back on your experiences, is there anything you have learned that you would want to pass on to a talented younger manager who desires a career in international business?

Appendix B

Methodology

Our interviews followed the questionnaire in appendix A, as far as possible in the order that the questions are presented. We took extensive notes, rather than record the interviews per se, later transcribing our notes for coding and analysis.

We followed a rule in the interviews that when all else fails—as it sometimes does in such far-flung travels—the two essential questions are the key-events question and the derailment question (numbers 1 and 2). As preparation, we had sent our questions to the executives well ahead of our scheduled meetings (and in most cases they had received them), and we asked them to prepare, if nothing else, these two areas (and in most cases they did).

Both the key-events and derailment questions have long histories in executive development. The key-events question served as the basis for *The Lessons of Experience,* by Morgan McCall, Michael Lombardo, and Ann Morrison[1]; the derailment question for research conducted at the same time and first published in *Psychology Today* in 1983.[2] Both these studies, conducted at the Center for Creative Leadership in the mid-1980s and widely used as a foundation for the center's programs, emphasized the crucial role of experience in developing executives. The lessons-of-experience studies focused on success, the derailment studies on failure.

The interviews produced 332 key events and 952 lessons learned from those events. Our process of analysis was essentially the same as that reported by Lindsay et al., 1987.[3] From the 332 events, we inductively developed the eighteen categories of experience presented in chapters 5 and 6, and from the 952 lessons, we inductively developed twenty-seven categories of lessons (chapter 4). Our team of four

. . . . .

researchers coded the events and lessons into their respective categories. We found some events too complex to be assigned a single code, so we then assigned a secondary code that we used for additional analyses.

Although we conducted a variety of analyses—from simple counts and percentages to cross tabulations and multidimensional scaling, this book is not intended to be a report of research per se, but rather as a book more generally about global executive development. We found that whenever we strayed too far from the stories of our executives, the lessons of the research were lost—data failed to capture the reality. The reality we found was a complex one indeed with few simple answers, as we have emphasized throughout. We have amply used quotes from our interviews. Given our method (interviews to notes to transcriptions), these "quotes" are rarely the exact words used by executives and are not presented as such. They represent our best efforts at catching the meaning from the interview. In most cases we have made additional changes to disguise names, companies, and any other features that might threaten the anonymity of our study executives. Brian's story is an exception. Brian and Royal Dutch/Shell permitted us to use his story as identified.

The derailment question produced 121 stories of executive failure. With good reason to believe that global derailment shared much with the original U.S. studies (see, for example, *A Look at Derailment Today*[4]), we examined our stories in terms of those derailment dynamics. After becoming familiar with the whole set of stories, we extended the previous framework to reflect the differences we found in the international setting (chapter 7).

The remaining interview questions were content-analyzed into appropriate categories and examined in terms of percentage of executives responding. The number of executives answering varied from question to question across interviews—sometimes interview time was short, sometimes an executive might give a different interpretation to the question. For questions other than the key-events and derailment questions, the interviewers had considerable latitude to conduct the interview in a way that did not compromise our basic data.

Although we present throughout our book various pieces of data and analysis, we came to believe that the basis for developing global leaders

· · · · ·

resides in the stories of global executives. It is in the stories of our executives that we are able to provide meaning to the complex tapestries of global careers and apply it to organizational practice. Our task has been to preserve the intensity and interest of the stories while taking advantage of the power of statistics and analysis where it can be useful. Our intention is not to lose the benefits of either approach.

Appendix C

Supplementary Tables

Table C-1   The Foundation Assignments

Definition	EARLY WORK EXPERIENCES Examples	Lessons Taught
These were jobs and assignments that occurred early in a career, sometimes even a first job, that typically laid a foundation for later development. These events often had a functional or technical focus, or reflected very early exposure to the ways of organizations or to cultural differences. These early jobs frequently carried with them significant culture shock.	• head of legal service program • started out as an accountant • unstructured sales job • in the export business very young and away from home country • a buyer for a British company working in Germany • a technical job with international reach • Swede selling engineering products in Holland	The lessons learned here laid a foundation for future growth. Executives tended to learn the value of listening to other people and seeing the world through other people's eyes. Often these early experiences were in other countries, and working directly with people in those countries in lower-level jobs forced the person to learn to do business in the native language.

Definition	FIRST MANAGERIAL RESPONSIBILITY Examples	Lessons Taught
The focus of these experiences was managing for the first time, often complicated by contextual factors such as difficult relationships with bosses, being in a new culture, being promoted over or supervising older or more experienced subordinates, or having to establish credibility. The jobs were frequently confounded by a huge increase in the scope of responsibility and influenced positively by another person who helped.	• first managerial job . . . with difficult boss • supervising older subordinates • an expatriate in Portugal • a Brazilian supervising manufacturing in Mexico • an expatriate in Hong Kong	Overwhelmingly, the challenges of these experiences taught these people to believe in themselves and to take responsibility for themselves and their situations. This often involved learning to speak for the company as well as oneself, sometimes under intense media pressure. When the person lived in another culture, the experience also offered lessons in living and working in that culture.

• • • • •

Table C-2   Major Line Assignments

BUSINESS TURNAROUNDS		
Definition	**Examples**	**Lessons Taught**
Fixing a business or function in trouble. Often compounded by culture shock, career shift, and occasionally an educational or a developmental event.	• turnaround in France • general manager sent to Norway to fix business • Brit sent to Australia to fix a lemon • sent to U.S. to grow a company that was in trouble • took over research organization that was doing bad science • sent to reorganize business in China • sent to get costs under control in Africa • sent to fix operation in Australia • big turnaround project in Sweden • turning a business around in Japan • fixing problems in Belgium left by former expatriate manager • U.S. manager sent to Sweden to fix things • Swede sent to turn around operations in China	Lessons cover all five themes and include belief in oneself, learning to listen to others and see the world through their eyes, running a business, staying focused, building a team, making tough calls on people, managing the interface with headquarters, and managing one's own career. An event with one of the largest repertoires of possible learning.

BUSINESS START-UPS		
Definition	**Examples**	**Lessons Taught**
Starting up a new business or organization. A particularly exciting assignment. Often compounded by culture shock and a significant other person (good or bad). See joint ventures, below, as many start-ups were carried out under that organizational structure.	• four colleagues and I set up our own company • built a finance department from scratch • started U.S. subsidiary in Asia • set up office in Prague • started the business in Canada	Surprisingly narrow range of lessons. A lot is learned about the specific culture in which the start-up takes place and about being open, fair, and respectful of others (probably because getting the job done requires establishing a feeling of "we are all in this together").

Definition	**BUILDING OR EVOLVING A BUSINESS** Examples	Lessons Taught
Running an organization where the challenge is growing or building a business, product, or organization that is performing adequately. This includes organizations that are past the initial start-up as well as organizations that need a transformation or change to continue growing. These assignments are often confounded by a dramatic increase in the scope of responsibility and are often career shifts into general management.	• ran business in Oman • built the organization in Venezuela • grew the business in Argentina • vice president/general manager of global business • developed the European market • built the business in Africa • grew the company in Thailand • Italian expatriate who grew the business in Brazil • Swedish expatriate who grew the business in Indonesia	Lessons include both strategic perspective (how the business fits into the larger corporation and seeing the business as worldwide) and running the business (structure, process, etc.). Also many lessons on getting focused and motivating people. Success generates a lot of confidence.

Definition	**JOINT VENTURES, ALLIANCES, MERGERS, OR ACQUISITIONS** Examples	Lessons Taught
These events involve working with another organization, individual, or group, typically from a very different culture, with different goals or perspectives, and often with considerable conflict or misunderstandings. Often confounded with culture shock, and frequently a start-up.	• joint venture (JV) with Brazilian firm • expatriate general manager of JV in Portugal • expatriate to run Korean JV • expatriate to run JV in Taiwan • vice president to carry out JV between U.S. firms in Asia • ran JV between Brazilians and Swedes • ran British JV in Russia • headed JV between U.S. and Japanese companies	Not surprisingly, learning to run the business is supplemented by learning to manage difficult relationships—the skills of negotiation, dealing with governments, etc. Many lessons learned about the specific culture in which the enterprise is set up.

Table C-3   Shorter-Term Experiences

| SPECIAL PROJECTS, CONSULTING ROLES, AND STAFF ADVISORY JOBS | | |
Definition	Examples	Lessons Taught
These events include temporary and short-term assignments and special projects, often on top of a regular job, or as a regular job in themselves. They usually involved giving advice or doing a study rather than bottom-line responsibility, were often limited in duration, and were usually well defined. They often occurred in conjunction with early work and often contained culture shock or a confrontation with reality.	• head of consultancy unit during a reorganization • chaired an international committee on standards • numerous cross-functional task forces • marketing manager given benchmarking project to do in Europe • appointed group counsel to senior executives • deeply involved in valuing a company for sale or merger • sent to close a plant • corporate adviser on capital proposals • troubleshooter in Latin America • global business coordinator • adapted U.S. marketing plan to Europe • developed overseas marketing plan	Lessons covered how to run a business from both a strategic and an operational perspective; how to have confidence in oneself. Specific knowledge is based on the content of the task.

| STINT AT HEADQUARTERS | | |
Definition	Examples	Lessons Taught
A job at the corporate headquarters, often for exposure or developmental purposes, intended to be temporary, and often involving a foreign national. Frequently confounded by culture shock.	• Colombian sent to headquarters and given lower level job than promised • Brazilian sent to headquarters and given lower-level job • expatriate to headquarters in the U.S. • expatriate to headquarters in Sweden • repatriation to headquarters • given terrible job in headquarters • moved to headquarters to run human resources • expatriate to headquarters in the U.K. and given lower-level job	Obvious learning was around managing the interface with the home office. From mistreatment or the occasional act of support, person learned how important it is to treat outsiders with fairness and respect. Foreign nationals learned about living in a new culture. Executives learned about running a business from headquarters perspective. Surviving built confidence.

NEGOTIATIONS

Definition	Examples	Lessons Taught
Negotiating with an outside party, often reluctant if not hostile, to arrive at a contract, a price, or an agreement. Usually short-term, specific, and formal, and usually with a customer, government, or union. Includes negotiations around joint ventures, alliances, etc., when the person was only involved in the negotiation and not in the running of it.	• contract negotiation team in Africa • negotiated secret acquisition that fell through • implementation of union contract and tedious arguments over meaning of details • negotiated acquisition in Brazil • negotiated customer contract in Europe • U.K. expatriate handles union negotiation in the U.S.	Executives obviously learned many lessons in how to negotiate, and related lessons in listening carefully to another's point of view and persevering through adversity and setback. Less obviously there were many lessons in building and motivating the negotiating team.

DEVELOPMENTAL AND EDUCATIONAL EXPERIENCES

Definition	Examples	Lessons Taught
Formal educational experiences and jobs or projects that had primarily an educational or exposure purpose. Included here are rotational programs, internal training programs, and various external programs (e.g., Harvard, INSEAD, Center for Creative leadership), both degree and non-degree. Frequently compounded by culture shock.	• internal program on leading change • lived with American family while on AFS scholarship to U.S. • required army service in Korea • sales training course • Harvard management development program • global executive development program or executive program • got M.B.A. in the U.S. • attended graduate school in the U.S. • went to British Foreign Office School in Lebanon • attended IMEDE • attended the executive program at INSEAD • sent as trainee to Malaysia • rotational program across functions • training course in Switzerland • rotation across departments • studied executives in Australia	Lessons were largely about culture in programs in a country other than one's own or in programs with multicultural participants. Executives learned how to be flexible and adapt, both to the people and to the demands. From a content perspective, they learned about international business. When the program involved action learning or projects, they learned about building teams. Some academic programs taught something about developing people.

(continued)

Table C-3   Shorter-Term Experiences *(continued)*

| SIGNIFICANT OTHER PEOPLE | | |
Definition	Examples	Lessons Taught
These experiences resulted from a relationship with another person or people, whether good or bad. These most frequently involve bosses, superiors, peers, subordinates, customers, friends, or spouses. Frequently confounded by early work and clashes with organizational reality.	• head of research presented a stiff challenge • boss's boss gave opportunities and held me accountable • Chinese businessman gave advice • chairman created learning environment • business partner became friend and gave lots of guidance • high-powered father of girlfriend made negative impression • boss in Madrid showed how to deal with change • peer demonstrated that you could still be a woman in a man's world • Asian boss was always calm, widely respected • boss took me on customer calls • chairman kept me from resigning • Australian business partner • pressure-cooker boss • ineffective boss • French boss who screwed up the business • English colleague in Madrid • Danish boss • Armenian boss • wonderful boss in Singapore • wild scientist	One could see examples of almost anything in the good and bad behavior of significant other people. The most frequently reported lessons involved learning about one's own likes and dislikes, strengths and weaknesses. Support from others increased confidence. Bad experiences with bosses could improve one's skill in dealing with superiors. Good bosses taught lessons in developing others. Other people could be particularly important early in a career and whenever learning about international context was important. Particularly valuable were good bosses from another culture.

Table C-4   Perspective-Changing Experiences

CRISES

Definition	Examples	Lessons Taught
The manager is involved in a major crisis, usually involving intense pressure, media exposure, and external parties (governments, terrorists, regulators). Can be confounded with negotiations.	• terrorists threaten to poison our products • the company was charged with making bribes • a key brand almost tanked in Europe • product tampering • thwarted attempt to shut down a plant	Crises confront a person with his or her strengths and weaknesses. Success bolsters belief in self and willingness to accept responsibility. Important lessons in business strategy to prepare for, prevent, and recover from crises. It also involves some lessons about dealing with the media.

CAREER SHIFTS

Definition	Examples	Lessons Taught
A major change in career direction, for example, changing organizations or vocations, or switching to a new function. Such moves often involved considerable risk or personal sacrifice. These events are commonly associated with family stress, changes in scope, and even joint ventures.	• left secure job to take a gamble in a different part of the business • uprooted my family to work for a big company in Frankfurt • chose between going to school in U.S. and taking a job • turned 50 and kept promise to myself by going to Korea, leaving home for the first time • left job I loved to be with my husband and daughter • left R&D to go into marketing • left planning for manufacturing • left Austria for Germany and a new career • switched from manufacturing to product development • gave up engineering for management • left to start my own business • left research to become a product manager	Most career shifts involved responsibility for something new and therefore taught lessons in running a business. Most involved a change in culture, so lessons in culture also came with it. Depending on the nature of the change, lessons about managing the family, taking risks, or developing people might follow. Successful transition was a big confidence builder.

(continued)

Table C-4   Perspective-Changing Experiences *(continued)*

CHANGES IN SCOPE OR SCALE		
Definition	**Examples**	**Lessons Taught**
These events were job shifts that significantly increased the complexity of the job, its scope, or the scale of responsibility. These changes often went from relatively small and simple to large and complex, or from domestic to global, or from local to global. These shifts were often sudden and dramatic. They tended to be associated with turnaround or build-the-business assignments, and often another person was instrumental.	• became a worldwide business area manager • the marketing director was fired and I got the job . . . had to deal with twenty markets, partners, and businesses I didn't know • I became an expatriate country manager to Spain • at thirty-two, I was expatriated to Saudi Arabia to run a large project • made vice president/general manager of global business • repatriated to Malaysia with full responsibility for a multicultural workforce	A leap in the scope of a job teaches many lessons in running a business. Other common lessons involved learning to listen to others who knew something about the new demands, and learning to establish one's credibility in the face of inexperience. Because of the large scope of some of these jobs, some executives had to learn to deal with local governments. Successful transition was a big confidence builder.

CULTURE SHOCK		
Definition	**Examples**	**Lessons Taught**
These events focused almost exclusively on the impact of being in a new or different culture, where the reason for being there took a backseat to the cultural learning. Most often the cultural discontinuity was a surprise or even a shock. These experiences were frequently associated with turnarounds and joint ventures.	• in Nigeria was shocked by the way people live • had to cope the with macho culture in Argentina • as an expatriate I was treated with condescension • coped with corruption while making sales deals • Swedish expatriate sent to India to set up a company run by Indians • Indian expatriate to the Philippines • as an expatriate to Thailand, I learned to eat flies • U.S. expatriate to Europe surprised by nationalism • unwelcome U.S. expatriate in Sweden • family culture shock in Asia	Culture shock is the primary source of lessons about culture—all three categories are heavily represented (learning a foreign language, specific cultural lessons, and generic cultural lessons). Related lessons include listening, seeing the world through others' eyes, being open and genuine, being flexible and adapting to the situation, and establishing credibility.

CONFRONTATIONS WITH REALITY

Definition	Examples	Lessons Taught
These experiences were usually unpleasant surprises, such as confrontations with organizational politics, arbitrary actions by others, tests of values or ethics, or perceptions of exile, unfairness, or betrayal. These were often in conjunction with a negative experience with another person and sometimes involved the family or personal stress as well.	• the position I was promised disappeared when I got to France because I was an Italian • my first time face to face with politics • I discovered an error in the books and was pressured to change the figures; I took the blame to protect my people from a witch hunt • difficult Indian chairman demoted me arbitrarily • I was betrayed by senior people • had an unethical partner in JV • had an idea stolen, and credit was given to the thief • faced sexism in Australia • betrayed and demoted by boss • demoted by tyrant boss • disillusioned by politics	People often learned that if they persevered they would eventually get through it and come out OK. They also learned a lot about politics, and through negative example how important it is to be genuine and fair in dealing with others. This experience confronted executives with their likes and dislikes (often values-oriented), and their survival bolstered their belief in themselves.

MISTAKES AND ERRORS IN JUDGMENT

Definition	Examples	Lessons Taught
These were experiences in which a person's own actions or misjudgment caused things to go wrong, eventually resulting in his or her learning from the mistake and sometimes from resurrection after the consequences. They included various kinds of assignments that failed because of actions or poor judgment by the manager.	• acted without consulting union leader • business failed in a few months • didn't listen to advice • handled reduction in force poorly and faced open hostility • an expatriate to Indonesia had things fall apart in a few years—I had to stay and fix his mistakes • hired the wrong person and suffered the consequences • bulldozed the board, and they got him later • chose the wrong people and almost got fired	Because the mistakes frequently involved a person's misunderstanding of a different culture, many lessons were about the specific culture. Mistakes also taught the importance of listening and being open and genuine oneself. Some people learned lessons about the differences in what motivates others. Surviving a mistake gave people confidence.

(continued)

Table C-4   Perspective-Changing Experiences *(continued)*

| FAMILY AND PERSONAL CHALLENGES | | |
Definition	Examples	Lessons Taught
Personal and/or family stress, challenges, and sacrifices caused by career events or vice versa. Also included are external events in the family or life that impact the career or perspective of the executive (e.g., a religious conversion, a peer killed in a plane crash, an irate spouse, or an illness). These are often confounded by culture shock.	• moved family (with a new baby) to Paris and left them for long periods while on the road • left a good job to follow spouse • accepted Christ • colleague was killed in a plane crash • endured severe competition for school admission in Japan	Key lessons include understanding what support one needs from others and how to mange a family situation under great ambiguity and stress. Many lessons about the specific cultures in which the events took place. Also learning to persevere— to stick with it even when things get very painful.

· · · · ·

**Table C-5   Key Events in the Lives of International Executives
versus U.S. Executives**

International Sample[a]	U.S. Sample[b]
Significant Other People (12 percent of events, 32 percent of people) These experiences resulted from a relationship with another person or people, whether good or bad. These most frequently involved bosses, superiors, peers, subordinates, customers, friends, or spouses.	*Role Models* (7.5 percent of events, 18.3 percent of people) *Values Playing Out** (10.6 percent of events, 24.6 percent of people)
Business Turnarounds (11 percent of events, 30 percent of people) A business turnaround meant fixing a business or function in trouble.	*Fix-It* (10.9 percent of events, 29.3 percent of people)
Culture Shock (9 percent of events, 27 percent of people) These events focused almost exclusively on the impact of being in a new or different culture, where the reason for an executive's being there takes a backseat to the cultural learning. Most often this experience was a surprise or even a shock.	No direct comparison, though there are some parallels with "Personal Trauma" (below)
Developmental and Educational Experiences (9 percent of events, 23 percent of people) These experiences included all formal educational experiences and jobs or projects that had primarily an educational or exposure purpose. Included here were rotational programs, internal training programs, and various external programs (e.g., Harvard, INSEAD, Center for Creative Leadership).	*Coursework* (6.2 percent of events, 18.3 percent of people)
Career Shift (8 percent of events, 21 percent of people) A major change in career direction, for example, changing organizations or vocations, or switching to a new function, often involved considerable risk or personal sacrifice.	*Breaking a Rut* (3.9 percent of events, 10.5 percent of people)
Special Projects, Consulting Roles, and Staff Advisory Jobs (8 percent of events, 24 percent of people) These events included temporary and short-term assignments and special projects, often on top of a regular job, but they could have been a regular job in themselves. They usually involved giving advice or doing a study rather than bottom-line responsibility, were often limited in duration, and were usually well defined.	*Project/Task Force* (12.3 percent of events, 28.8 percent of people) *Line to Staff Switch* (2.1 percent of events, 6.8 percent of people)

(continued)

. . . . .

Table C-5   Key Events in the Lives of International Executives versus U.S. Executives *(continued)*

International Sample[a]	U.S. Sample[b]
Building or Evolving a Business (6 percent of events, 16 percent of people) This involved running an organization where the challenge was growing or building a business, a product, or an organization that was not in trouble (has not yet become a turn-around). This included organizations that were past the initial start-up stage and organizations that needed a transformation or change to continue growing.	See "Change in Scope" (below), which included running a large operation as well as the increase in scope or scale.
Confrontations with Reality (6 percent of events, 18 percent of people) These experiences were usually unpleasant surprises, such as confrontations with organizational politics, arbitrary actions by others, tests of values or ethics, or perceptions of exile, unfairness, or betrayal.	*Demotions/Missed Promotions/Lousy Jobs*** (4.4 percent of events, 12 percent of people) *Subordinate Performance Problems*** (3.4 percent of events, 10.5 percent of people) *Personal Trauma*** (1.8 percent of events, 5.8 percent of people) See also "Values Playing Out" (above)
Changes in Scope or Scale (6 percent of events, 17 percent of people) These events were job shifts that significantly changed the complexity of the job, its scope, or the scale of its responsibility. These changes often went from relatively small and simple to large and complex, or from domestic to global. The shifts were often sudden and dramatic.	*Change in Scope* (16.9 percent of events, 40.8 percent of people)
Early Work Experiences (4 percent of events, 12 percent of people) These were jobs and assignments that occurred early in a career, sometimes even a first job that typically laid a foundation for later development. These events often had a functional or technical focus, or reflected very early exposure to the ways of organizations or to cultural differences.	*Early Work Experiences* (3.2 percent of events, 9.9 percent of people)
Joint Ventures, Alliances, Mergers, or Acquisitions (4 percent of events, 11 percent of people) These events involved working with another organization, individual, or group—typically from a very different culture, with different goals or perspectives, and often with considerable conflict or misunderstanding.	See "Project/Task Force" (above)

International Sample[a]	U.S. Sample[b]
Mistakes and Errors in Judgment (4 percent of events, 10 percent of people) These were experiences in which a person's own actions or misjudgment caused things to go wrong, eventually resulting in learning from the mistake and sometimes in resurrection after the consequences. They included various kinds of assignments that failed because of actions or poor judgment of the manager.	*Business Failures and Mistakes* (3.9 percent of events, 11 percent of people)
Business Start-Up (3 percent of events, 10 percent of people) Starting up a new function, department, business subsidiary, or organization.	*Starting from Scratch* (5.5 percent of events, 16.8 percent of people)
Negotiations (3 percent of events, 8 percent of people) Executives negotiated with an outside party, often reluctant if not hostile, to arrive at a contract, price, or agreement. The negotiations were usually short-term, specific, and formal and were usually with a customer, government, or union. We include negotiations around joint ventures, alliances, etc., only when the person was involved in the negotiation and not in the running of the venture.	See "Project/Task Force" (above)
Crises (2 percent of events, 7 percent of people) The manager was involved in a major crisis, usually involving intense pressure, media exposure, and external parties (governments, terrorists, regulators).	See "Personal Trauma" (above)
Family and Personal Challenges (2 percent of events, 8 percent of people) Personal and/or family stress, challenges, and sacrifices were caused by career events or vice versa. Also included are external events in the family or life that impact the career or perspective of the executive (e.g., a religious conversion, a peer killed in a plane crash, an irate spouse, and an illness).	*Purely Personal* (2.6 percent of events, 8.4 percent of people)

(continued)

. . . . .

Table C-5   Key Events in the Lives of International Executives versus U.S. Executives *(continued)*

International Sample[a]	U.S. Sample[b]
First Managerial Responsibility (2 percent of events, 7 percent of people) The focus of these experiences was on a person's managing for the first time, often complicated by contextual factors such as difficult relationships with bosses, being in a new culture, being promoted over or supervising older or more experienced subordinates, or having to establish credibility.	*First Supervision* (4.9 percent of events, 15.7 percent of people)
Stint at Headquarters (2 percent of events, 7 percent of people) The stints involved a job at corporate home office, often for exposure or developmental purposes, intended to be temporary, and often involving a foreign national.	See "Line to Staff Switch" (above) See "Demotions/Missed Promotions/Lousy Jobs" (above)

[a] International sample included 332 events and 101 people.

[b] U.S. sample included 616 events and 191 people. U.S. data from Esther H. Lindsey, Virginia Homes, and Morgan W. McCall, Jr., *Key Events in Executives' Lives,* technical report no. 32 (Greensboro, NC: Center for Creative Leadership, 1987).

 *Matched with more than one experience.

** Not a perfect match, but close.

Notes

Preface
1. Joseph Campbell, *The Hero with a Thousand Faces,* 2nd edition (Princeton, NJ: Princeton University Press, 1972).
2. John Steinbeck, *The Log from the Sea of Cortez* (New York: Viking, 1951), 61.

Chapter 1: Introduction
1. Heraclitus, *Fragments: The Collected Wisdom of Heraclitus,* translated by B. Haxton (New York: Viking, 2001).
2. See, for example, Christopher A. Bartlett and Sumantra Ghoshal, *Managing Across Borders* (Boston: Harvard Business School Press, 1998).
3. See, for example, Manfred F. R. Kets de Vries, *The New Global Leaders: Richard Branson, Percy Barnevik, and David Simon* (San Francisco: Jossey-Bass, 1999).
4. Jay Galbraith, *Designing the Global Corporation* (San Francisco: Jossey-Bass, 2000).
5. J. Stewart Black, Allen J. Morrison, and Hal B. Gregersen, *Global Explorers: The Next Generation of Leaders* (New York: Routledge, 1999).
6. George P. Hollenbeck, "A Serendipitous Sojourn through the Global Leadership Literature," in *Advances in Global Leadership,* vol. 2, ed. William Mobley and Morgan W. McCall, Jr. (Stamford, CT: JAI Press, 2001).
7. See, for example, John Fulkerson, "Growing Global Executives," in *The 21st Century Executive: Innovative Practices for Building Leadership at the Top,* ed. Rob Silzer (San Francisco: Jossey-Bass, 2002); and Douglas T. Hall, Gurong Zhu, and Amin Yan, "Developing Global Leaders: To Hold On to Them, Let Them Go!" in *Advances in Global Leadership,* vol. 2, ed. William Mobley and Morgan W. McCall, Jr. (Stamford, CT: JAI Press, 2001).
8. Morgan W. McCall, Jr., Michael Lombardo, and Ann Morrison, *The Lessons of Experience* (New York: Free Press, 1988).
9. Morgan W. McCall, Jr., *High Flyers: Developing the Next Generation of Leaders* (Boston: Harvard Business School Press, 1998).
10. Black, Morrison, and Gregersen, *Global Explorers,* 10, 11.
11. Galbraith, *Designing the Global Corporation,* 2.

. . . . .

Chapter 2: What Is a Global Executive?

1. Bartlett and Ghoshal, *Managing Across Borders*.
2. Christopher A. Bartlett and Sumantra Ghoshal, "What Is a Global Manager?" *Harvard Business Review* 70, no. 5 (1992): 125.
3. Christopher A. Bartlett and Sumantra Ghoshal, "Matrix Management: Not a Structure, a Frame of Mind," *Harvard Business Review* 68, no. 4 (July–August 1990): 138–145.
4. Although people frequently use the word *country* to define the borders we cross, the term is a convenient but imperfect proxy for *culture*, which is, in fact, the crossing of greatest interest.
5. See, for example, Z. Aycan, *Expatriate Management: Theory and Research* (Greenwich, CT: JAI Press, 1997).
6. *Culture* has many definitions. See, for example, William B. Gudykunst, *Bridging Differences: Effective Intergroup Communication*, 3rd ed. (Thousand Oaks, CA: Sage Publications, 1998), 69. We focus here on the beliefs, attitudes, and behaviors that characterize, knowingly or not, some group.
7. Bartlett and Ghoshal, "What Is a Global Manager?"
8. For this argument, see Hollenbeck, "A Serendipitous Sojourn through the Global Leadership Literature"; for a practical illustration, see "Churning at the Top," *The Economist*, 17 March 2001, 67–69.
9. See Hollenbeck, "A Serendipitous Sojourn through the Global Leadership Literature," for several competency lists from companies and consulting firms.
10. W. Taylor, "The Logic of Global Business: An Interview with ABB's Percy Barnevik," *Harvard Business Review* 69, no. 2 (March–April 1991): 91–105.

Chapter 3: Global Journeys

1. We couldn't resist filching this chapter opening quote by Dickens from Warren Bennis's classic, *On Becoming a Leader* (Reading, MA: Addison-Wesley, 1989). In addition to Warren's own wisdom, this book contains a number of irresistible quotes about learning from notable places, including the following excerpt from Mark Twain's *Life on the Mississippi:* "Two things seemed pretty apparent to me. One was that in order to be a [Mississippi River] pilot a man had got to learn more than any one man ought to be allowed to know; and the other was, that he must learn it all over again in a different way every 24 hours."
2. According to *Fortune* ("The Triumph of English," 18 September 2000, 209–212), there are 322 million native English speakers, give or take, and perhaps another billion who speak it with some degree of competence. With the world's population in excess of 6.1 billion, we are looking at something between 5.3 and 21.6 percent English speaking, depending on how loose the criterion.

Chapter 4: The Lessons of International Experience

1. Craig Storti, *The Art of Crossing Cultures* (Yarmouth, ME: Intercultural Press, 1990), 15.

2. McCall, Lombardo, and Morrison, *The Lessons of Experience;* and Esther H. Lindsey, V. Holmes, and Morgan W. McCall, Jr., *Key Events in Executives' Lives,* technical report no. 32 (Greensboro, NC: Center for Creative Leadership, 1987).

3. Morgan W. McCall, Jr., Gretchen M. Spreitzer, and J. Mahoney, *Identifying Leadership Potential in Future International Executives: A Learning Resource Guide,* final report on phase 2 of this research project (Lexington, MA: International Consortium for Executive Development Research, 1994); and Gretchen M. Spreitzer, Morgan W. McCall, Jr., and J. Mahoney, "Early Identification of International Executives," *Journal of Applied Psychology* 82, no. 1 (1997): 6–29.

4. McCall, Lombardo, and Morrison, *The Lessons of Experience.*

5. The data on which the U.S. results are based was collected from a sample of 191 executives from five U.S. corporations and the U.S. subsidiary of a Canadian firm. Eighty-nine of those executives were interviewed, the remainder responded via a written survey. When that study was designed, the authors were not concerned with international issues and did not consider or collect data on the nationalities of the executives. By our best estimate, fewer than 5 percent of the total were non-U.S., so for all practical purposes this can be considered a domestic U.S. sample. For convenience we will use that shorthand throughout this book rather than repeatedly qualify it with phrases like "virtually all" or "for all practical purposes." Although the sample was U.S., some of the executives in the original study had expatriate experience. The power of those out-of-country experiences rather than the nationality of the executives may partially explain some of the similarities in the lessons they learned with those of our global sample.

6. McCall, Spreitzer, and Mahoney, *Identifying Leadership Potential.*

7. McCall, *High Flyers.*

8. Douglas T. Hall and Philip H. Mirvis, "The New Protean Career," in Douglas T. Hall and Associates, *The Career Is Dead, Long Live the Career: A Relational Approach to Careers* (San Francisco: Jossey-Bass, 1996), 15–45.

9. McCall, *High Flyers;* and McCall, Spreitzer, and Mahoney, *Identifying Leadership Potential.*

10. Hall, Zhu, and Yan, "Developing Global Leaders."

11. Hollenbeck, "A Serendipitous Sojourn through the Global Leadership Literature," 15–47.

12. Ibid.

13. Hall, Zhu, and Yan, "Developing Global Leaders."

Chapter 5: Experiences That Teach Global Executives

1. McCall, *High Flyers,* 62.

2. Steinbeck, *Sea of Cortez,* 158.

3. Campbell, *Hero with a Thousand Faces.*

4. Morgan W. McCall, Jr., Michael Lombardo, and Ann Morrison, "Great Leaps in Career Development," *Across the Board* (March 1989): 61.

5. Hall, Zhu, and Yan, "Developing Global Leaders."

. . . . .

6. Campbell, *Hero with a Thousand Faces.*

7. Hall, Zhu, and Yan, "Developing Global Leaders."

Chapter 6: Making Sense of Culture

1. Mary Catherine Bateson, *Peripheral Visions: Learning along the Way* (New York: HarperCollins, 1994).

2. Kalvero Oberg, "Culture Shock: Adjustment to New Cultural Environments," *Practical Anthropology* 7 (1960): 177–182, as referenced in Joyce S. Osland, *The Adventure of Working Abroad* (San Francisco: Jossey-Bass, 1995).

3. Lindsey, Holmes, and McCall, *Key Events in Executives' Lives.*

4. Joyce S. Osland, *The Adventure of Working Abroad* (San Francisco: Jossey-Bass, 1995), 141 and 154.

5. Storti, *The Art of Crossing Cultures,* 106.

6. Black, Morrison, and Gregersen, *Global Explorers.*

7. Bartlett and Ghoshal, *Managing Across Borders,* 114.

8. In fact, family issues are no doubt more important than our key experiences question revealed. It was a central topic in answers to other questions in the interview.

9. See, for example, Monica Rabe, *Culture Shock: A Practical Guide* (Portland, OR: Graphic Arts Publishing, 1997).

10. Storti, *The Art of Crossing Cultures,* 11.

11. Barbara W. Tuchman, *The March of Folly: From Troy to Vietnam* (New York: Ballantine, 1984).

Chapter 7: When Things Go Wrong

1. McCall, *High Flyers.* See also Morgan W. McCall, Jr., and Michael M. Lombardo, "Off the Track: Why and How Successful Executives Get Derailed," Technical Report 21 (Greensboro, NC: Center for Creative Leadership, 1983).

2. McCall, *High Flyers.*

3. John J. Gabarro, *The Dynamics of Taking Charge* (Boston: Harvard Business School Press, 1987).

4. See, for example, Osland, *The Adventure of Working Abroad.*

Chapter 8: Developing Global Executives

1. McCall, *High Flyers.*

2. See, for example, Bartlett and Ghoshal, *Managing Across Borders.*

3. See, for example, Galbraith, *Designing the Global Corporation,* on the increased complexity of such designs; and Lynn Isabella and Robert Spekman, "Alliance Leadership: Template for the Future," in *Advances in Global Leadership,* vol. 2, ed. William Mobley and Morgan W. McCall, Jr. (Stamford, CT: JAI Press, 2001), on the alliances and joint ventures that often accompany global expansion.

4. Bartlett and Ghoshal, *Managing Across Borders.*
5. Isabella and Spekman, "Alliance Leadership."
6. Laree S. Kiely, "Overcoming Time and Distance: Virtual International Executive Teams"; and Alison Eyring, "The Challenges of Long-Distance Leadership: A View from Asia." Both articles are in *Advances in Global Leadership,* vol. 2, ed. William Mobley and Morgan W. McCall, Jr. (Stamford, CT: JAI Press, 2001).
7. Spreitzer, McCall, and Mahoney, "Early Identification of International Executives."
8. McCall, *High Flyers.*

Chapter 9: Building a Global Career

1. Hall and Mirvis, "The New Protean Career," in Hall and Associates, *The Career Is Dead, Long Live the Career.*
2. Yumiko Ono and Bill Spindle, "Japan's Long Decline Makes One Thing Rise: Individualism," *Wall Street Journal,* 29 December 2000.
3. Douglas T. Hall and Jonathan E. Moss, "The New Protean Career Contract: Helping Organizations and Employees Adapt," *Organizational Dynamics* (winter 1998).
4. Hall and Mirvis, "The New Protean Career," in Hall, *The Career Is Dead, Long Live the Career,* 20.
5. A very readable description of the uncertainty and anxiety of experiencing other cultures, as well as tools for learning from it, is found in Storti, *The Art of Crossing Cultures.* We have recommended it to executives working in a variety of situations (e.g., an American working for a Japanese company).
6. David A. Thomas and John J. Gabarro, *Breaking Through: The Making of Minority Executives in Corporate America* (Boston: Harvard Business School Press, 1999).
7. "Few Female Executives Posted Overseas," *Houston Chronicle,* 24 November 2000, 4C.
8. John P. Kotter, *The New Rules: How to Succeed in Today's Post-Corporate World* (New York: Free Press, 1995); Thomas and Gabarro, *Breaking Through*; Stefan Wills and Kevin Barham, "Being an International Manager," *European Management Journal* 12, no. 1 (1994): 49–58.
9. Books that describe and prescribe dealing with culture shock are widespread. Our favorite is Storti, *The Art of Crossing Cultures.* Simple, straightforward, easy to read, the book is recommended for anyone dealing with other cultures. Gudykunst, *Bridging Differences,* provides a quite readable description of the anxiety attendant in confronting the different and how it can be dealt with.
10. The well-known tendency of global executives to feel inadequately compensated and to make seemingly unreasonable demands (well-known at least to any international compensation manager) is, we suspect, about appreciation for the hardship, not about money. Stories are legion, from demands to transport a thousand-bottle wine cellar to moving a stable of jumping horses!

· · · · ·

Chapter 10: Epilogue

1. Finding past London/Singapore airline schedules started with a creative lead from Jane Fama at Harvard Business School Library, which led to Bill Demarest at the World Airline Historical Society, which in turn then led to WAHS members David Keller, Jim "Jet" Thompson, and Steve Caisse, notable collectors of airline timetables who were most generous with their help.

2. The staying power of both the methodology and results of the experiences/lessons approach (originally published in 1987) was confirmed recently by two replications and extensions, one study carried out at The Boeing Company in the United States and the other a cross-organizational study done in Japan. See Paul R. Yost, Mary Mannion Plunkett, Robert McKenna, and Lori Homer, "Lessons of Experience: Personal and Situational Factors That Drive Growth," paper presented at the annual meeting of the Society for Industrial and Organizational Psychology, San Diego, CA, April 27–29, 2001; and Works Institute, "Research Project: 'The Lessons of Experience' in Japan," unpublished research report, Tokyo, Japan, June 2001.

3. Thomas L. Friedman, *The Lexus and the Olive Tree* (New York: First Anchor Books, 2000).

4. G. Pascal Zachary, *The Global Me* (New York: Public Affairs, 2000).

5. Bruce Tulgan, *Winning the Talent Wars* (New York: W. W. Norton, 2001).

6. "The Staff of Life," *The Economist,* 3 February 2001, 87.

Appendix B: Methodology

1. McCall, Lombardo, and Morrison, *The Lessons of Experience.*

2. Morgan McCall, Jr., and Michael M. Lombardo, "What Makes a Top Executive," *Psychology Today* 17, no. 2 (February 1983): 26–31.

3. Lindsey, Holmes, and McCall, *Key Events in Executives' Lives.*

4. Jean Brittain Leslie and Ellen Van Velsor, *A Look at Derailment Today: North America and Europe* (Greensboro, NC: Center for Creative Leadership, 1996).

References

Aycan, Z. *Expatriate Management: Theory and Research.* Greenwich, CT: JAI Press, 1997.

Bartlett, Christopher A. and Sumantra Ghoshal. "Matrix Management: Not a Structure, a Frame of Mind." *Harvard Business Review* 68, no. 4 (July–August 1990): 138–145.

_____. "What Is a Global Manager?" *Harvard Business Review* 70, no. 5 (September–October 1992): 125.

_____. *Managing Across Borders.* Boston: Harvard Business School Press, 1998.

Bateson, Mary Catherine. *Peripheral Visions: Learning along the Way.* New York: HarperCollins, 1994.

Bennis, Warren. *On Becoming a Leader.* Reading, MA: Addison-Wesley, 1989.

Black, J. Stewart, Allen J. Morrison, and Hal B. Gregersen. *Global Explorers: The Next Generation of Leaders.* New York: Routledge, 1999.

Campbell, Joseph. *The Hero with a Thousand Faces,* 2nd ed. Princeton, NJ: Princeton University Press, 1972.

Eyring, Alison. "The Challenges of Long-Distance Leadership: A View from Asia." In *Advances in Global Leadership,* vol. 2, ed. William Mobley and Morgan W. McCall, Jr. Stamford, CT: JAI Press, 2001.

Friedman, Thomas L. *The Lexus and the Olive Tree.* New York: First Anchor Books, 2000.

Fulkerson, John. "Growing Global Executives." In *The 21st Century: Innovative Practices for Building Leadership at the Top,* ed. Rob Silzer. San Francisco: Jossey-Bass, 2002.

Gabarro, John J. *The Dynamics of Taking Charge.* Boston: Harvard Business School Press, 1987.

Galbraith, Jay. *Designing the Global Corporation.* San Francisco: Jossey-Bass, 2000.

Gudykunst, William B. *Bridging Differences: Effective Intergroup Communication,* 3rd ed. Thousand Oaks, CA: Sage Publications, 1998.

Hall, Douglas T. and Jonathan E. Moss. "The New Protean Career Contract: Helping Organizations and Employees Adapt." *Organizational Dynamics* (Winter 1998).

Hall, Douglas T. and Philip H. Mirvis. "The New Protean Career." In Douglas T. Hall and Associates, *The Career Is Dead, Long Live the Career: A Relational Approach to Careers.* San Francisco: Jossey-Bass, 1996.

Hall, Douglas T., Gurong Zhu, and Amin Yan. "Developing Global Leaders: To Hold On to Them, Let Them Go!" In *Advances in Global Leadership,* vol. 2, ed. William Mobley and Morgan W. McCall, Jr. Stamford, CT: JAI Press, 2001.

Heraclitus. *Fragments: The Collected Wisdom of Heraclitus,* translated by B. Haxton. New York: Viking, 2001.

Hollenbeck, George P. "A Serendipitous Sojourn through the Global Leadership Literature." In *Advances in Global Leadership,* vol. 2, ed. William Mobley and Morgan W. McCall, Jr. Stamford, CT: JAI Press, 2001.

Isabella, Lynn and Robert Spekman. "Alliance Leadership: Template for the Future." In *Advances in Global Leadership,* vol. 2, ed. William Mobley and Morgan W. McCall, Jr. Stamford, CT: JAI Press, 2001.

Kets de Vries, Manfred F. R. *The New Global Leaders: Richard Branson, Percy Barnevik, and David Simon.* San Francisco: Jossey-Bass, 1999.

Kiely, Laree S. "Overcoming Time and Distance: Virtual International Executive Teams." In *Advances in Global Leadership,* vol. 2, ed. William Mobley and Morgan W. McCall, Jr. Stamford, CT: JAI Press, 2001.

Kotter, John P. *The New Rules: How to Succeed in Today's Post-Corporate World.* New York: Free Press, 1995.

Leslie, Jean Brittain and Ellen Van Velsor. *A Look at Derailment Today: North America and Europe.* Greensboro, NC: Center for Creative Leadership, 1996.

Lindsey, Esther H., V. Holmes, and Morgan W. McCall, Jr. *Key Events in Executives' Lives.* Technical report no. 32. Greensboro, NC: Center for Creative Leadership, 1987.

McCall, Jr., Morgan W. *High Flyers: Developing the Next Generation of Leaders.* Boston: Harvard Business School Press, 1998.

McCall, Jr., Morgan W. and Michael M. Lombardo. "What Makes a Top Executive." *Psychology Today* 17, no. 2 (February 1983): 26–31.

McCall, Jr., Morgan W., Michael Lombardo, and Ann Morrison. "Great Leaps in Career Development." *Across the Board* (March 1989): 61.

_____. *The Lessons of Experience.* New York: Free Press, 1988.

McCall, Jr., Morgan W., Gretchen M. Spreitzer, and J. Mahoney. *Identifying Leadership Potential in Future International Executives: A Learning Resource Guide.* Lexington, MA: International Consortium for Executive Development Research, 1994.

Oberg, Kalvero. "Culture Shock: Adjustment to New Cultural Environments." *Practical Anthropology* 7 (1960): 177–182.

Ono, Yumiko and Bill Spindle. "Japan's Long Decline Makes One Thing Rise: Individualism." *Wall Street Journal,* 29 December 2000.

Osland, Joyce S. *The Adventure of Working Abroad.* San Francisco: Jossey-Bass, 1995.

Rabe, Monica. *Culture Shock: A Practical Guide.* Portland, OR: Graphic Arts Publishing, 1997.

Spreitzer, Gretchen M., Morgan W. McCall, Jr., and J. Mahoney. "Early Identification of International Executives." *Journal of Applied Psychology* 82, no. 1 (1997): 6–29.

Steinbeck, John. *The Log from the Sea of Cortez.* New York: Viking, 1951.

Storti, Craig. *The Art of Crossing Cultures.* Yarmouth, ME: Intercultural Press, 1990.

Taylor, W. "The Logic of Global Business: An Interview with ABB's Percy Barnevik." *Harvard Business Review* 69, no. 2 (March–April 1991): 91–105.

Thomas, David A. and John J. Gabarro. *Breaking Through: The Making of Minority Executives in Corporate America.* Boston: Harvard Business School Press, 1999.

Tuchman, Barbara W. *The March of Folly: From Troy to Vietnam.* New York: Ballantine, 1984.

Tulgan, Bruce. *Winning the Talent Wars.* New York: W. W. Norton, 2001.

Wills, Stefan and Kevin Barham. "Being an International Manager." *European Management Journal* 12, no. 1 (1994): 49–58.

Works Institute. "Research Project: 'The Lessons of Experience' in Japan." Unpublished research report, Tokyo, Japan, June 2001.

Yost, Paul R., Mary Mannion Plunkett, Robert McKenna, and Lori Homer. "Lessons of Experience: Personal and Situational Factors that Drive Growth." Paper presented at the annual meeting of the Society for Industrial and Organizational Psychology, San Diego, CA, April 27–29, 2001.

Zachary, G. Pascal. *The Global Me.* New York: Public Affairs, 2000.

Index

About the Authors

Morgan W. McCall, Jr. is a Professor of Management and Organization in the Marshall School of Business at the University of Southern California and teaches in USC's International Business Education and Research (IBEAR) program. He is the author of *High Flyers: Developing the Next Generation of Leaders,* coauthor of *The Lessons of Experience,* and, with Bill Mobley, editor of *Advances in Global Leadership,* Volume 2. He holds a B.S. from Yale and a Ph.D. from Cornell, and was elected a Fellow of the Society for Industrial and Organizational Psychology. Prior to joining USC, Morgan was Director of Research and a Senior Behavioral Scientist at the Center for Creative Leadership.

George P. Hollenbeck is an organizational psychologist who writes, consults, and teaches about executive leadership development. His career has included executive positions at Merrill Lynch in New York and at Fidelity Investments, and he was Senior Director, Executive Education, at the Harvard Business School. After receiving his Ph.D. from the University of Wisconsin, he joined IBM, and he worked at The Psychological Corporation. He was a James McKeen Cattell Fund Fellow at the University of California, Berkeley, and as a Merrill Lynch executive, he attended Harvard Business School's Advanced Management Program. His consulting is primarily in the area of individual executive coaching.